Lecture Notes in Computer Science 1583
Edited by G. Goos, J. Hartmanis and J. van Leeuwen

Springer

Berlin
Heidelberg
New York
Barcelona
Hong Kong
London
Milan
Paris
Singapore
Tokyo

Daniel Scharstein

View Synthesis Using Stereo Vision

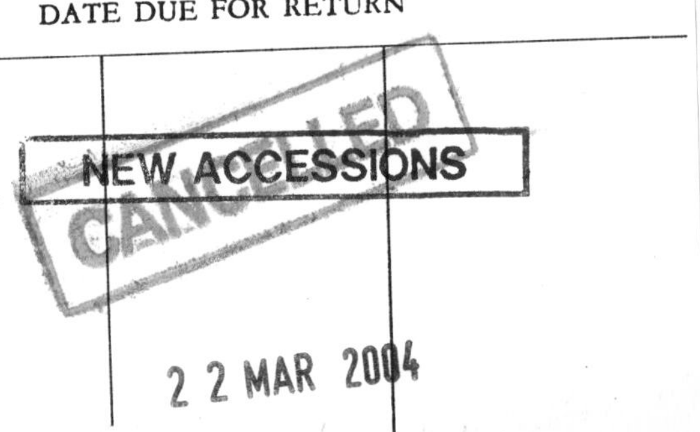

Springer

Series Editors

Gerhard Goos, Karlsruhe University, Germany
Juris Hartmanis, Cornell University, NY, USA
Jan van Leeuwen, Utrecht University, The Netherlands

Volume Author

Daniel Scharstein
Middlebury College
Department of Mathematics and Computer Science
Middlebury, VT 05753, USA
E-mail: schar@panther.middlebury.edu

Cataloging-in-Publication data applied for

Die Deutsche Bibliothek - CIP-Einheitsaufnahme

Scharstein, Daniel:
View synthesis using stereo vision / Daniel Scharstein. - Berlin ; Heidelberg ; New York ; Barcelona ; Hong Kong ; London ; Milan ; Paris ; Singapore ; Tokyo : Springer, 1999
(Lecture notes in computer science ; Vol. 1583)
ISBN 3-540-66159-X

CR Subject Classification (1998): I.4, I.3, H.5.1, I.2.10

ISSN 0302-9743
ISBN 3-540-66159-X Springer-Verlag Berlin Heidelberg New York

Typesetting: Camera-ready by author
SPIN: 10703155 06/3142 – 5 4 3 2 1 0 Printed on acid-free paper

To Amy, with all my love

Foreword

Over the past few years the fields of computer vision and computer graphics, two well-established but distinct areas of computer science, have begun to investigate some common problems. As computer vision techniques have matured they have found applications to problems in many areas, including computer graphics. At the same time, the field of computer graphics has become more concerned with the use of image data for producing realistic, synthetic images.

The area of overlap between graphics and vision, now commonly termed image-based rendering, uses computer vision techniques to aid in synthesizing new views of scenes. Image-based rendering methods are having a substantial impact on the field of computer graphics, and also play an important role in the related field of multimedia systems, for applications such as teleconferencing, remote instruction and surgery, virtual reality and entertainment.

The recent interest in image-based rendering methods has brought with it a renewed investigation of some well-established computer vision techniques, in particular stereo vision and structure from motion. Using these computer vision techniques in the context of rendering new views creates new requirements that are just beginning to be understood. This book, which grew out of Daniel Scharstein's doctoral thesis, provides a rigorous introduction to some of these new requirements, and develops new computer vision techniques to address them.

In this book, Daniel Scharstein provides an introduction to the field of image-based rendering, including a broad survey of the state-of-the-art literature. Besides providing a well-written introduction to this area, this text makes several important research contributions. First, it develops a novel way of formalizing the view synthesis problem under the full perspective model, yielding a clean, linear warping equation. Second, it provides new techniques for dealing with visibility issues such as partial occlusion and "holes", problems that have received little attention in the literature. In addition, it provides a thorough re-evaluation of the requirements that view synthesis places on stereo algorithms. Finally, the book introduces two novel stereo algorithms specifically tailored to the application of view synthesis.

Image-based rendering has become an important research area only fairly recently. From the beginning, however, Daniel was firmly convinced that the new application area of image synthesis would result in a substantially different formulation of the stereo problem, which would then require new solutions. His insight was certainly right on. Moreover, Daniel sought out collaborators such as Richard Szeliski, who had established themselves as leaders at the boundary of computer vision and computer graphics. Students like Daniel really lead their faculty advisors, rather than the other way around.

December 1998

Daniel P. Huttenlocher
Associate Professor of Computer Science
and Weiss Presidential Fellow
Cornell University

Preface

The topic of this volume is an investigation of the use of stereo vision for the application of view synthesis. View synthesis – the problem of creating images of a scene as it would appear from novel viewpoints – has traditionally been approached using methods from computer graphics. These methods, however, suffer from low rendering speed, limited achievable realism, and, most severely, their dependence on a global scene model, which typically needs to be constructed manually.

Motivated by the shortcomings of traditional computer graphics methods, we present a new approach to view synthesis that avoids the above problems by synthesizing new views from existing images of a scene. Using an image-based representation of scene geometry computed by stereo vision methods, a global model can be avoided, and realistic new views can be synthesized quickly using image warping.

The first part of this book focuses on the view synthesis problem. Chapter 1 introduces and motivates the problem, and provides a brief review of stereo vision. Chapter 2 contains an in-depth survey of related work in image-based rendering and stereo vision. In Chapter 3, we formalize the view synthesis problem under the full perspective model and derive a linear warping equation using a special rectification step. We discuss how to resolve visibility, and how "holes" resulting from partially occluded areas can be filled. We also discuss how the view synthesis method can be used in a larger framework for image-based scene representations, and present experiments demonstrating that it is possible to efficiently synthesize realistic new views even from inaccurate and incomplete depth information.

The new application of stereo for view synthesis makes it necessary to re-evaluate the requirements on stereo algorithms. In Chapter 4, we compare view synthesis to several traditional applications of stereo and conclude that stereo vision is better suited for view synthesis than for applications requiring explicit 3D reconstruction. In particular, limited achievable depth resolution and matching ambiguities due to lack of texture are less of a problem for view synthesis. Other issues become more important, such as the correct recovery of depth discontinuities. We also discuss ways of dealing with partially occluded regions of unknown depth and with completely occluded regions of unknown texture.

The second part of the book presents several novel stereo algorithms that are motivated by the specific requirements imposed by view synthesis. In Chapter 5, we introduce a new evidence measure based on intensity gradients for establishing correspondences between images. This measure combines the notions of similarity and confidence, and allows stable matching and easy assigning of canonical depth interpretations in image regions of insufficient information. In Chapter 6, we present new diffusion-based stereo algorithms that are motivated by the need to correctly recover object boundaries. Our algorithms are based on iteratively diffusing support at different disparity hypotheses and locally controlling the amount of diffusion based on the current quality of the disparity estimate. In particular, we develop a novel Bayesian estimation technique that significantly outperforms area-based algorithms using fixed-sized windows. We provide experimental results for all algorithms on both synthetic and real images.

Chapter 7 concludes the volume with a summary and a discussion of possible directions for future work.

This book is based on my Ph.D. thesis, which was submitted to Cornell University in January of 1997. The original document has been revised and updated thoroughly; in particular, Chapter 2 now provides a comprehensive review of related work through December 1998. Some of the material in this volume is based on work that has been published previously. The view-synthesis method in Chapter 3 and some of the material in Chapter 4 was first presented in Scharstein [1996]. The stereo method in Chapter 5 is an extension of work described in Scharstein [1994a, b]. Finally, the material presented in Chapter 6 is based on joint work with Richard Szeliski [Scharstein and Szeliski, 1996; Scharstein and Szeliski, 1998].

Acknowledgements

I would first like to thank Dan Huttenlocher, who has been a great friend and advisor. He gave me a lot of support and freedom while I was trying to find my own path as a researcher, and did not mind when I picked a different area of research from his own. (And I did eventually manage to convince him that stereo is an interesting problem.) Many thanks to Sheila Hemami, Nick Trefethen, and Ramin Zabih, all of whom served on my Ph.D. committee and gave many valuable comments, suggestions, and corrections. Thanks especially to Ramin, who got me interested in the problem of synthesizing new views from real images in the first place. He also contributed many valuable ideas and insights during numerous interesting research discussions. I would also like to thank Amy Briggs for tirelessly reading and correcting countless drafts of this document, and for finding (hopefully) all the typos. (She also deserves the credit for the good English.)

I am indebted to Rick Szeliski, who has had a tremendous influence on my career as a researcher and has taught me a lot about effectively conducting research. Thanks to Rick for a wonderful collaboration, which started with a week-long visit at DEC's Cambridge Research Lab in June, 1995, and which has contributed an important part to the work presented here.

Thanks to everyone who helped me during my last two years of working on my dissertation "remotely" from Vermont, including Karl Böhringer, Mark Hayden, and Nikos Pitsianis, and also the members of the great support staff at Cornell. I would also like to thank my colleagues in the Department of Mathematics and Computer Science at Middlebury College, for their support and friendship.

Finally, I would especially like to thank my family for their love, support, and confidence, and for putting up with my "emigration" in such a good-natured way. It is nice to know that someone is happy about me being happy.

And, most important of all, I thank my wife, Amy, who has made my life so wonderful. This book is dedicated to her.

Middlebury, January 1999 *Daniel Scharstein*

Contents

1. Introduction 1
1.1 The problem 2
1.1.1 Applications 2
1.1.2 The computer graphics approach 5
1.1.3 Avoiding the model 6
1.2 A review of stereo vision 8
1.2.1 Camera model and image formation 8
1.2.2 Stereo geometry 10
1.2.3 The correspondence problem 13
1.2.4 The epipolar constraint 14
1.2.5 A simple stereo geometry 16
1.2.6 Rectification 17
1.2.7 Example: SSD 19
1.3 Contributions and outline 22

2. A Survey of Image-Based Rendering and Stereo 23
2.1 Image-based rendering 23
2.1.1 View synthesis based on stereo 24
2.1.2 View interpolation 27
2.1.3 Mosaics and layered representations 29
2.2 Stereo 32
2.2.1 A framework for stereo 32
2.2.2 Preprocessing 33
2.2.3 Matching cost 33
2.2.4 Evidence aggregation 34
2.2.5 Disparity selection 35
2.2.6 Sub-pixel disparity computation 35
2.2.7 Diffusion-based techniques 36
2.2.8 Other techniques 37
2.2.9 Promising recent approaches 37
2.3 Computer vision books 38

3. View Synthesis ... 41
3.1 Geometry ... 41
3.1.1 Three-view rectification ... 42
3.1.2 The linear warping equation ... 44
3.1.3 Computing the rectifying homographies ... 45
3.2 Synthesizing a new view ... 47
3.2.1 Resolving visibility ... 47
3.2.2 Holes and sampling gaps ... 47
3.2.3 Combining information from both images ... 48
3.2.4 Adjusting intensities ... 49
3.2.5 Filling holes ... 50
3.2.6 The view synthesis algorithm ... 51
3.2.7 Limitations of the approach ... 52
3.3 Experiments ... 53
3.4 Image-based scene representations ... 60
3.5 Summary ... 61

4. Re-evaluating Stereo ... 63
4.1 Traditional applications of stereo ... 63
4.1.1 Automated cartography ... 64
4.1.2 Robot navigation ... 64
4.1.3 3D Reconstruction ... 65
4.1.4 3D Recognition ... 66
4.1.5 Visual servoing ... 66
4.1.6 Full vs. weak calibration ... 67
4.1.7 Comparison of requirements ... 68
4.2 Stereo for view synthesis ... 68
4.3 Accuracy ... 69
4.4 Correct vs. realistic views ... 71
4.5 Areas of uniform intensities ... 72
4.5.1 Geometric constraints ... 73
4.5.2 Interpolated views ... 75
4.5.3 Extrapolated views ... 77
4.5.4 General views and the aperture problem ... 79
4.5.5 Assigning canonical depth interpretations ... 80
4.5.6 Does adding more cameras help? ... 80
4.6 Partial occlusion ... 81
4.7 Summary ... 85

5. Gradient-Based Stereo ... 87
5.1 Similarity and confidence ... 88
5.2 Displacement-oriented stereo ... 89
5.3 The evidence measure ... 90
5.3.1 Comparing two gradient vectors ... 91
5.3.2 Comparing gradient fields ... 93

5.3.3 Computing gradients of discrete images 94
5.4 Accumulating the measure 96
5.5 Experiments 97
5.5.1 Observing E_δ for interesting displacements 98
5.5.2 Stereo: 1D search range 98
5.5.3 General motion: 2D search range 105
5.6 Computing disparity maps for view synthesis 105
5.6.1 Occlusion boundaries 107
5.6.2 Detecting partially occluded points and uniform regions 109
5.6.3 Extrapolating the disparities 109
5.7 Efficiency 109
5.8 Discussion and possible extensions 110
5.9 Summary 111

6. Stereo Using Diffusion 113
6.1 Disparity space 114
6.2 The SSD algorithm and boundary blurring 116
6.3 Aggregating support by diffusion 121
6.3.1 The membrane model 122
6.3.2 Support function for the membrane model 123
6.4 Diffusion with local stopping 125
6.5 A Bayesian model of stereo matching 127
6.5.1 The prior model 127
6.5.2 The measurement model 129
6.5.3 Explicit local distribution model 131
6.6 Experiments 134
6.7 Discussion and possible extensions 141
6.8 Summary 144

7. Conclusion 145
7.1 Contributions in view synthesis 145
7.2 Contributions in stereo 146
7.3 Extensions and future work 146

Bibliography 149

1. Introduction

View synthesis is the problem of generating images of a scene as it would appear from certain viewpoints. *Stereo vision* is the problem of inferring scene structure from two images taken from slightly different viewpoints. In many ways these are complementary problems: the former derives images from a scene description, while the latter derives a scene description from images.

Although closely related, the two problems have traditionally been studied by two different research communities. View synthesis is considered a *computer graphics* problem, while stereo vision is a problem in *computer vision.* In general, the field of computer graphics is concerned with creating two-dimensional images from three-dimensional scene models, while computer vision is concerned with extracting information about the three-dimensional world from two-dimensional images.

Both view synthesis and stereo vision are hard problems. The basic limitation of images created by computer graphics methods is the degree of realism that can be achieved. In stereo vision, on the other hand, the computed scene structure is inherently uncertain and noisy, and has only limited accuracy.

In this volume we examine the two problems in combination: we use stereo vision to synthesize new views. Surprisingly, we will see that both problems become easier when considered in combination than they are in isolation. The key insight is that the difficulties of either problem are intimately related to the dependence on a *global scene model.* By synthesizing new views from stereo data directly, using an *image-based* representation of scene structure, an explicit model of scene geometry can be avoided. In other words, we propose deriving new images from existing images without ever recovering a complete scene description.

Image-based scene representations have received much recent interest. In the last several years, other methods for synthesizing new views from existing images have also been proposed, contributing to the emerging field of *image-based rendering* (a term coined by McMillan and Bishop [1995b]). This text makes several new contributions:

First, making use of a special rectification step, a purely two-dimensional way of phrasing view synthesis as local image warping is presented. This enables the efficient generation of exact views under the full perspective model, while in many other approaches only an approximation of the new view is achieved.

Second, possible ways of dealing with insufficient information in the images are proposed. Occlusion and ambiguities in the stereo matching process can make the accurate prediction of new views impossible. While other authors have proposed adding more cameras and using more images (which is not always possible and creates other problems), we investigate what can be done in the basic case where only two images are available as input.

Third, the assumptions underlying traditional approaches to view synthesis and stereo vision are examined critically, and the requirements on stereo vision in light of the application of view synthesis are re-evaluated.

Finally, two new stereo methods that are motivated by these new requirements are presented.

1.1 The problem

The basic problem considered is the following: "Given a number of images of a scene, can we predict the appearance of the scene from a new viewpoint?" For example, consider the two images in Figure 1.1, showing a man and two children playing in a courtyard. These two images were taken simultaneously by two cameras from two slightly different viewpoints. The top image was taken from a viewpoint on the left; the bottom image was taken from a viewpoint on the right. Given these images, can we predict the view from a new viewpoint? Can we create a synthetic view corresponding to, say, a viewpoint lying above the original left view, or one lying halfway in between the original two views? The answer is yes – although with certain limitations. How this can be achieved is the topic of a large part of this volume. For now, to prove the point, Figure 1.2 shows a synthetic view corresponding to the center viewpoint. Before discussing how new views can be synthesized, however, we will briefly motivate why this is an important problem.

1.1.1 Applications

The problem of synthesizing new views from existing images is motivated by applications in *tele-reality* (a term coined by Szeliski [1994]). The concept of tele-reality is similar to that of virtual reality. In virtual reality, the idea is to convey the impression of a different reality to an observer, who can actively explore a (virtual) environment. This can be achieved with a head-mounted display that displays new views of a scene in accordance with the head movements of the user, thereby providing the illusion of immersion in the scene. In contrast with virtual reality, tele-reality communicates real, existing scenes (which can be remote either in space or time), while virtual reality typically refers to synthetic, nonexistent environments (e.g., video games and simulation).

Fig. 1.1. The *kids* image pair. The figure shows two images taken simultaneously by two cameras from slightly different viewpoints.

Fig. 1.2. A synthetic center view from a new viewpoint lying halfway in between the two views from Figure 1.1. This view has been synthesized only from the two existing views, without any additional knowledge about the scene geometry.

The emphasis in tele-reality is on realism: the synthetic views should resemble as closely as possible the real views of the existing scene. Such realism is not easily achieved with existing techniques from computer graphics, which are often restricted to simple environments composed from geometric primitives such as polyhedra or cylinders. It is possible to achieve higher realism using texture-mapping, i.e., by projecting pieces of real images onto the geometric model. The approach proposed here goes yet a step further, by constructing the synthetic views solely from the set of existing views without requiring any scene model.

Tele-reality, i.e., virtual presence in real scenes, has many applications. Some applications require real-time presence at remote sites, for example, teleconferencing, remote instruction, and remote medical diagnosis and surgery. Other applications require virtual presence in previously "recorded" environments, for purposes ranging from training in the use of expensive equipment (e.g., flight simulation) to remote shopping (e.g., purchase of a new house in a different country) to entertainment.

Fast methods for view synthesis are essential for tele-reality applications. These will become increasingly important in the next decade, following the shift from passive consumption of information (such as from conventional television) to interactive media. Besides the full immersion into a virtual environment via a head-mounted display, simpler forms of active exploration are also possible. This might include, for example, "low-cost virtual reality" capability on home TV sets equipped with a tracker that senses the position of the viewer's head. (To facilitate this task, the viewer could wear a small infrared transmitter.) Depending on the viewer's position, new views can then be synthesized to simulate a three-dimensional impression. This has been termed "fish-tank VR", as the virtual world is observed through the "window" of the screen in much the same way as one observes the fish in an aquarium.

1.1.2 The computer graphics approach

The synthesis of new views, in particular for virtual reality applications, has traditionally been a topic of the computer graphics community. Computer graphics is concerned with creating synthetic images from a 3D scene model by simulating the physics of light. Besides an explicit model of the scene geometry (e.g., a CAD model), this also requires models of illumination and surface reflectance properties. Given these models, synthetic images can then be rendered by tracing single rays of light (*ray tracing*), or by estimating the illumination distribution of all surface patches in parallel (*radiosity*). These processes are computationally very expensive, and, depending on the complexity of the scene, might take minutes or even hours for a single image, even when specialized hardware is employed.

For images of man-made objects, such as the interiors of buildings, the achieved realism is often quite impressive. The synthetic nature of images of people and of outdoor scenes, however, is usually obvious. Since the rendering time depends on scene complexity, this "synthetic look" is even worse for images generated by the relatively simple models and methods necessary to achieve real-time performance. As mentioned above, a partial remedy is *texture-mapping*, i.e., projecting real images onto the model surfaces. By "painting" parts of synthetic images with real textures, realism can be improved to some extent (which demonstrates the importance of real images for synthesizing realistic views).

Even if we gloss over the problems of low rendering speed and limited realism, the central problem with the computer graphics approach is its dependence on a global scene model. Acquiring such a model is non-trivial: how can one achieve accurate measurements of all the 3D coordinates in the scene? Yet another problem is that modeling techniques need to be updated whenever a new type of object or surface is encountered.

In many cases, scene models are constructed manually,[1] although considerable effort has been directed towards automating the process. For man-made scenes or objects, this is often referred to as "reverse engineering". It involves taking measurements with passive methods such as cameras (which is the subject of much work in computer vision and photogrammetry), or

[1] The modeling for the computer-animated movie "Toy Story" took over 10 person-years [Lasseter and Daly, 1995].

active methods such as laser-range finders. For some objects, such as trees or waterfalls, however, it can be infeasible or even impossible to construct an explicit model.

1.1.3 Avoiding the model

The discussion above illustrates that the traditional computer graphics approach has several shortcomings. Ideally, for tele-reality applications, a view synthesis method should be fast (independent of scene geometry), yield high realism, and should avoid the problems associated with acquiring global models. This motivates the approach taken in this volume. The key idea is to use a set of images to represent a scene or an object. Between pairs of images, *correspondence maps* can be computed with stereo vision techniques. Such correspondence maps give direct information about the relative depth of the visible scene points. Thus, each map constitutes an *image-based* representation of scene geometry; its information can be used to warp the existing images into new images corresponding to new viewpoints. *Warping* refers to a (not necessarily continuous) transformation of image coordinates, i.e., each image point (or *pixel*) is mapped to a new position. Figure 1.1.3 illustrates this idea.

Synthesizing new views from a single stereo pair is the basic building block of a larger framework for view synthesis, in which a scene is represented by a graph consisting of images and correspondence maps. The vertices in this graph are views from physical locations in the scene, while the edges in the graph are the correspondence maps between adjacent views. This approach has the advantage that a global model is not necessary, as new views can be synthesized from two nearby reference images and their correspondence map. Also, warping can be performed much faster than image rendering, and the warping time is largely independent of scene complexity. An additional advantage of using only a small number of local images to synthesize new views is that we only need to know the relative configurations between adjacent views, which do not need to be globally consistent. For example, images could be acquired with a hand-held camera and be labeled with rough global coordinates.

A disadvantage of the approach is that stereo provides only limited information about the scene, in particular due to occlusion. A view synthesis method based on stereo must be able to deal with previously invisible scene points, and also with partially occluded points, i.e., with points that are only visible in one reference view, and whose depth is unknown. Missing information due to occlusion can make it impossible to synthesize the *correct* view, but, using heuristics, it is often possible to synthesize a *plausible* view that looks convincing to an observer. To avoid visual artifacts (i.e., noticeable rendering errors such as single miscolored pixels), the sampling of reference

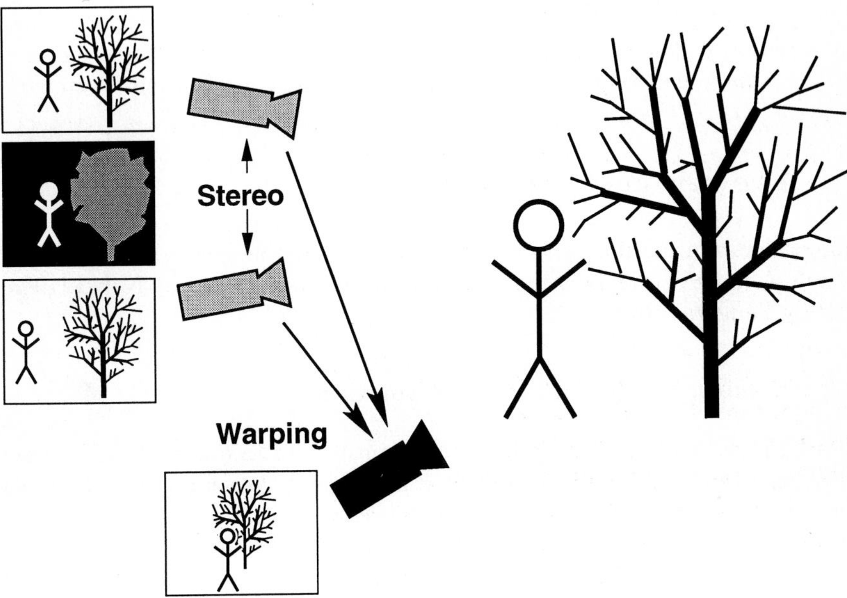

Fig. 1.3. View synthesis using stereo and warping. Two real cameras (shown in gray) observe a scene. Their images together with a *depth map* computed by stereo vision techniques constitute an image-based scene representation, from which a new view corresponding to a hypothetical camera (shown in black) can be synthesized by *image warping*.

images needs to be reasonably dense, so that only small changes in viewpoint are required.[2]

Another problem is that stereo suffers from certain well-known problems: it only yields limited depth resolution, and the matching process is prone to errors, in particular in the presence of repetitive patterns and uniform regions. It turns out, however, that many of these traditional shortcomings of stereo have less significance in view synthesis. The reason is that the output of stereo is not used to create an explicit three-dimensional scene model, but only to predict the local image changes between the existing reference views and the new synthetic views. For example, the geometry of a uniform image region can not be recovered, but a new view can usually be predicted. Thus, by avoiding a global model, both stereo vision and view synthesis become easier. This makes view synthesis an interesting new application for stereo.

1.2 A review of stereo vision

For readers not familiar with computer vision, we now give a brief review of stereo. A more detailed discussion can be found in the books by Nalwa [1993] and by Faugeras [1993].

1.2.1 Camera model and image formation

Throughout this text, we use perspective projection as our geometric model of image formation: an image is formed by projecting each scene point along a straight line through the *center of projection* onto an image plane. This is commonly referred to as the pinhole camera model (see Figure 1.4): light originating from the scene passes through a pinhole in the front of an opaque box onto a transparent surface at the rear of the box, where it creates a reversed image of the scene. The pinhole camera is a powerful model that resembles very closely the operation of real cameras. The only principal differences are that real cameras have a lens instead of a simple hole, and the imaging surface is an array of sensors. Geometric distortions introduced by the lens are not accounted for by the pinhole model, but can be corrected by an initial image transform. Also not modeled are blurring due to limited depth of field and lens aberrations.

Mathematically, perspective projection is most easily described using *homogeneous coordinates* (also called *projective coordinates*). In homogeneous coordinates, each point is extended by a dummy coordinate $w \neq 0$ that maps the point to a line through the origin in a space whose dimension is one higher than that of the original space. For example, a two-dimensional (image) point

[2] A denser sampling, while requiring that more views be stored, also allows a higher degree of compression [Levoy and Hanrahan, 1996].

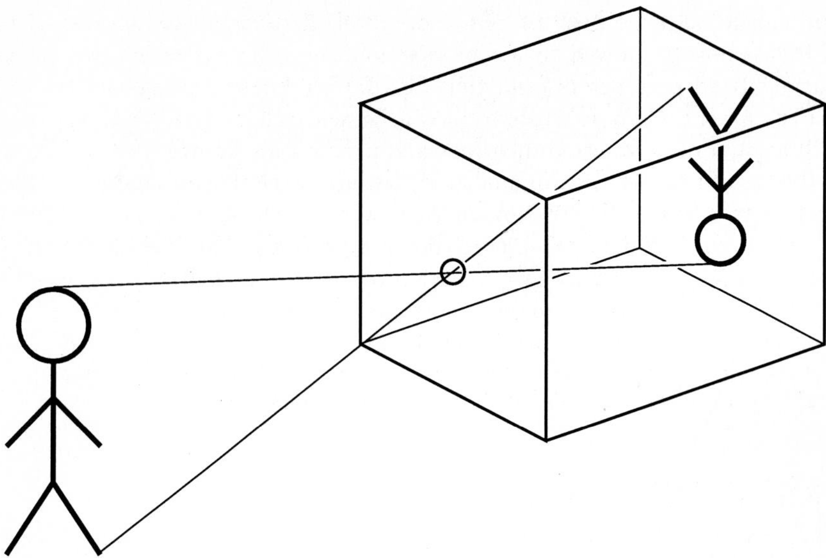

Fig. 1.4. The pinhole camera model. A 2D image of a 3D object is formed by perspective projection: each ray of light passes through a common *center of projection* and intersects the *image plane* at a unique position.

(x, y) is represented by the set of vectors $[wx \;\; wy \;\; w]^T$, $w \neq 0$ in homogeneous coordinates. Similarly, a three-dimensional (scene) point (X, Y, Z) is represented by the set of vectors $[wX \;\; wY \;\; wZ \;\; w]^T$, $w \neq 0$.[3] Although homogeneous coordinates are redundant, they are very useful as they allow us to express otherwise non-linear transformations linearly. In particular, the perspective projection of a 3D scene point onto a 2D image plane can be written with the following linear equation using homogeneous coordinates:

$$\begin{bmatrix} u \\ v \\ w \end{bmatrix} = \begin{bmatrix} & & \\ & \mathbf{P} & \\ & & \end{bmatrix} \begin{bmatrix} X \\ Y \\ Z \\ 1 \end{bmatrix} . \qquad (1.1)$$

In this equation, (X, Y, Z) are the coordinates of a scene point (in an arbitrary 3D coordinate system), and $(x, y) = (u/w, v/w)$ are the coordinates of its projection (in an arbitrary 2D image coordinate system). The *projection matrix* $\mathbf{P}$ is a 3×4 matrix defined up to a scalar factor that captures both the *extrinsic* and *intrinsic* camera parameters. The extrinsic parameters specify the position and orientation of the camera with respect to the scene coordinate system, while the intrinsic parameters specify the focal length, the

[3] We use upper and lowercase letters for scene and image quantities, respectively. Matrices and vector quantities (including points and lines) are typeset in boldface.

aspect ratio, and the position of the origin of the image coordinate system. (If the camera is moved to a new position, only the extrinsic parameters change.) If all parameters (and thus also **P**) are known, we speak of a *calibrated* camera. Camera calibration can be achieved by observing a special calibration object, whose dimensions and position are known.

To transform the optical, analog image into an electrical, digital one, the continuous intensity distribution on the image plane is both *sampled* spatially on a rectangular grid, and *quantized* into integer values. This yields the typical representation of an image as a 2D array of discrete intensity values, usually called *pixels* (short for picture element). See Figure 1.5 for an example. Color images can be encoded by three such intensity images, each representing one of three color components (usually red, green, and blue). In this case, each pixel is a triplet of integers.

1.2.2 Stereo geometry

Stereo vision (or stereopsis) is the process of estimating the depth of scene points from their change in position between two images. This is done effortlessly by the human visual system, which translates the differences between the views from the two eyes into a three-dimensional impression of the scene. Figure 1.6 illustrates how the *disparity*, or change of image location, of a point is related to its depth for two identical parallel cameras. The figure shows a scene point **P** and its two images $\mathbf{p}_L$ and $\mathbf{p}_R$ in the left and right images, respectively. Let us denote the *focal length* (i.e., the distance of the center of projection to the image plane) by f and the *baseline* (i.e., the distance between the two cameras) by b. Then, given that the scene point **P** has distance Z and lateral offset X (with respect to the left camera), and given further that **P**'s images $\mathbf{p}_L$ and $\mathbf{p}_R$ have coordinates x_L and x_R, we can conclude from consideration of similar triangles that

$$\frac{x_L}{f} = \frac{X}{Z} \quad \text{and} \quad \frac{x_R}{f} = \frac{X+b}{Z}.$$

The *disparity* d, i.e., the change in image location is

$$d = x_R - x_L = \frac{fb}{Z}. \tag{1.2}$$

Note that the disparity of a point is proportional to focal length and baseline, and inversely proportional to its depth. Since focal length and baseline are constant over the entire image, the disparity map provides a direct (but inverse) encoding of scene depth. The following simple experiment illustrates this inverse relationship between disparity and depth: hold up one finger and blink between the left and right eyes while fixing the gaze on a distant object. The closer the finger is held to the eyes (i.e., the smaller the depth), the further the image of the finger jumps (i.e., the higher the disparity).

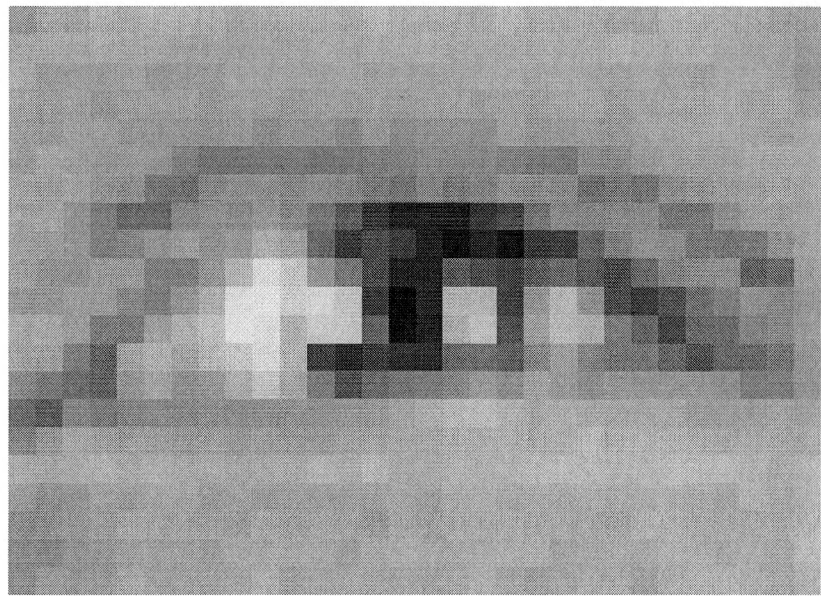

152	166	165	181	171	181	182	181	171	177	181	181	178	193	182	183	181	178	193	182	178	181	171	166	182	178	171	168	165	159
168	171	171	181	171	168	166	171	173	171	177	181	178	181	181	187	181	178	181	181	181	181	187	181	181	178	173	168	168	156
171	159	165	163	167	157	161	163	178	171	171	171	178	168	171	177	178	178	181	171	178	171	171	177	168	163	173	171	168	152
166	163	168	158	166	166	171	167	171	168	166	171	173	177	168	177	178	168	173	168	177	178	168	173	177	177	178	168	181	163
159	160	167	167	157	159	160	159	163	150	156	157	147	163	150	156	160	152	168	160	161	165	165	168	177	171	178	168	166	171
157	171	165	157	159	157	138	127	127	133	133	127	133	138	140	147	147	145	138	133	127	147	147	160	166	165	165	171	177	171
168	166	171	159	152	127	127	147	154	154	147	152	147	138	133	147	140	145	157	152	147	127	138	127	150	160	165	167	177	168
165	168	152	133	117	116	145	152	147	157	145	127	109	87	75	75	74	87	99	127	145	145	147	147	127	127	147	165	165	167
159	160	152	133	138	152	163	152	157	181	166	117	87	99	87	75	62	75	62	87	91	117	138	152	147	127	123	127	152	163
159	150	147	157	157	133	133	154	190	229	206	152	127	99	74	74	109	99	93	109	116	108	99	117	138	145	147	109	116	157
147	150	160	156	138	127	150	178	231	234	213	224	210	86	47	74	193	190	91	152	193	150	99	87	99	117	127	145	138	147
166	171	160	123	123	159	181	199	235	227	181	210	210	108	47	68	182	201	99	161	193	181	133	109	91	109	109	133	138	152
163	163	133	109	166	182	166	193	206	226	187	87	75	87	79	79	116	116	108	139	161	138	127	123	109	99	109	109	123	147
140	127	117	109	152	166	147	156	182	201	168	127	99	116	123	133	140	156	145	166	156	147	156	152	152	152	147	127	133	147
117	108	138	127	138	138	140	150	145	145	150	147	152	156	166	181	193	193	181	171	181	171	171	168	168	157	157	159	166	161
138	156	171	166	163	160	156	165	157	161	160	156	163	166	171	171	182	178	181	181	178	190	183	181	182	171	166	171	168	168
166	166	173	181	168	173	166	171	167	168	168	181	171	187	168	171	181	177	181	187	187	187	183	181	187	187	187	177	168	182
152	147	152	165	160	163	167	159	165	157	161	158	161	163	168	163	171	177	167	171	168	178	177	171	178	168	165	181	171	178
140	147	152	157	166	165	167	167	160	168	163	163	167	157	168	165	171	171	178	171	171	171	168	181	181	171	168	168	173	181
138	138	147	150	157	160	163	160	168	168	168	167	160	168	178	171	168	171	177	178	165	171	177	168	181	178	168	171	168	187
138	152	147	150	163	157	159	160	165	171	160	161	165	165	163	165	167	171	165	159	165	171	171	160	177	178	181	171	168	182

Fig. 1.5. An *image* is represented on a computer by a rectangular array of *pixels*. Each pixel is an integer value representing the intensity at that point.

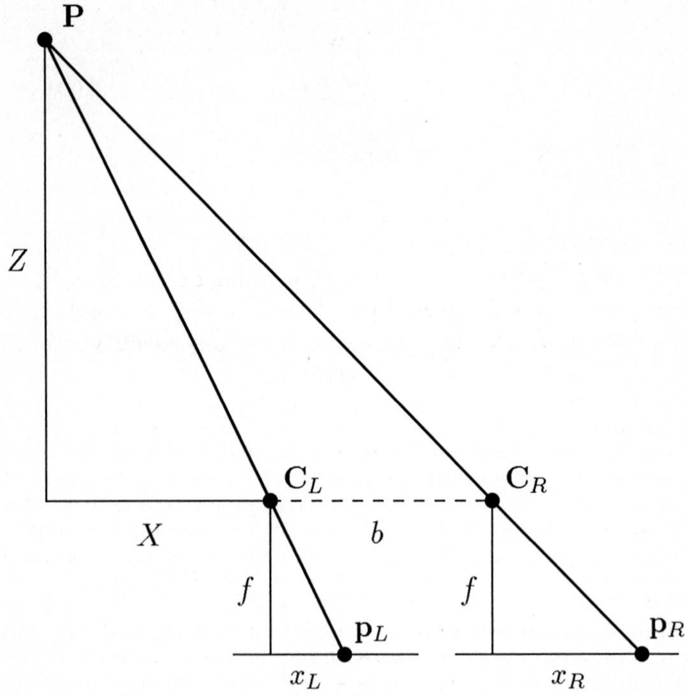

Fig. 1.6. Stereo geometry. The figure shows a top-down view of two identical parallel cameras with focal length f and at distance b to each other. The disparity of a scene point $\mathbf{P}$ of depth Z is $d = x_R - x_L = fb/Z$.

1.2.3 The correspondence problem

How do we know that $\mathbf{p}_L$ and $\mathbf{p}_R$ *correspond*, that is, that they are really the projections of the same scene point $\mathbf{P}$? Solving this *correspondence problem*, i.e., finding for each point in one image the matching point in the other image, is the hard part of stereo. Difficulties include matching ambiguities due to repetitive patterns and locally uniform intensities, as well as uncertain intensity values due to noise introduced by the imaging process. Also, we are implicitly assuming that corresponding points have the same intensity in both images. In technical terms, this is equivalent to assuming that the scene is composed of *Lambertian* surfaces, i.e., perfectly matte surfaces whose brightness depends only on the angle of incident light (which remains constant for two images taken simultaneously) and not on the angle of observation. Obviously, this need not be true, and specularities or reflections typically present problems for stereo algorithms (as do semi-transparent surfaces). Even when the Lambertian assumption holds, matching points can have different intensities if the cameras differ in *bias* or *gain* (i.e., constant additive or multiplicative intensity factors), or due to *vignetting* (i.e., an uneven brightness distribution in the image, yielding darker corners).

Yet another problem are partially occluded points (i.e., points visible from only one camera) that can not be matched. Correctly identifying and dealing with partially occluded points is especially important in the context of view synthesis, and will be discussed in detail in Chapter 4. Excluding occlusion from our discussion for now, the main reason that establishing correspondences is difficult is that the amount of information available at a single pixel (i.e., its intensity, which is typically corrupted by noise) is usually not enough for finding an unambiguous match. Since matching of single pixels is an unstable process, it is necessary to consider small local neighborhoods around each pixel to reduce the ambiguity. Even so, often only image locations with a large amount of information, such as intensity edges or corners, can be matched unambiguously.

There are two common approaches to this dilemma. The first approach is to deal only with points that can be matched unambiguously. This is the idea behind *feature-based* stereo algorithms, which first extract points of high local information (e.g., using an edge detector), and then restrict the correspondence search to those pre-selected *features*. This has the obvious drawback of yielding only a sparse disparity map, and disparity estimates for non-feature points have to be interpolated.

A different possibility is to consider larger image regions (or *areas*) that contain enough information to yield unambiguous matches. This second approach is usually called *area-based* stereo matching, and has the advantage of yielding a dense disparity map. It relies on the assumption, however, that most points in the area under consideration have the same disparity, which is not necessarily the case. Still, as the application of view synthesis requires a disparity estimate at every pixel, the focus of this volume is on area-based

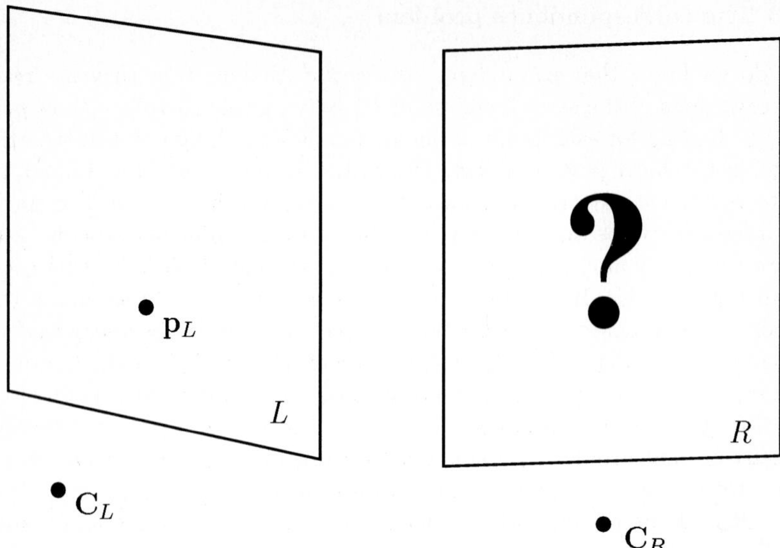

Fig. 1.7. Searching for correspondences. Given two cameras $(\mathbf{C}_L, L)$ and $(\mathbf{C}_R, R)$ and an observed point $\mathbf{p}_L$, where do we search for the corresponding point $\mathbf{p}_R$?

stereo methods. We present several new area-based approaches in Chapters 5 and 6. These have been motivated by shortcomings of previous methods, and also by the particular requirements imposed by the application of view synthesis.

1.2.4 The epipolar constraint

So far we have discussed how matching image locations can be found. We now turn to the question of *where* to look for potential matches. This problem is illustrated in Figure 1.7: Suppose we have two cameras, specified by their centers of projection $\mathbf{C}_L$ and $\mathbf{C}_R$ and their image planes L and R. Given that we observe the image $\mathbf{p}_L$ of a scene point in the left image, where do we search in the right image for its corresponding point $\mathbf{p}_R$? It turns out that instead of having to search the entire image, we can restrict the search to a single line, the *epipolar line* $\mathbf{e}_R$ corresponding to $\mathbf{p}_L$. This reduces the search from 2D to 1D, which is an enormous help in establishing correspondences.

To see why the corresponding point $\mathbf{p}_R$ must lie on a line, observe that any scene point $\mathbf{P}$ projecting to $\mathbf{p}_L$ has to lie on the *projection ray* defined by $\mathbf{p}_L$, i.e., the line through $\mathbf{C}_L$ and $\mathbf{p}_L$. Assuming for a moment that this ray is visible from the right camera, $\mathbf{p}_R$ must lie on the *image* of this ray in the right image plane. We call this image the *epipolar line* $\mathbf{e}_R$ defined by $\mathbf{p}_L$. In other words, the epipolar line $\mathbf{e}_R$ is the image (in the right camera) of all possible locations of a scene point $\mathbf{P}$ that would project to $\mathbf{p}_L$ in the left

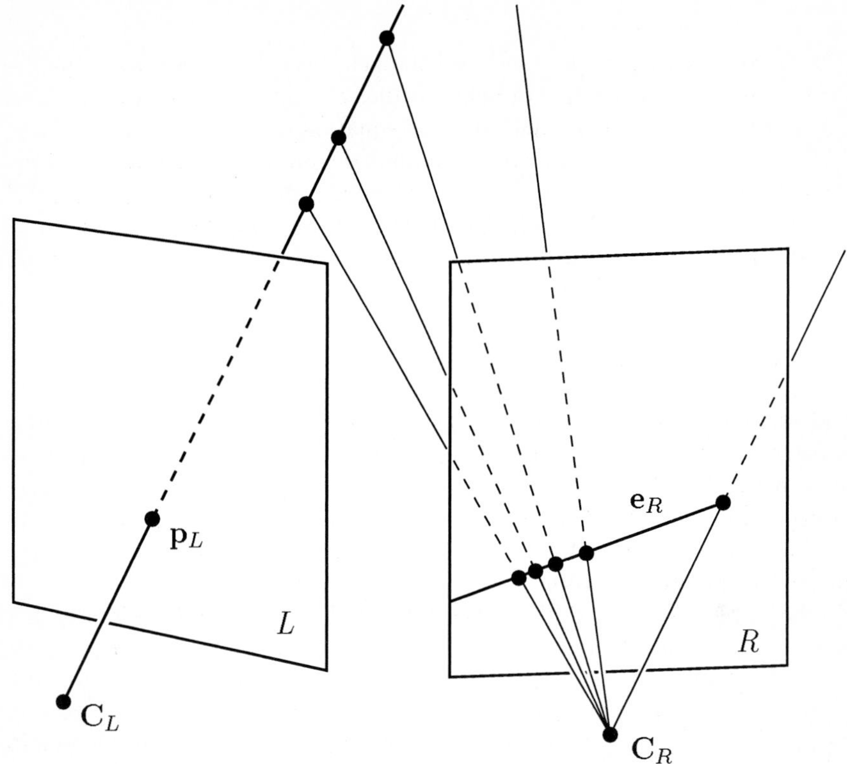

Fig. 1.8. The epipolar constraint. The point corresponding to $\mathbf{p}_L$ must lie on $\mathbf{p}_L$'s *epipolar line* $\mathbf{e}_R$, the *image* of the projection ray defined by $\mathbf{p}_L$.

camera. This is illustrated in Figure 1.8. Note that, geometrically, $\mathbf{e}_R$ is the intersection of the plane defined by $\mathbf{p}_L$, $\mathbf{C}_L$, and $\mathbf{C}_R$ with the right image plane R.

The epipolar geometry, that is, the relationship between points in one image and their corresponding epipolar lines in the other, can easily be computed if the configurations of both cameras (the positions of centers of projection $\mathbf{C}_L$ and $\mathbf{C}_R$ and image planes L and R) are known (in some global coordinate system). This is called a *fully calibrated* stereo setup, and the 3D coordinates of a scene point $\mathbf{P}$ can be computed from the coordinates of its two images $\mathbf{p}_L$ and $\mathbf{p}_R$.

To establish correspondences between the two images, however, it is sufficient to know only the epipolar geometry, which can be characterized concisely with the *fundamental matrix* $\mathbf{F}$, a 3×3 matrix defined up to a scalar factor. This matrix $\mathbf{F}$ relates a point $\mathbf{p}$ (in homogeneous coordinates) in one image with its corresponding epipolar line $\mathbf{e}$ in the other image via the equation

$$\mathbf{F}\mathbf{p} = \mathbf{e}. \tag{1.3}$$

Recall that a point $\mathbf{p} = [u \;\; v \;\; w]^T$ in homogeneous coordinates describes the point $(x, y) = (u/w, v/w)$. We define a *line* $\mathbf{e} = [a \;\; b \;\; c]^T$ in homogeneous coordinates to describe the line with the equation $ax + by + c = 0$.[4]

The fundamental matrix can be computed from the two images directly, by establishing a small number of point-to-point correspondences [Luong and Faugeras, 1996; Zhang, 1998a]. If we know only the epipolar geometry (i.e., the fundamental matrix), but not the explicit camera configurations, we speak of a *weakly calibrated* setup.

1.2.5 A simple stereo geometry

A particularly simple epipolar geometry results from two identical, parallel cameras whose image planes coincide and whose x-axes are parallel to the baseline (the line connecting their centers of projection). In this case, corresponding epipolar lines are horizontal and have the same y-coordinate (i.e., they are corresponding *scanlines*). In fact, this is the situation that was depicted in Figure 1.6.

The stereo matching problem is much easier in this simple geometry, because matching points must have identical y-coordinates (and the explicit computation of epipolar lines is not required). Furthermore, rectangular image regions (or regions of any shape) can be compared directly, whereas in the general case (for example, with verging cameras), a rectangular region in one image can correspond to any quadrilateral in the other image.

For these reasons, most stereo algorithms assume the simple stereo geometry of parallel identical cameras with coinciding image planes. The fundamental matrix describing this scenario (up to a scalar multiplier) is

$$\mathbf{F}_{\text{simple}} = \begin{bmatrix} 0 & 0 & 0 \\ 0 & 0 & 1 \\ 0 & -1 & 0 \end{bmatrix}. \tag{1.4}$$

(One can easily verify that this matrix maps a point $[wp_x \;\; wp_y \;\; w]^T$ to the line $[0 \;\; w \;\; -wp_y]^T$, i.e., the line with the equation $y = p_y$.)

Note that our definitions of *depth* and *disparity* as well as the inverse relationship between them only apply in this simple geometry. In particular, the depth of a (scene) point is its distance to the plane through the two camera

[4] Using this representation for points and lines has several advantages. It requires no special cases for vertical lines or points at infinity, and allows easy checks: for example, a point $\mathbf{p}$ lies on a line $\mathbf{e}$ if and only if their dot-product $\mathbf{p}^T\mathbf{e}$ is zero. The notation also captures the duality between points and lines in the plane in an elegant way: the line $\mathbf{g}$ defined by two points $\mathbf{p}$ and $\mathbf{q}$ is simply their cross-product $\mathbf{g} = \mathbf{p} \times \mathbf{q}$; analogously, the point $\mathbf{p}$ defined by the intersection of two lines $\mathbf{g}$ and $\mathbf{h}$ is $\mathbf{p} = \mathbf{g} \times \mathbf{h}$. Note that in equations involving homogeneous vectors, we use the equal sign "=" to denote equality up to a scalar factor.

Fig. 1.9. A stereo rig with two identical, parallel cameras.

centers parallel to the (common) image plane, and the disparity of a point is its difference in image coordinates (using two identical image coordinate systems offset in x-direction by a baseline of length b).

In the general case with different, non-parallel cameras, there is no longer a single obvious direction with respect to which depth can be defined. It is also more difficult to define disparity given two independent image coordinate systems in general position to each other.

Instead of trying to extend our definitions to the general case, we go a different way: we *only* consider the simple geometry. Obviously, one way of achieving the simple camera geometry is to mount and carefully adjust two cameras in such a way that they are perfectly parallel. Such a *stereo rig* with two parallel cameras is shown in Figure 1.9. However, even for two cameras in general position, the simple geometry can be achieved by *rectification*.

1.2.6 Rectification

Rectification is the process of *reprojecting* the two images onto a common image plane that is parallel to the baseline. This is illustrated in Figure 1.10. Note that no knowledge of scene geometry is required in order to reproject an image, since only the image plane changes position, while the center of projection and all projection rays remain stationary. Mathematically, any

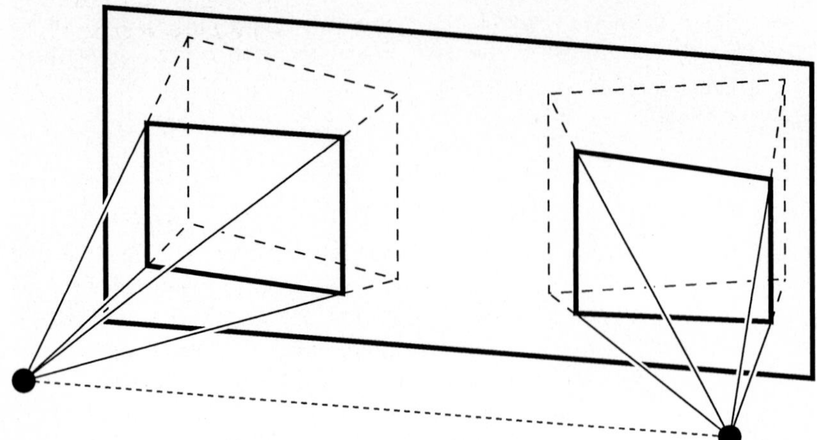

Fig. 1.10. Rectification. The simple stereo geometry can be derived from a general configuration by reprojecting the two images onto a plane parallel to the baseline.

such reprojection onto a new plane can be described by a 3×3 projection matrix (or *homography*) $\mathbf{H}$, again defined up to a scalar factor. This matrix constitutes a *coordinate transform* (in homogeneous coordinates) from the original image to the reprojected image:

$$\begin{bmatrix} u' \\ v' \\ w' \end{bmatrix} = \mathbf{H} \begin{bmatrix} u \\ v \\ w \end{bmatrix} . \tag{1.5}$$

Thus, rectification of a stereo pair can be achieved by applying two appropriate homographies $\mathbf{H}_L$ and $\mathbf{H}_R$ to the two images. In a calibrated setup, $\mathbf{H}_L$ and $\mathbf{H}_R$ can easily be derived from the known position and orientation of the two cameras. Rectification is also possible in a weakly calibrated setup, i.e., if only the fundamental matrix $\mathbf{F}$ is known [Robert *et al.*, 1995; Seitz and Dyer, 1996a].

Note that the only requirement for the new common image plane is that it must be parallel to the baseline. This leaves two free parameters: its distance and its orientation (i.e., angle of rotation). The distance is less interesting, since it only amounts to globally scaling the coordinates. The rotation angle, on the other hand, affects the distortion of the rectified images. This parameter plays an important role in the view synthesis procedure presented in Chapter 3. For traditional stereo applications it is often chosen so as to minimize some measure of overall image distortion.

Finally, explicit rectification requires the re-sampling of the images, usually using backward mapping. For each pixel (x', y') in the rectified image, the corresponding image position (x, y) in the original image is computed using $\mathbf{H}^{-1}$. Since these coordinates are real-valued, an intensity value must be interpolated from the four nearest pixels (at integer-valued coordinates). Bi-linear interpolation is the simplest choice, but more complicated methods such as cubic spline interpolation are also possible. More information on image transforms can be found in the book by Wolberg [1990].

1.2.7 Example: SSD

We finish our brief review of stereo with an example: the classic sum-of-squared differences (SSD) algorithm. This is a very simple example of an area-based stereo algorithm. Assuming rectified images, the best match for a point in one image is found by comparing a square window centered at this point against windows of equal size centered at points that lie on the corresponding scanline in the other image. The sum of the squared intensity differences across the window is used as a measure of dissimilarity. The location that minimizes this measure is selected as the best match, and the disparity, i.e., the horizontal offset between the matching locations, is stored. Figure 1.11 shows pseudocode for the SSD algorithm.

Note that the algorithm in the figure does not handle the image boundaries: it is assumed that the images extend sufficiently beyond the area over which the disparity map is computed. A real implementation needs to make sure that the window does not extend beyond the image boundaries. Also, assuming a window size of $w \times w$, the running time of the algorithm can be improved by a factor of w^2, by accumulating the squared differences by convolution with two one-dimensional box filters.

Figure 1.12 shows disparity maps computed by the SSD algorithm. The top half of the figure shows the stereo pair used as input. These are images 18 and 24 from the Stanford *tree* sequence (provided by Harlyn Baker and Bob Bolles at SRI), which was taken by a single camera mounted on a horizontal motion stage (yielding the simple stereo geometry). The bottom half shows two disparity maps using two different window sizes: 3×3 (left) and 7×7 (right). The disparities are displayed using a graylevel encoding. Close points (large disparities) are shown light; far points (small disparities) are shown dark.

The figure illustrates the basic trade-off involved in selecting the best window size, which is a problem for all window-based techniques. A small window results in many wrong matches due to ambiguities and noise, but preserves object shapes in relatively fine detail. A large window cuts down on the wrong matches, but also starts to blur the object boundaries. This problem of selecting the best window size is the motivation behind the diffusion-based stereo techniques in Chapter 6.

SSD

Input: *two intensity images* ImL[x, y], ImR[x, y]

Output: *disparity map* Disp[x, y] *w.r.t. the left image*

Parameters: *disparity range* dmin..dmax
window size wsize

```
for x := xmin to xmax do
   for y := ymin to ymax do
      best_ssd := MAXINT;
      for d := dmin to dmax do
         ssd := 0;
         for xx := x-wsize/2 to x+wsize/2 do
            for yy := y-wsize/2 to y+wsize/2 do
               diff := ImL[xx, yy] - ImR[xx+d, yy];
               ssd := ssd + diff*diff
            end for yy
         end for xx;
         if (ssd < best_ssd) then
            best_ssd := ssd;
            best_d := d
         end if
      end for d;
      Disp[x, y] := best_d
   end for y
end for x
```

Fig. 1.11. Pseudocode for the SSD algorithm.

Fig. 1.12. Disparity maps computed by the SSD algorithm. The image pair is shown at the top; two disparity maps computed with different window sizes are shown at the bottom. Disparities are encoded with graylevels: dark represents far, light represents close.

1.3 Contributions and outline

In this volume, we show that stereo vision is well-suited for the application of view synthesis, and demonstrate that it is possible to efficiently synthesize realistic new views from existing images using stereo data. The main contributions with respect to view synthesis are:

- a purely two-dimensional way of formalizing view synthesis under the full perspective model as rectification, linear warping, and derectification;
- possible ways of dealing with regions of unknown geometry due to partial occlusion and regions of unknown intensities due to total occlusion;
- a re-evaluation of the requirements on stereo algorithms in light of the new application of view synthesis.

Additional contributions are several novel stereo algorithms that are motivated by the requirements imposed by view synthesis, including:

- a new gradient-based stereo method combining the notions of similarity and confidence, offering an easy way to deal with image regions of uniform intensity;
- several new diffusion-based stereo algorithms motivated by the problem of boundary blurring, including a Bayesian estimation technique that significantly outperforms traditional window-based techniques such as SSD.

After a review of related work in Chapter 2, the main focus of this text is on two topics: view synthesis (Chapters 3 and 4), and actual stereo algorithms (Chapters 5 and 6).

Chapter 3 presents the algorithm used to synthesize new views from a stereo pair. Chapter 4 contains an evaluation of stereo in light of the requirements imposed by the application of view synthesis, including possible ways of dealing with occlusion. Chapter 5 introduces a new stereo method based on comparing image gradients. In Chapter 6 we explore different stereo algorithms based on diffusion, including an algorithm derived from a Bayesian model of stereo matching. We conclude in Chapter 7 with a summary and a discussion of possible directions for future work.

2. A Survey of Image-Based Rendering and Stereo

The purpose of this chapter is to provide a compact overview of work done by others relating to the topics presented in this volume. We first discuss work relating to the topic of view synthesis from real images (image-based rendering). We then give a broader overview of related work in stereo vision. The chapter concludes by providing a list of books on computer vision and related areas.

While much of the discussion in this chapter is at a general level, there are several passages that make reference to concepts that will not be explained until later chapters. These sections are aimed at readers who are familiar with computer vision, and may safely be skipped by others.

2.1 Image-based rendering

View synthesis from real images is a topic that has received much recent interest. Creating new views without a scene model is also an emerging field in the computer graphics community, where it is called *image-based rendering.* Recent surveys of image-based rendering methods are provided by Kang [1997] and Zhang [1998b]. An overview of recent developments from a computer graphics perspective is given by Lengyel [1998].

In discussing work related to the view synthesis problem, we distinguish between three different approaches. The first – the one pursued in this volume – is to synthesize new views from few reference images using stereo vision techniques. The aim of methods following this approach is to construct correct synthetic views for a wide range of viewpoints (in the vicinity of the original views). These methods can be further subdivided into those that construct new views directly from the given images, and those that first build an explicit 3D model from which new views can be rendered using traditional computer graphics techniques (e.g., texture mapping).

The second approach is called *view interpolation.* The idea is to synthesize only those views lying on the straight line connecting two reference views. Many view interpolation methods do not solve the exact reconstruction problem (under perspective projection), but only *approximate* the intermediate view. Furthermore, depth discontinuities and occlusion are often not considered by these methods.

The third approach is to utilize the information from many images, typically an image sequence taken with a video camera. Example applications include constructing a layered representation of scene structure, or combining all images into a single 3D-corrected *mosaic*.

We consider each approach in turn.

2.1.1 View synthesis based on stereo

The earliest papers that describe methods for synthesizing new views using stereo data are motivated by the application of 3D teleconferencing and the creation of "virtual eye contact". Skerjanc and Liu [1991] use a calibrated trinocular setup and an edge-based stereo algorithm to synthesize intermediate views. Ott *et al.* [1993] create a virtual center view from two off-center views provided by cameras mounted on either side of a teleconferencing monitor using a dynamic-programming stereo method [Cox *et al.*, 1992a].

Laveau and Faugeras [1994] describe a method for constructing a new view directly from weakly calibrated images, without any reconstruction in three dimensions. A new viewing configuration is specified by manually selecting four points in each of the existing images. These points correspond to the images of the focal point and of three points defining the retinal plane of the virtual camera. Assuming a given disparity map, the authors then present two ways of constructing the new view using either forward or backward remapping of pixels.

McMillan and Bishop [1995b] introduce the term *image-based rendering* (now widely used for the field of view synthesis from real images). They describe a method for synthesizing new views from two cylindrical panoramic views created by mosaicing (see also McMillan [1995a]). Image-based rendering is characterized as "reconstructing a continuous representation of the plenoptic function from a set of discrete samples of that function."[1] Disparity maps are computed between adjacent cylindrical panoramas using a cylindrical variant of the epipolar constraint, and new views are synthesized by warping (forward-mapping) the existing panoramas based on the disparities. The method does not deal with partially occluded points, and holes in the new view are simply filled by interpolation. More information about this method can be found in McMillan's dissertation [McMillan, 1997].

In other work [McMillan and Bishop, 1995a], the authors describe an implementation of (almost) real-time viewpoint generation in a head-mounted display using image warping based on a generalized depth map (which is assumed to be given). The authors also present a simple algorithm for visibility resolution based on forward mapping (given parallel viewing planes), which is employed in the view synthesis method described in Chapter 3.

[1] The plenoptic function [Adelson and Bergen, 1991] describes the (visual) information available to an observer at any possible viewpoint.

Fuchs *et al.* [1994] describe the concept of teleconferencing using "a sea of cameras," in which a user wearing a head-mounted display observes synthetic views of a scene that are generated in real time corresponding to the motion of the user. The authors describe a prototype system based on multiple-baseline stereo [Okutomi and Kanade, 1993]. Images are mapped onto the polygonally-meshed depth map and re-rendered using standard computer graphics techniques.

Kanade *et al.* [1995] describe a similar system for "virtualized reality," also based on re-rendering real images that have been mapped onto polygonal meshes. The meshes are computed from hand-edited depth maps acquired by multiple-baseline stereo. Both Fuchs *et al.* and Kanade *et al.* describe the vision of a complete tele-reality scenario using a large number of reference views, and give preliminary results to show the feasibility of the proposed framework. Using a real-time stereo machine [Kanade *et al.*, 1996], another proposed application is *Z keying*: merging the real image with a virtual (computer graphics) image. The two images are combined, and visibility is resolved by comparing their depths in real time.

Satoh *et al.* [1996] present a 3D imaging system with motion parallax. Correct new views are generated depending on the position of the viewer's head, both for fixed and head-mounted screens. The 3D scene information is derived using a 3×3 camera matrix, which allows robust detection of occlusion and precise localization of object boundaries [Nakamura *et al.*, 1996; Satoh and Ohta, 1996].

The approaches discussed above represented the state of the art when the view synthesis method presented in this volume was first published [Scharstein, 1996]. Many of these approaches do not deal with problems related to depth discontinuities and occlusion, and few recognize the importance of the changed requirements on stereo algorithms, issues that are addressed in Chapters 3 and 4. Discussed below are more recent methods, several of which have made significant progress on these issues.

Kanade, Narayana, and Rander [Kanade *et al.*, 1997; Rander *et al.*, 1997; Narayanan *et al.*, 1998] present several new results in the context of their virtualized reality project. The input data are synchronized video streams taken in the "3D Dome", a spherical studio with 51 calibrated cameras. New image sequences of dynamic scenes can be generated from two different scene representations: either from local *visible surface models*, which are purely image-based, or from a global texture-mapped polygonal *complete scene model*. They also present experiments in which virtual objects are introduced into the synthesized images.

Chang and Zakhor [1997] build an image-based scene representation from an image sequence acquired with a hand-held camcorder. Similar to the approach presented here, new views are generated from dense depth maps associated with selected reference viewpoints along the camera trajectory. The depth maps are constructed from multiple images with a stereo algorithm that uses variable-sized support regions and cubic spline interpolation in low-confidence image regions. New views are generated from the three closest views by rendering each pixel as a rectangular patch. Holes in the resulting view are filled by interpolation.

Avidan and Shashua [1997] present a new algorithm for view synthesis based on Shashua's trilinear tensor framework [Shashua, 1995]. In contrast to methods based on epipolar line intersection [Laveau and Faugeras, 1994; Faugeras and Robert, 1996], the tensor approach does not suffer from singular configurations that arise when the camera centers are collinear. Avidan *et al.* [1997] apply their method to the synthesis of novel views of flexible 3D objects, in particular human faces, using the learning techniques developed by Beymer and Poggio [1993; 1996].

Chen, Medioni, Havaldar, and Lee [Chen and Medioni, 1997; Havaldar *et al.*, 1996; Havaldar *et al.*, 1997] present a system for generating new views from uncalibrated existing images based on projective reprojection of texture-mapped scenes. With human assistance, corners and edges are first extracted and put into correspondence. The scene (assumed to be polygonal) is then triangulated, and each triangle is reprojected based on its projective depth [Shashua, 1993].

Genc and Ponce [1998] describe a novel method for image synthesis under an affine projection model. Taking Euclidean constraints under consideration, it is possible to construct correct new views of a sparse set of feature points that were tracked through a sequence of images. New images can then be synthesized using triangulation and texture mapping.

In the remainder of this section we describe approaches that explicitly recover 3D scene structure by integrating stereo data from one or more image pairs. These methods can be considered hybrid image- and model-based approaches.

Koch [1995] describes a system that builds texture-mapped 3D surface models using stereo, segmentation, and interpolation. New views can be synthesized with computer graphics methods.

Kang and Szeliski [1996; 1997] present a system to recover 3D scene structure from a sequence of images spanning a 360° field of view. Similar to the approach by McMillan and Bishop [1995b], they first create cylindrical panoramas from image streams taken with cameras rotating about a vertical axis. The 3D scene structure is then recovered from several such cylindrical panoramas using a structure-from-motion algorithm and multiple-baseline stereo. Using texture mapping, new views of the recovered scene can be generated with standard computer graphics methods.

Kang and Desikan [1998] describe a method for virtual navigation of complex environments using clusters of panoramic images. New views are generated using forward-mapping based on geometric information derived from a spline-based registration of the different mosaics [Szeliski and Coughlan, 1994].

Debevec *et al.* [1996] describe a hybrid geometry- and image-based approach for modeling and rendering existing architectural scenes from a sparse set of images. A geometric model is first constructed manually by a human operator using a photogrammetric modeling system. A model-based stereo algorithm then computes the deviation of the real scene from the model. Using the model, the images can be reprojected, which enables the stereo matcher to process widely-spaced image pairs. This has the advantage that a scene can be modeled from only few reference images. In subsequent work, Debevec [1998] shows how synthetic objects can be rendered into real scenes using a high dynamic range light model.

Izquierdo and Kruse [1998] present a system for synthesizing new views for video-conferencing applications. They employ a stereo algorithm that interleaves matching with object segmentation. New views are rendered from a texture-mapped wire frame model.

Zhang *et al.* [1998] use domain knowledge to recover Euclidean structure from uncalibrated images (see also Faugeras *et al.* [1995]). The technique is applied to the synthesis of new facial images.

A voxel-based approach to view synthesis is presented by Seitz and Dyer [1997a]. Proceeding from many calibrated input images (on the order of 20), a colored 3D model is constructed, from which new views can be synthesized. In subsequent work, Seitz and Kutulakos [1998] show how such a representation allows manual editing of an image while simultaneously maintaining three-dimensional consistency with other images of the same scene.

A related approach is the one by Moezzi *et al.* [1997], who create new views from multiple video sequences of a dynamic scene using a volume occupancy method.

2.1.2 View interpolation

In contrast to view synthesis methods, which can handle arbitrary new viewpoints, *view interpolation* methods (also called *image interpolation* methods) require the new viewpoint to lie on the straight line connecting two reference views. While this may seem restrictive, it is sufficient for applications in which the new viewpoint follows a fixed (piecewise straight) trajectory. Given many images of a scene, it is also possible to generate arbitrary new views using a sequence of interpolation steps. For example, the view from a point in the interior of a triangle defined by three reference views can be generated with two interpolation steps. Similarly, generating a new view in the interior of a tetrahedron defined by four reference views requires three interpolation steps.

Chen and Williams [1993] introduce image interpolation in the context of efficient image rendering in computer graphics. They assume that the depth of points is known from an available 3D scene model, and focus on ways to improve rendering speed. Although their framework extends to real images, they only present experiments using synthetic images. They discuss a simple way of filling holes in the synthesized views without giving special treatment to depth boundaries. Chen and Williams also note that linear image interpolation only produces the correct perspective view if the baseline is parallel to the image planes. For general viewing configurations, image interpolation thus only results in an approximation of the intermediate view.

Also in the computer graphics domain, Mark *et al.* [1997] describe a similar technique for speeding up rendering by warping pre-rendered images using McMillan and Bishop's warping algorithm. This technique extends Chen and Williams' work in that the images are rendered correctly for all viewpoints, and holes are filled using more than two reference images.

Skerjanc [1994] describes a stereo algorithm for a multiview 3D TV system using a specialized calibrated rig with five cameras. New views can be generated for intermediate viewpoints.

Katayama *et al.* [1995] describe view generation based on the interpolation of epipolar-plane images. Epipolar-plane image analysis [Bolles *et al.*, 1987] uses multiple images taken along a common baseline (as in multiple-baseline stereo) and computes disparities by fitting lines in x-d space. The paper describes a way of synthesizing new views along the baseline by interpolating the detected lines. The authors also discuss how new views corresponding to a forward motion of the camera can be synthesized. The vertical pixel motion, however, is only approximated.

Werner *et al.* [1995] use view interpolation to generate new views of an object on a turntable. Matching points between reference views are established using the stereo method by Cox *et al.* [1992a], and new intermediate views are synthesized by interpolating the motion field. Partially occluded points can not be tolerated, and the method is restricted to purely intermediate views. The authors have also investigated how a small set of reference views can be selected from a larger initial set of images so as to minimize the error for interpolated views [Hlaváč *et al.*, 1996]. They propose an optimization procedure based on the number of occluded pixels detected by the stereo algorithm.

Seitz and Dyer [1995], under an affine projection model, derive criteria under which image interpolation yields the correct synthetic view. They show that a particular range of views can be synthesized correctly if the reference images are first rectified. They also show that the view synthesis problem is theoretically well-posed under the additional assumption of monotonicity (which basically excludes occlusion). They propose a view interpolation algorithm that matches and shifts uniform patches of intensity as a whole. In subsequent work [Seitz and Dyer, 1996a], they extend the method to perspective projection, and also to more than two images using a sequence of interpolation operations. They also propose a method called *view morphing* that combines geometric image interpolation and user specified *image morphing* [Seitz and Dyer, 1996b; Seitz and Dyer, 1997b]. For a summary of all of this work see Seitz' dissertation [Seitz, 1997].

The view synthesis method proposed by Seitz and Dyer consists of three steps: rectification, linear disparity interpolation, and derectification. This is conceptually very similar to our view synthesis algorithm (presented in the next chapter), which was developed independently. The main difference between the two approaches is that Seitz and Dyer only consider purely intermediate views, while our method allows arbitrary new viewpoints. Furthermore, they employ a different model of stereo matching that relies on *monotonicity*, while our method imposes fewer constraints. This is discussed in more detail in Chapter 4.

Two recent approaches in the computer graphics community, the "lumigraph" [Gortler *et al.*, 1996] and "light field rendering" [Levoy and Hanrahan, 1996], phrase view synthesis as sampling and reconstructing the plenoptic function. As opposed to McMillan and Bishop [1995b], who introduced the concept of *plenoptic modeling*, both approaches construct an explicit 4D data structure containing a subset of the plenoptic function that captures the complete flow of light in a bounded region of space. This data structure contains the intensity (and color) for all lines of sight intersecting a closed volume (e.g., a cube) around an object. New views of this object can be synthesized by reconstructing the light rays passing through the new (virtual) camera center from a set of discrete samples. Both the lumigraph and the light field are constructed from a large number of images (with known parameters) of the object. The approaches rely solely on resampling the visual information, without the need to establish correspondences. Thus, they can be characterized as interpolation methods. Since a discontinuous function can not be reconstructed from sparse samples, depth discontinuities and occlusion can yield artifacts in the synthesized views.

View synthesis and interpolation have also been used in the context of recognition. Ullman and Basri [1991] show that, under orthographic projection, a new view can be expressed as a linear combination of other views. This property is used in a recognition system to test whether a viewed object is a linear combination of views of different models. Beymer and Poggio [1995; 1996] describe learning networks that can analyze pose and expression parameters of facial views. New views corresponding to novel parameter settings can then be synthesized and used to recognize other faces (see also Vetter and Poggio [1997]).

Another way of incorporating new parameters (other than just the viewpoint) into a view synthesis framework has been proposed by Jägersand [1997], who describes a method for image-based view synthesis of articulated agents, such as a human arm or a robot arm.

2.1.3 Mosaics and layered representations

Multiple overlapping images of the same scene can be combined into a single larger image, a so-called *mosaic*. Before the images can be combined, it is necessary to apply transforms to the original images that bring the overlapping parts into alignment. Finding such a transform is referred to as *image registration*. Brown [1992] gives a survey of image registration techniques; see also [Kuglin and Hines, 1975; Tian and Huhns, 1986]. Image registration is also a central problem in the field of photogrammetry [Moffitt and Mikhail, 1980; Slama, 1980; Wolf, 1983].

The difficulty of registering two images depends on the number of parameters that need to be estimated. If two images are taken from the same viewpoint (i.e., only under different rotation and zoom), they are related by a single projective transform, which depends on at most 8 parameters. The same is true if a *planar* scene is observed from different viewpoints. A global optimization (e.g., Levenberg-Marquardt minimization [Press *et al.*, 1992]) can be used to compute these parameters such that the residual between the registered images is minimized. Since the number of parameters to be estimated (i.e., 8) is much smaller than the number of input variables (i.e., the number of pixels), panoramic mosaics from a single viewpoint can be constructed robustly [Szeliski, 1994; Szeliski, 1996; McMillan and Bishop, 1995b; Kang and Szeliski, 1997]. This is also the basic idea behind Apple's QuickTime VR [Chen, 1995]. Note that no knowledge of the scene geometry is required to register different images taken from the same viewpoint.

It is also possible to create mosaics from video sequences. Such *video stills* can be used to represent the information contained in a whole sequence of images in a single frame [Teodosio and Bender, 1993; Mann and Picard, 1994]. Other applications of mosaicing include image stabilization [Burt and Anandan, 1994; Hansen *et al.*, 1994], improving image resolution [Irani and Peleg, 1991], and image compression and video enhancement [Irani *et al.*, 1995].

The problem of registering two views is much harder if a (non-planar) scene is observed from two different viewpoints. The number of parameters to be estimated is now of the same order as the number of input variables: besides the 8 parameters specifying the relative camera configurations, it is necessary to estimate the depth at every pixel. To be able to solve this underconstrained problem, either additional constraints need to be imposed, or the number of input variables needs to be increased by utilizing many images.[2] Szeliski and Coughlan [1994] reduce the number of parameters to be estimated by representing the depth map using a tensor-product spline, and only estimate the depth of the spline control vertices.

The second approach, increasing the number of input variables by utilizing a whole image sequence, has recently been taken by several authors. The key idea is to represent the depth of the scene in a way that is independent of the viewpoint.

Kumar *et al.* [Kumar, 1994; Kumar *et al.*, 1994; Kumar *et al.*, 1995] use a global optimization to recover the parameters of a virtual reference

[2] Stereo algorithms take the former approach by imposing smoothness or ordering constraints.

plane and the parallax field describing the residual parallax with respect to this plane. This has also been termed estimating *projective depth* [Shashua, 1993; Shashua and Navab, 1994]. The method is an extension to the direct estimation framework introduced by Hanna [1991] and by Bergen *et al.* [1992]. Once the parameters have been estimated, new views can be synthesized from this representation, and multiple views can be combined into a 3D-corrected mosaic.

A similar approach has been taken by Sawhney *et al.* [Sawhney, 1994b; Sawhney, 1994a; Sawhney *et al.*, 1995; Sawhney and Ayer, 1996]. As in Kumar's work, the parameters of a reference plane and of a parallax field are directly estimated. Using robust estimators, motion outliers (corresponding to independently moving objects) can be tolerated and detected.

Yet another approach is to decompose the scene into components with different motions. Adelson [1995] describes how such a *layered* representation of video sequences can be computed using the motion segmentation method by Wang and Adelson [1993; 1994]. Starting with an image sequence, the scene is divided into layers containing independent motions that can be described by affine motion models. The idea is similar to the work by Sawhney and Ayer on dominant motion detection [Sawhney *et al.*, 1995] and on layered representations of video [Ayer and Sawhney, 1995; Sawhney and Ayer, 1996]. Using a whole image sequence as input has the advantage that deciding which pixel belongs to which layer is relatively robust, yielding sharp object boundaries. The disadvantage is that these methods only work well for scenes that can be decomposed into few layers, each of which has a globally consistent motion.

More recent work in mosaicing includes the work by Szeliski and Shum [Szeliski and Shum, 1997; Shum and Szeliski, 1998], who present a system for creating and displaying panoramic mosaics constructed from images taken with a hand-held camera. Employing a novel "deghosting" technique, slight changes in viewpoint can be tolerated without resulting in visual artifacts. Shum *et al.* [1998] show how texture-mapped 3D models can be constructed interactively from one or more such mosaics.

Sawhney and Kumar [1997] present a technique for mosaicing with simultaneous estimation and correction of radial lens distortion. Zoghiami *et al.* [1997] present a method for aligning images that differ significantly in rotation and zoom. A different mosaicing technique with super-resolution zoom is presented by Capel and Zisserman [1998]. Panoramic mosaics can also be constructed using few images taken with a fish-eye lens [Xiong and Turkowski, 1997], or using manifold projection by simulating a sweeping strip camera [Peleg and Herman, 1997].

The latter approach is related to a new image-based scene representation, proposed by Rademacher and Bishop [1998], termed "multiple-center-of-projection images". This representation allows arbitrary views of a scene to be combined into a single image, by sweeping a strip camera along a continuous path. The technique is better suited for synthetic than real images, due to the difficulty of obtaining accurate depth measurements and camera calibration data.

Shade *et al.* [1998] describe a different representation for image-based rendering, termed "layered depth images". They also propose efficient forward-rendering methods based on splatting [Westover, 1990] to avoid sampling gaps.

2.2 Stereo

Stereo vision – inferring scene geometry from two or more images taken simultaneously from slightly different viewpoints – is the other central topic of this text. Stereo vision is one of the earliest and most thoroughly investigated topics in the computer vision community, and an exhaustive discussion of related work in stereo vision is beyond the scope of this volume. For general (though slightly dated) surveys of the stereo literature, see Dhond and Aggarwal [1989], and Barnard and Fischler [1982].

In the rest of this section we discuss stereo methods that are relevant to the methods presented in this volume in the context of view synthesis. We start by outlining a framework for stereo, in order to better categorize the existing related work.

2.2.1 A framework for stereo

All stereo methods must address the *correspondence problem*, that is, the problem of finding matching points in two images of the same scene. Two image points *match* if they result from the projection of the same point in the scene. The desired output of a stereo correspondence algorithm is a *disparity map*, specifying the relative displacement of matching points between images.

The stereo correspondence problem is inherently underconstrained and further complicated by the fact that the images typically contain noise. Traditional approaches thus either recover only a subset of matches, or make additional assumptions. *Feature-based* approaches, belonging to the former category, only match points with a certain amount of local information (such as intensity edges). *Area-based* approaches match small image patches as a whole, relying on the assumption that nearby points usually have similar displacements. The disadvantage of feature-based methods is that they only yield sparse disparity maps, and that disparities at locations between features need to be estimated by interpolation. The disadvantage of area-based methods is that the computed disparity map is more likely to contain errors, in particular near depth discontinuities (where not all nearby points have the same displacement). Since the application of view synthesis requires dense depth maps, however, we will focus on area-based approaches, which compute disparity estimates at every pixel.

A typical area-based stereo matching algorithm proceeds in the following way: An optional preprocessing step (e.g., band-filtering) can be used to accommodate global intensity changes, or to extract dense feature vectors. Then, for each location in one image, the displacement is found that aligns this location with the best matching location in the other image. The quality of a match is measured by comparing windows centered at the two locations, for example, using the sum of squared intensity differences (SSD).

A more general, *displacement-oriented,* way of characterizing area-based algorithms is the following:

1. Preprocess images (optional)
2. For each disparity under consideration, compute a per-pixel matching cost (e.g., squared intensity difference)
3. Aggregate support spatially (e.g., by summing over a window, or by diffusion)
4. Across all disparities, find the best match
5. Compute a sub-pixel disparity estimate (optional)

We now discuss the related work using this characterization of the different processing stages of area-based algorithms.

2.2.2 Preprocessing

The reason that a preprocessing step is often necessary is that images contain high-frequency noise introduced by the imaging process, and low-frequency variations due to different camera characteristics, such as differences in bias and gain, and vignetting (uneven intensity distributions). These undesirable frequency components can be filtered out using *low-pass* and *band-pass* image transforms [O'Gorman and Sanderson, 1987]. Such filtering operations are *image processing* tasks [Pratt, 1992]. (Generally, in image processing the focus is on transforming images, while in computer vision the focus is on extracting information from images.) Other examples for preprocessing include the computation of binary features such as edges [Canny, 1986] or the sign of the Laplacian [Nishihara, 1984], the computation of high-dimensional feature vectors [Jones and Malik, 1992a], and the rank and census transforms [Zabih, 1994; Zabih and Woodfill, 1994].

2.2.3 Matching cost

At the base of any matching algorithm is a matching cost that measures the (dis-)similarity of a pair of locations, one in each image. Matching costs can be defined locally (at the pixel level), or over a certain area of support. Examples of local costs are absolute intensity differences [Kanade, 1994; Kanade *et al.*, 1996], squared intensity differences [Hannah, 1974; Anandan, 1989; Matthies *et al.*, 1989; Simoncelli *et al.*, 1991], filter-bank responses [Marr and Poggio,

1979; Kass, 1988; Jenkin *et al.*, 1991; Jones and Malik, 1992a], and measures based on gradients [Seitz, 1989] (see also Chapter 5). Binary matching "costs" (i.e., match / no match) are also possible [Marr and Poggio, 1976], based on binary features such as edges [Baker, 1980; Grimson, 1985; Canny, 1986] or the sign of the Laplacian [Nishihara, 1984]. Matching costs that are defined over a certain area of support include correlation [Ryan *et al.*, 1980] and non-parametric measures [Zabih and Woodfill, 1994]. These can be viewed as a combination of the matching cost and aggregation stages.

Assuming only Gaussian noise, using intensity differences as a cost to minimize is optimal [Anandan, 1989; Matthies *et al.*, 1989; Simoncelli *et al.*, 1991]. As mentioned in the previous section, however, this assumption is easily violated: two cameras can differ in bias and gain, and intensities can depend on the position in the image due to vignetting. Gradient-based costs (see Chapter 5) are less sensitive to these problems. Non-parametric measures as used by Zabih and Woodfill [1994] are a different way of addressing these problems. Another possibility is using methods from robust statistics [Black and Anandan, 1993; Black and Rangarajan, 1994; Black and Rangarajan, 1996].

2.2.4 Evidence aggregation

Aggregating support is necessary for stable matching. A support region can be either two-dimensional at a fixed disparity (favoring fronto-parallel surfaces), or three-dimensional in x-y-d space (supporting slanted surfaces). Two-dimensional evidence aggregation has been implemented using square windows or Gaussian convolution (traditional), multiple windows anchored at different points [Intille and Bobick, 1994], and windows with adaptive sizes [Arnold, 1983; Okutomi and Kanade, 1992; Kanade and Okutomi, 1994]. Three-dimensional support functions that have been proposed include limited disparity difference [Grimson, 1985], limited disparity gradient [Pollard *et al.*, 1985], and Prazdny's coherence principle [Prazdny, 1985], which can be implemented using two diffusion processes [Szeliski and Hinton, 1985].

As mentioned above, measures defined over a fixed support region, such as correlation and rank statistics, combine the cost and aggregation steps into one. Measures that can be accumulated in a separate step have the following advantages:

- efficiency: the measure can be aggregated with a single convolution (or box-filter) operation [Kanade, 1994];
- parallelizability: the aggregation step can be implemented by local iterative diffusion, making the algorithm suited for highly parallel architectures [Szeliski and Hinton, 1985];
- adaptability: the measure can be aggregated over locally different support regions using either adjustably-sized windows [Kanade and Okutomi, 1994] or a non-uniform diffusion process (see Chapter 6).

Instead of collecting support for all different disparities, it might also be desirable to only find points at the depth of fixation (the so-called *horopter*), for example in the context of active vision. This is similar to Marr's model of the human stereo system involving a set of disparity pools [Marr, 1982]. Coombs and Brown [1993] describe an active stereo vision system that finds such points by means of a feature-based *zero-disparity filter* (see also Coombs *et al.* [1992]). Olson and Lockwood [1992] describe a different way of disparity filtering using a multi-scale correlation method to extract points at zero disparity.

2.2.5 Disparity selection

The easiest way to choose the best disparity is to select at each pixel the minimum aggregated cost across all disparities under consideration ("winner-take-all"). A problem with this is that uniqueness of matches is only enforced for one image (the *reference image*), while points in the other image might get matched to multiple points. Cooperative algorithms employing symmetric uniqueness constraints are one attempt to solve this problem [Marr and Poggio, 1976]. Using dynamic-programming techniques is another way of selecting unique and consistent disparities [Arnold, 1983; Ohta and Kanade, 1985; Belhumeur and Mumford, 1992; Cox *et al.*, 1992a; Cox *et al.*, 1992b; Geiger *et al.*, 1992; Cox, 1994; Intille and Bobick, 1994]. Dynamic-programming approaches to stereo work by computing the minimizing path through the matrix of all pairwise matching costs between two corresponding scanlines. Partial occlusion is handled explicitly by assigning a group of pixels in one image to a single pixel in the other image (see Figure 2.1 for an example). Problems with dynamic-programming stereo include the selection of the right cost for occluded pixels and the difficulty of enforcing inter-scanline consistency. In addition, dynamic-programming stereo requires the strict enforcement of the *monotonicity* or *ordering constraints* [Yuille and Poggio, 1984]. This constraint requires that the relative ordering of pixels on the scanline remains the same between the two views, which is usually not the case in real scenes containing narrow occluding objects.

2.2.6 Sub-pixel disparity computation

Sub-pixel disparity estimates can be computed in a variety of ways, including by iterative gradient descent, or by fitting a curve to the matching costs at the discrete disparity levels [Lucas and Kanade, 1981; Tian and Huhns, 1986; Matthies *et al.*, 1989; Kanade and Okutomi, 1994]. This provides an easy way to increase the resolution of a stereo algorithm with little additional computation. However, to work well, the intensities being matched must vary smoothly.

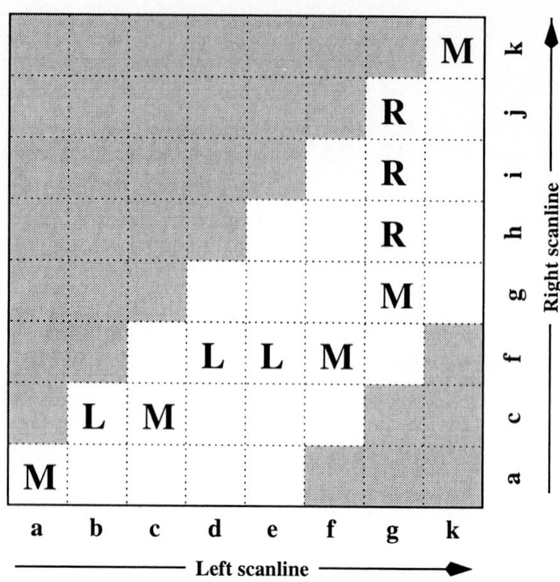

Fig. 2.1. Stereo matching using dynamic programming. For each pair of corresponding scanlines, a minimizing path through the matrix of all pairwise matching costs is selected. Lowercase letters (**a**–**k**) symbolize the intensities along each scanline. Uppercase letters represent the selected path through the matrix. Matches are indicated by **M**, while partially occluded points (which have a fixed cost) are indicated by **L** and **R**, corresponding to points only visible in the left and right image, respectively. Usually, only a limited disparity range is considered, which is 0–4 in the figure (indicated by the squares that are not shaded).

2.2.7 Diffusion-based techniques

In Chapter 6 we introduce several diffusion-based stereo algorithms. *Diffusion* refers to an aggregating (or averaging) operation that is implemented by repeatedly adding to each pixel the (weighted) values of its neighboring pixels. Non-linear and anisotropic diffusion has been proposed for a variety of early vision tasks, including edge detection [Perona and Malik, 1990; Nordström, 1990]. Proesmans *et al.* [1994] detect discontinuities in optical flow by comparing forward and backward flow estimates and then using a diffusion process to smooth the discontinuity maps. (Similar ideas of comparing left-to-right and right-to-left estimates in stereo have also been used by Fua [1993] and others.) Proesman *et al.* and Fua also use an anisotropic diffusion process (mediated by intensity gradients) to smooth out the flow or disparity estimates. Shah [1993] has also used non-linear diffusion in conjunction with a gradient descent algorithm for stereo matching.

2.2.8 Other techniques

Other stereo techniques include hybrid and iterative techniques, such as stochastic search [Marroquin *et al.*, 1987; Barnard, 1989] and joint matching and surface reconstruction [Hoff and Ahuja, 1989; Olsen, 1990; Stewart *et al.*, 1996; Fua, 1997]. Jones and Malik [1992b] propose the recovery of surface orientation from the difference in local texture distortion directly, instead of estimating surface orientation from the disparity map (see also Robert and Hébert [1994]). Hierarchical (coarse-to-fine) matching is another important technique that allows for a larger range of disparities to be matched without excessive search [Quam, 1984; Witkin *et al.*, 1987]. An implementation of a hybrid method utilizing both area-based and feature-based approaches is described by Cochran and Medioni [1992].

More than two images are used in multiframe stereo to increase stability of the algorithm [Bolles *et al.*, 1987; Matthies *et al.*, 1989; Kang *et al.*, 1995]. A special case is *multiple-baseline stereo*, where all images have identical epipolar lines [Okutomi and Kanade, 1993]. In this case, the similarity measures between the reference image and all other images can be combined by summation into a single measure before the aggregation step.

Finally, occlusion is an important issue. Many approaches ignore the effects of occlusion; others try to minimize them using a cyclopean disparity representation [Barnard, 1989], or try to recover occluded regions after the matching by cross-checking [Cochran and Medioni, 1992; Fua, 1993]. Several authors have developed methods for dealing with occlusion explicitly, using Bayesian models and dynamic programming [Belhumeur and Mumford, 1992; Belhumeur, 1996; Cox *et al.*, 1992a; Cox, 1994; Geiger *et al.*, 1992; Intille and Bobick, 1994].

2.2.9 Promising recent approaches

In the last few years, several new stereo algorithms have been proposed that are potentially well-suited for use in view synthesis applications.

Boykov *et al.* [1997] propose a new way of implementing variable support regions: using a maximum likelihood argument, the plausible matches at each disparity level are grouped into connected components. The disparity at each pixel is then selected to be the one with the largest connected component of support.

Birchfield and Tomasi [1998a] present a stereo algorithm designed to recover depth discontinuities precisely. A dynamic programming algorithm is used in conjunction with a dissimilarity measure that is insensitive to image sampling [Birchfield and Tomasi, 1998b]. The method can deal with untextured objects and backgrounds and employs a postprocessing step that propagates highly reliable matches into neighboring regions. Sharp object boundaries are recovered, although at the price of diminished accuracy of the recovered scene depth.

Szeliski and Golland [1998] describe a new multiframe stereo algorithm that simultaneously recovers the disparity, true color, and opacity at each pixel. Similar to the method described in Chapter 6, an initial set of matches is computed by iteratively diffusing support in a disparity space. These matches are then validated by reprojection into the original images, resulting in a visibility map, from which color and opacity estimates can be derived. Finally, these estimates are refined using global minimization.

Along similar lines, Baker *et al.* [1998] propose a layered approach to stereo reconstruction. Using techniques from parametric motion estimation, the scene is divided into planar layers. Each layer consists of a plane equation, a color image with opacity (a *sprite* [Torborg and Kajiva, 1996]), and a residual depth at each pixel. Similar to the work by Szeliski and Golland, opacity and color estimates are refined by taking into account occlusion using re-synthesis.

Roy and Cox [1998] phrase stereo correspondence as a maximum-flow problem. An algorithm that finds the corresponding minimum cut, can be viewed as a generalization of dynamic programming algorithms with better inter-scanline coherence. A different minimum-cut approach to stereo is presented by Boykov *et al.* [1998], who model the stereo correspondence problem with a Markov Random Field.

Wei *et al.* [1998] present a new stereo algorithm based on minimizing a global cost function that uses both intensity and gradient constraints. Disparities are parameterized using a hierarchy of Gaussians, and differences in camera parameters are compensated for during the iterative minimization process.

Lee and Medioni [1998] present a stereo algorithm that directly computes a segmented surface description.

2.3 Computer vision books

A number of good books on computer vision are available for readers who wish to learn more about the field.

A Guided Tour of Computer Vision by Nalwa [1993] is an excellent introduction to computer vision. *Three-Dimensional Computer Vision: A Geometric Viewpoint* by Faugeras [1993] provides an in-depth coverage of the use of projective geometry in computer vision. The book chapter "Computer Vision" by Huttenlocher in the *Handbook of Computer Science and Engineering* provides a compact overview of the state of the art in the field [Huttenlocher, 1996].

Classic texts in computer vision include *Robot Vision* by Horn [1986], *Vision* by Marr [1982], and *Computer Vision* by Ballard and Brown [1982]. *Readings in Computer Vision*, a collection of important papers in computer vision, has been published by Fischler and Firschein [1987].

A treatment of Bayesian techniques in computer vision can be found in *Bayesian Modeling of Uncertainty in Low-Level Vision* by Szeliski [1989]. *Digital Image Warping* by Wolberg [1990] provides a good overview of techniques related to image synthesis. *Computer Graphics: Principles and Practice* by Foley *et al.* [1990] is the classic text in computer graphics. Finally, *Foundations of Vision* by Wandell [1995] is a nice recent introduction to the human visual system.

3. View Synthesis

We are now ready to discuss our proposed method for view synthesis. In this chapter we assume that the stereo problem is solved, and that precomputed disparity maps are available for our experiments. In the next chapter we evaluate what is required from a stereo algorithm whose output is to be used for view synthesis. Actual stereo algorithms used for the results presented in this chapter will then be discussed in Chapters 5 and 6.

The proposed application of view synthesis using stereo data has the goal of generating realistic new views with minimal visual artifacts. This restricts the new viewpoints to be reasonably close to the existing reference views. Even so, we will have to deal explicitly with regions of unknown geometry or texture, since "black holes" in the new views can not be tolerated. To support real-time applications such as tele-reality, new views need to be synthesized efficiently.

Our new method for view synthesis addresses these issues by warping the existing images based on local depth information. The method is based on *three-view rectification*, a special rectification step that both aids in stereo matching and allows an easy formulation of fast exact view synthesis. The method also incorporates ways of dealing with partially occluded regions of unknown depth and with completely occluded regions of unknown texture, which are issues not addressed in most previous approaches.

In Section 3.1 we introduce the three-view rectification step, and derive the linear warping equation. Section 3.2 describes in detail the various steps of the view synthesis algorithm, which include rectifying the original images, warping the rectified images into the new view, adjusting the intensities and combining the warped images, filling holes, and derectifying the combined image into the final view. In Section 3.3 we present experiments demonstrating the viability of our method. In Section 3.4 we outline how our method for view synthesis from two reference images can be used in the larger framework of image-based scene representations. We summarize the chapter in Section 3.5.

3.1 Geometry

In this section we develop the geometric foundations that will allow us to synthesize a new, *virtual view* from two existing *reference views*. Let I_1 and I_2

denote the existing images (left and right respectively), and let I_3 denote the new image to be synthesized. We develop coordinate transforms that enable us to formulate view synthesis as linear disparity interpolation, allowing fast generation of new views by a local warping algorithm. Note that we solve the exact view synthesis problem as opposed to other work in which the term "view interpolation" refers to an approximation of the correct synthetic view.

We assume that the geometry of the two existing views is known, either by explicit calibration or by self-calibration [Deriche *et al.*, 1994], and that the desired configuration of the third (virtual) camera is specified relative to the existing two.

In the case of "pure" weak calibration, i.e., where we only know the fundamental matrix $\mathbf{F}$ relating the epipolar geometries, specifying the new viewpoint presents a problem [Laveau and Faugeras, 1994]. We therefore assume that we have at least a rough estimate of the full (external) calibration (see also Section 3.4).

3.1.1 Three-view rectification

Using *three-view rectification*, we achieve a simple geometry allowing the synthesis of a new view by a *linear* warping algorithm. The key step is choosing a convenient global coordinate system. See Figure 3.1 for an illustration of the rectification process.

We choose our global coordinate system in such a way that all three focal points $\mathbf{C}_1$, $\mathbf{C}_2$, $\mathbf{C}_3$ lie in the plane $Z = 0$. In particular, we let the first camera center define the origin of this coordinate system, and we let the second camera center lie on the x-axis at unit distance from the origin (i.e., at $(1, 0, 0)$). This defines the position, scale and orientation of the new coordinate system, except for the angle of rotation around the x-axis. We can choose this rotation such that the plane $Z = 0$ contains the synthetic camera center. This defines the coordinates of the synthetic view (X_S, Y_S) in the new coordinate system (the subscripts S indicate the synthetic view). In summary, the three camera centers have the coordinates

$$\mathbf{C}_1 = \begin{bmatrix} 0 \\ 0 \\ 0 \end{bmatrix}, \quad \mathbf{C}_2 = \begin{bmatrix} 1 \\ 0 \\ 0 \end{bmatrix}, \quad \mathbf{C}_3 = \begin{bmatrix} X_S \\ Y_S \\ 0 \end{bmatrix}. \tag{3.1}$$

We use homographies (i.e., projective coordinate transforms) $\mathbf{H}_i$, $(i = 1, 2, 3)$, to project the original images I_i onto the plane $Z = 1$, the plane at unit distance from the *tri-focal plane* $Z = 0$ containing the three camera centers. This yields the rectified images I_i'. The homographies $\mathbf{H}_i$ are 3×3 matrices describing coordinate transforms in *homogeneous* image coordinates. That is, a point $\mathbf{q}_i = (u_i, v_i)$ in image I_i is projected to $\mathbf{q}_i' = (u_i'/w_i', v_i'/w_i')$, with

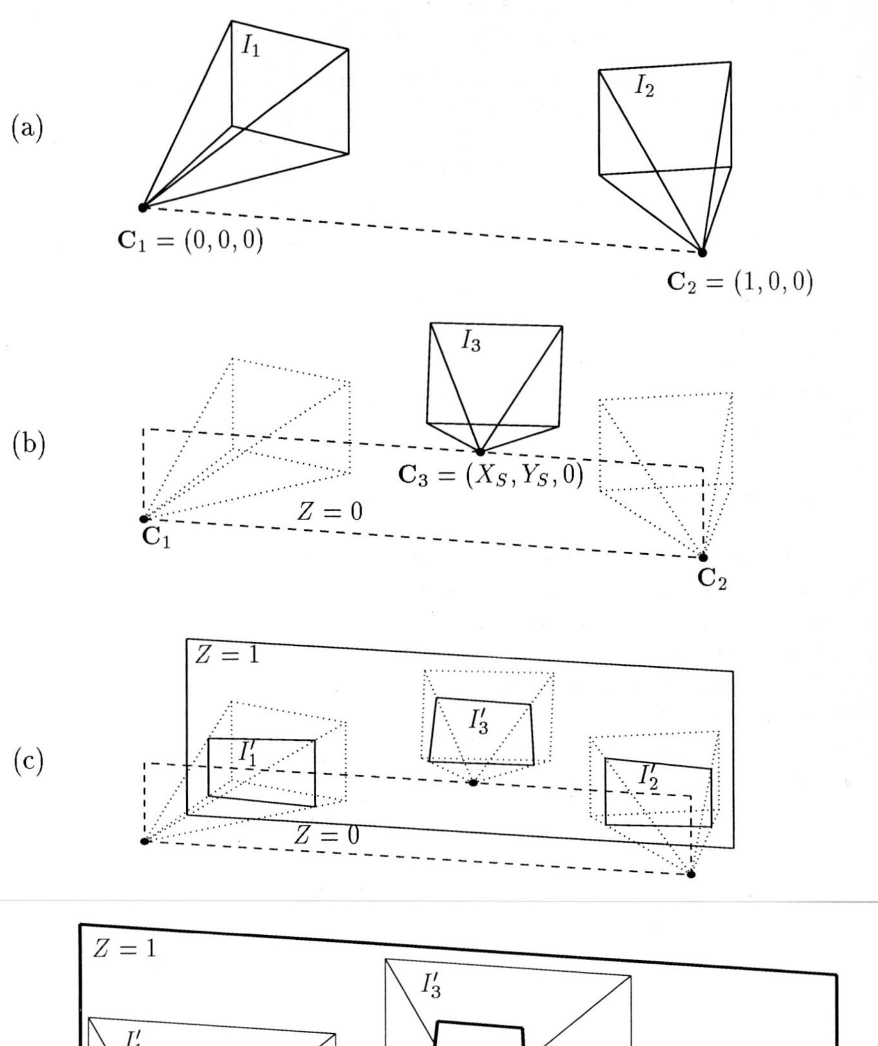

Fig. 3.1. Illustration of the rectification process: existing views (a), synthetic view (b), and reprojection onto plane $Z = 1$ (c). To achieve equal image sizes, larger actual image areas can be chosen to contain the reprojected images (d).

$$\begin{bmatrix} u_i' \\ v_i' \\ w_i' \end{bmatrix} = \mathbf{H}_i \begin{bmatrix} u_i \\ v_i \\ 1 \end{bmatrix}. \tag{3.2}$$

In the resulting rectified geometry, all three cameras have identical parameters, all image planes coincide, and all three coordinate systems are oriented the same way. In order to achieve equal image sizes, the image areas can be expanded to a common "bounding box" that is large enough to enclose each of the three rectified images. This is illustrated in Figure 3.1 (d). The reprojection of I_i to I_i' based on $\mathbf{H}_i$ can be done using a fast projective image warping algorithm [Wolberg, 1990].

Note that the rectification presented here is an extension of the "two-view" rectification commonly done in traditional stereo vision algorithms. To yield coinciding epipolar lines, the rectifying plane must be parallel to the baseline, but its orientation can be arbitrary. We have taken advantage of this fact and have chosen a plane that is parallel to *all three* baselines, yielding pairwise coinciding epipolar lines between all three images.

3.1.2 The linear warping equation

So far we have only rectified the original images and simplified the geometry in which the new view is to be synthesized. We now derive the linear warping equation specifying how each pixel needs to be displaced to generate the new view I_3'. The final step then consists of simply computing the derectified image I_3 from I_3' using the inverse transform $\mathbf{H}_3^{-1}$.

In images I_1', I_2', I_3', a scene point $\mathbf{P} = (X_P, Y_P, Z_P)$ has the coordinates

$$\mathbf{p}_1 = \begin{bmatrix} \frac{X_P}{Z_P} \\ \frac{Y_P}{Z_P} \end{bmatrix}, \quad \mathbf{p}_2 = \begin{bmatrix} \frac{X_P-1}{Z_P} \\ \frac{Y_P}{Z_P} \end{bmatrix}, \quad \mathbf{p}_3 = \begin{bmatrix} \frac{X_P-X_S}{Z_P} \\ \frac{Y_P-Y_S}{Z_P} \end{bmatrix}, \tag{3.3}$$

respectively. The positional offsets of point $\mathbf{P}$ in the new image I_3' with respect to images I_1' and I_2' are

$$\mathbf{p}_3 - \mathbf{p}_1 = \begin{bmatrix} -\frac{X_S}{Z_P} \\ -\frac{Y_S}{Z_P} \end{bmatrix} \quad \text{and } \mathbf{p}_3 - \mathbf{p}_2 = \begin{bmatrix} -\frac{X_S-1}{Z_P} \\ -\frac{Y_S}{Z_P} \end{bmatrix}. \tag{3.4}$$

Using a stereo algorithm, we get the point's *disparity*, i.e., its offset in position between images I_1' and I_2':

$$d_{12} = [\mathbf{p}_2 - \mathbf{p}_1]_x = -1/Z_P;$$

and, symmetrically, between images I_2' and I_1':

$$d_{21} = [\mathbf{p}_1 - \mathbf{p}_2]_x = 1/Z_P.$$

(We use the notation $[\mathbf{v}]_x$ to refer to the x-component of a vector $\mathbf{v}$. Note that the y-component in the above equations is zero due to rectification.)

Given the disparity, we can specify $\mathbf{p}_3$, the image coordinates of $\mathbf{P}$ in the virtual view, as a linear combination of its disparity and the position of the virtual camera (X_S, Y_S). This yields the *linear warping equation*

$$\mathbf{p}_3 = \mathbf{p}_1 + d_{12} \begin{bmatrix} X_S \\ Y_S \end{bmatrix},$$
$$\mathbf{p}_3 = \mathbf{p}_2 - d_{21} \begin{bmatrix} X_S - 1 \\ Y_S \end{bmatrix}. \tag{3.5}$$

3.1.3 Computing the rectifying homographies

We have yet to explain how to compute the rectifying homographies $\mathbf{H}_i$, $(i = 1, 2, 3)$. Let $\mathbf{O}_i$ be the origin, and let $\mathbf{R}_i$, $\mathbf{S}_i$ be the unit vectors of the original image coordinate system of I_i, specified with respect to the new global coordinate system. That is, a point (u_i, v_i) in the original image I_i has 3D coordinates

$$\mathbf{P}_i = u_i \mathbf{R}_i + v_i \mathbf{S}_i + \mathbf{O}_i .$$

Using the fact that Equation (3.3) can be rewritten

$$\mathbf{p}_i = \mathbf{P} - \mathbf{C}_i \tag{3.6}$$

(where $\mathbf{p}_i$ is expressed in homogeneous coordinates, while $\mathbf{P}$ and $\mathbf{C}_i$ are not), the projection of $\mathbf{P}_i$ in image I_i' is

$$\begin{aligned} \mathbf{p}_i &= \mathbf{P}_i - \mathbf{C}_i \\ &= u_i \mathbf{R}_i + v_i \mathbf{S}_i + \mathbf{O}_i - \mathbf{C}_i \\ &= \left[\mathbf{R}_i \,\middle|\, \mathbf{S}_i \,\middle|\, \mathbf{O}_i - \mathbf{C}_i \right] \begin{bmatrix} u_i \\ v_i \\ 1 \end{bmatrix} . \end{aligned} \tag{3.7}$$

Thus, the rectifying homographies $\mathbf{H}_i$ are simply composed from the original image unit vectors $\mathbf{R}_i$, $\mathbf{S}_i$ and the offset between camera center $\mathbf{C}_i$ to old image origin $\mathbf{O}_i$:

$$\mathbf{H}_i = \left[\mathbf{R}_i \,\middle|\, \mathbf{S}_i \,\middle|\, \mathbf{O}_i - \mathbf{C}_i \right] . \tag{3.8}$$

For illustration, Figure 3.2 shows the vectors defining the homography $\mathbf{H}_2$.

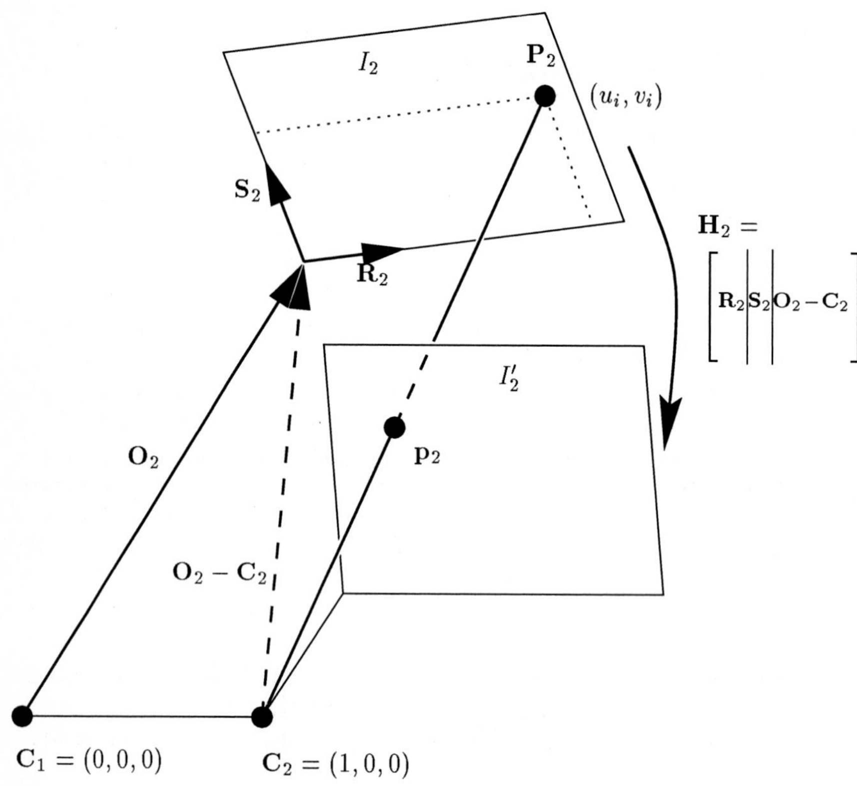

Fig. 3.2. The construction of the rectifying homographies. The figure shows the vectors $\mathbf{O}_2$, $\mathbf{R}_2$, $\mathbf{S}_2$ defining the original image I_2, which are used to construct the rectifying homography $\mathbf{H}_2$.

3.2 Synthesizing a new view

We assume in this chapter that a stereo algorithm has provided us with dense disparity maps $d_{12}(i,j)$ and $d_{21}(i,j)$ between the rectified images I'_1 and I'_2.[1] While many authors assume that the disparity maps are given, the problem of computing them is obviously not an easy one. In fact, it will be the topic of much of the remainder of this volume. In the next chapter, we will discuss the specific requirements that the application of view synthesis imposes on stereo algorithms, and we will then present our new stereo algorithms in Chapters 5 and 6.

Given a disparity map d_{12} or d_{21}, Equation (3.5) yields a fast way of synthesizing any new view at (X_S, Y_S) based on *forward mapping* [Wolberg, 1990]. That is, the existing image is warped into the synthetic view by shifting each pixel by the correct displacement. There are two issues that need to be dealt with: visibility and *holes.*

3.2.1 Resolving visibility

A visibility decision needs to be made whenever two different points map to the same location in the new view. A key advantage of the rectified geometry is that visibility resolution is easy, since the front-to-back ordering of the scene points is the same for all three views. In fact, visibility can be resolved automatically by *ordered forward mapping*, i.e., by simply mapping the pixels to their new positions in the correct sequence. The correct mapping sequence depends only on image coordinates and not on the depth values. This has the effect that closer pixels are mapped later, thus automatically overwriting pixels further away. For example, for a new viewpoint with $X_S > 0, Y_S > 0$, the correct order of mapping (for the left image) is left-to-right and bottom-to-top.

Visibility can still be resolved in this way for more general camera configurations, as long as the image planes stay parallel. The correct order in this case depends on the position of the epipole in the new image [McMillan, 1995b].

3.2.2 Holes and sampling gaps

Holes in the new view occur if the new viewpoint uncovers previously invisible scene points. We have to distinguish carefully between sampling gaps due to the forward-mapping process, and real holes caused by occlusion boundaries in the disparity map. Sampling gaps occur when the (small) disparity

[1] Recall that a disparity map is *dense* if it assigns a disparity to every pixel (i,j). We assume that we have disparity estimates even for partially occluded pixels (i.e., pixels only visible in one image). How such estimates can be computed will be discussed in Section 4.6.

difference between adjacent pixels is amplified in the remapping process. The same is true for holes, except that the disparity difference that causes the hole corresponds to a depth discontinuity. Since depth maps are discrete, distinguishing between the two cases can present a problem. One possibility is to impose a disparity gradient limit that acts as a threshold. For example, a gradient limit of 1 would mean that if two neighboring disparity values differ by an amount $d \leq 1$, then they are considered to belong to the same object (and forward mapping can create a sampling gap which needs to be filled). If they differ by $d > 1$, on the other hand, they would be considered to be separated by an occlusion boundary (and thus forward mapping can create a hole).

Given that we have distinguished between depth discontinuities and small disparity differences, we can counteract sampling gaps by increasing the sampling rate proportionally to the distance of the new camera to the reference camera. (Recall from Equation (3.5) that the disparities are multiplied by this distance.) Note that sampling gaps occur in areas that are viewed less obliquely from the new viewpoint than from the old one, and are therefore subject to less perspective foreshortening in the new view. We have to "stretch" the visual surface in these areas in order to avoid sampling gaps. A different approach is necessary to deal with holes, however, since we do not want to stretch surfaces across depth discontinuities.

3.2.3 Combining information from both images

Before addressing how holes can be filled explicitly, we will discuss how the size and number of holes can be reduced by combining the information from both reference images. Using two symmetric disparity maps d_{12} and d_{21}, we can warp each image I_1', I_2' separately, yielding two synthetic images $I_{3,1}'$, $I_{3,2}'$ for the same new viewpoint. Although displaying the identical view, these two images can differ in the following ways:

1. The global intensities can be different due to different camera characteristics of the original two cameras;
2. The quality can be different due to the different distortions created by the two warps;
3. The holes (i.e., locations of previously invisible scene points) are at different positions.

To compensate for the first two effects, it is useful to blend the intensities of the two images, possibly weighting the less-distorted image more (i.e., the one that is closer to the new viewpoint). For example, the weights could be proportional to the distance between the virtual viewpoint and the (respective other) reference viewpoint. This is discussed in more detail in Section 3.2.4 below. Similar approaches to blending images have recently been proposed, termed *view-dependent* or *depth-corrected* texture mapping [Debevec *et al.*, 1996; Gortler *et al.*, 1996].

The third way in which the warped images can differ, namely in the position of holes, deserves special attention. Given that both synthetic images are based on the same geometry, how can the holes be at different positions at all? The answer is that, if the new views are synthesized by remapping only those pixels whose depth is known (i.e., those that are visible in both images), then the holes will indeed be at the same positions in both new views. If we want to utilize the total intensity information available, however, we need to include areas that are only visible in one image (and whose depth is thus unknown). In Section 4.6 we will discuss ways of estimating disparities of such *partially occluded* regions. Given a disparity estimate for these regions, it is possible to fill some of the holes in one image with intensities of partially occluded (unmatched) regions of the other image. It is still possible, however, for both images to have a hole at the same position, which needs to be filled explicitly. This will be discussed in Section 3.2.5.

3.2.4 Adjusting intensities

Filling holes from one image can create visual artifacts, in particular if the two images have strong global intensity differences. The reason is that the filled hole has the intensity of a single image, while the surrounding has a blended intensity. Thus, it is advisable to perform a global intensity correction before the images are combined. There are two possibilities for intensity corrections. The first is to adjust the global intensities before any new views are synthesized. This has the advantage that the intensity stays constant if multiple views from different viewpoints are generated. The other possibility is to adjust the intensities depending on the new viewpoint, for example to achieve a smooth transition of views between the original (unadjusted) reference images.

In our implementation, the intensity correction is performed by computing a linear regression of image intensities using the warped views. Since the warped images are spatially consistent, a linear regression of intensity values corrects for cameras with different *bias* and *gain*. The idea is to fit the intensity values $I_L = \{l_i\}$ and $I_R = \{r_i\}$ to a straight-line model:[2]

$$I_R = a + bI_L. \tag{3.9}$$

The regression coefficients a and b can be computed using the following equations [Press *et al.*, 1992]:

$$a = \frac{S_{ll}S_r - S_l S_{lr}}{SS_{ll} - (S_l)^2}, \qquad b = \frac{SS_{lr} - S_l S_r}{SS_{ll} - (S_l)^2}, \tag{3.10}$$

where

[2] For simplicity, we will use the symbols I_L and I_R instead of $I'_{3,1}$ and $I'_{3,2}$ in this section.

$$S = \sum 1, \quad S_l = \sum l_i, \quad S_r = \sum r_i,$$
$$S_{lr} = \sum l_i r_i, \quad S_{ll} = \sum l_i^2, \quad S_{rr} = \sum r_i^2, \tag{3.11}$$

and all summations range over all pixels that are defined in both images (i.e., excluding locations for which there is a hole in one or both images).

Given the coefficients a and b, we can combine the intensities using a blending weight α and an intensity weight γ:

$$\begin{aligned} I_{\text{sum}} &= \alpha[\gamma I_L + (1-\gamma)(a + bI_L)] \\ &\quad + (1-\alpha)[\gamma((I_R - a)/b) + (1-\gamma)I_R]. \end{aligned} \tag{3.12}$$

What is the difference between the two weights? The blending weight α controls the "mixture" of the two images: If $\alpha = 1$, only the left image is used; if $\alpha = 0$, only the right image is used. These are the settings used at locations of single holes. At other locations, α should have a value between 0 and 1. According to the discussion above, one possibility is to choose α and $(1-\alpha)$ to be proportional to the distances between the new viewpoint and the reference viewpoints (so that the less-distorted image is weighted more), i.e.,

$$\alpha = \frac{d_R}{d_L + d_R}, \tag{3.13}$$

where d_L and d_R are the distances

$$d_L = |\mathbf{C}_3 - \mathbf{C}_1| = \sqrt{X_S^2 + Y_S^2},$$
$$d_R = |\mathbf{C}_3 - \mathbf{C}_2| = \sqrt{(X_S - 1)^2 + Y_S^2}. \tag{3.14}$$

The second weight, γ, controls whether the intensity of I_R is adjusted towards that of I_L ($\gamma = 1$), or whether the intensity of I_L is adjust towards that of I_R ($\gamma = 0$). If several different views need to be synthesized, it is usually best to use a constant weight (e.g., $\gamma = 0.5$). However, if a smooth transition between the original views is desired, one can choose $\gamma = \alpha$ (referring to Equation (3.13)). This way, if we synthesize a new view close to the left view, we mostly change the intensity of the right view, and vice versa.

3.2.5 Filling holes

Holes in the synthesized view occur when the new viewpoint reveals previously invisible scene points. We have seen that only holes occurring at the same position in both images need to be filled explicitly. Such coinciding holes correspond to scene points invisible from both cameras. These are quite likely observed from "extrapolated" viewpoints outside the original baseline, but are unlikely for "interpolated" viewpoints in between the reference viewpoints. The reason is illustrated in Figure 3.3: two different objects have to

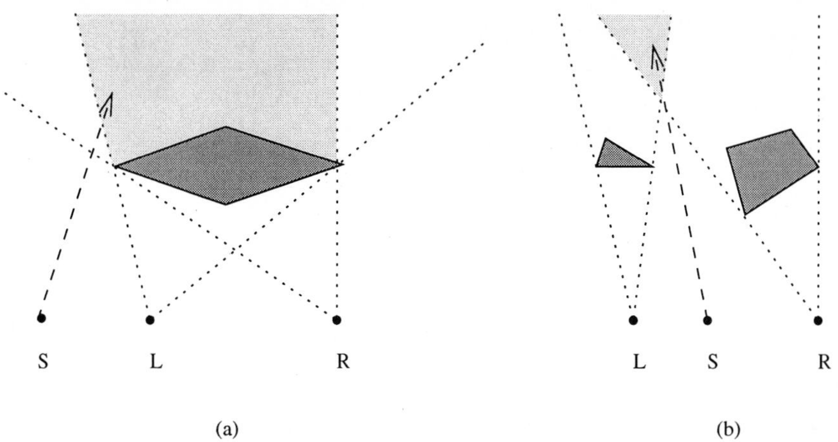

Fig. 3.3. The generation of holes. The illustration shows a top-down view of two cameras L and R observing a scene that contains occluding objects. A synthetic view S has holes due to the exposure of previously invisible scene points. Single objects can cause holes only for views outside the original baseline (a), while multiple objects can conspire to create holes even in intermediate views (b).

"conspire" in order for coinciding holes to occur in intermediate views. We can not exclude this case in natural environments, and thus holes can never be avoided completely.

Dealing with this situation involves synthesizing texture for the newly visible areas. An easy way to fill these holes is to spread the intensities of the neighboring pixels, but this often yields "blurry" regions. A different possibility is to mirror the intensities in the scanline adjacent to the hole, which gives noticeably better results than simple intensity spreading. It is very important to prevent intensities from being spread across occlusion boundaries, since holes are usually created by a close object that has uncovered part of the scene, and now bounds the hole on one side. The new texture should be based only on existing intensities on the close side of these boundaries, to avoid "smearing" of foreground and background. More sophisticated texture synthesis methods based on neighboring intensity distributions (again taking into account occlusion boundaries) are clearly possible, for example those developed in the context of *image restoration* [Hirani and Totsuka, 1996; Kokaram and Godsill, 1996].

3.2.6 The view synthesis algorithm

In summary, we can synthesize a new view I_3 from images I_1, I_2 using the following algorithm:

1. Compute rectified images I_1', I_2' using homographies $\mathbf{H}_1$, $\mathbf{H}_2$.

2. Using a stereo algorithm tailored to view synthesis,[3] compute dense disparity maps $d_{12}(i,j)$ and $d_{21}(i,j)$ between images $I_1'(i,j)$ and $I_2'(i,j)$.
3. Compute new images $I_{3,1}'$ and $I_{3,2}'$ by mapping points

$$I_1'(i,j) \rightarrow I_{3,1}'(i + X_S d_{12}(i,j), j + Y_S d_{12}(i,j))$$

$$I_2'(i,j) \rightarrow I_{3,2}'(i - (X_S - 1)d_{21}(i,j), j - Y_S d_{21}(i,j))$$

4. Adjust the intensities of images $I_{3,1}'$ and $I_{3,2}'$, and combine them into image I_3', filling single holes in the process.
5. Fill the remaining holes in I_3' using texture synthesis.
6. Compute the final derectified image I_3 from I_3' using inverse homography $\mathbf{H}_3^{-1}$.

Note that if many views need to be synthesized from the same original image pair, the first two steps of the algorithm, i.e., rectification and stereo matching, only need to be performed once. Even if the new views lie in different planes, which requires a new rectification step, the disparity map does not need to be recomputed, but can be reprojected using the appropriate homography (the disparity values need to be rescaled accordingly also).

Stereo matching is the most time-intensive step of the algorithm. A typical area-based stereo algorithm needs to perform a substantial number of operations per pixel. Depending on disparity range, size of the support region, and the desired quality, this number can range from a few hundred to several thousand. Rectification and view generation, in comparison, can be accomplished much faster, since only a few operations per pixel are necessary.

To give some actual running times, the computation of the disparity maps used for the synthetic view shown in Figure 1.2 using the stereo method described in Chapter 5 takes 38 seconds on a SPARCstation 5. The image size is 350×236, and the number of disparity levels is 45. Creating a new view (i.e., warping, adjusting intensities, filling holes, and combining the images) takes only 1.1 seconds. The reported times were obtained using an experimental implementation that was not optimized for speed.

This enables interesting applications, such as "low-cost virtual reality", where a single server with high computing power provides images and disparities in real time, and a large number of clients with less computing power could generate different viewpoints.

3.2.7 Limitations of the approach

The proposed method of view synthesis based on explicit rectification, warping, and derectification has certain drawbacks. First, each of the three steps involves resampling the image, which introduces blur. Second, the approach becomes impractical for viewing directions close to parallel to the *tri-focal*

[3] The specific requirements on such a stereo algorithm will be discussed in the next chapter.

plane, the plane containing the three camera centers. The reason is that explicit rectification for these directions results in distortions and large image sizes. If the tri-focal plane intersects the scene (caused, for example, by a pure forward or backward motion of the virtual camera), rectification becomes impossible.[4]

Blurring due to repeated resampling can be counteracted with more sophisticated interpolation techniques, or by super-sampling the intermediate images [Wolberg, 1990]. A different idea is to aggregate the three steps into a single warping operation. This has the effect that the image is resampled only once. Furthermore, as the image is never explicitly reprojected, large (or even infinite) intermediate image sizes are no longer a problem. Both ideas have also been proposed by Seitz and Dyer [Seitz and Dyer, 1996b; Seitz and Dyer, 1996a] in the context of their view morphing method. An aggregated warping step, however, can no longer be implemented using simple scanline operations. In particular, automatic visibility resolution by ordered forward mapping is no longer possible, and it is difficult to counteract sampling gaps. For these reasons, it would be preferable to implement a combined warping step using backward mapping, resulting in an algorithm similar to the "ray-tracing like" algorithm proposed by Laveau and Faugeras [1994].

3.3 Experiments

In this section we demonstrate the viability of our proposed method with experimental results. We synthesize new views from the *kids* image pair used by Intille and Bobick [1994] and the *birch* image pair from the JISCT data set [Bolles *et al.*, 1993]. Both image pairs are already rectified, making explicit rectification unnecessary.

Figure 3.4 shows (from top to bottom) the left and right image of the *kids* pair and the disparity maps d_{12} and d_{21}. The image pair is identical to the one in Figure 1.1, except that the images have been scaled vertically by 1/2.[5] The disparity maps shown in the figure are computed using the stereo method presented in Chapter 5. Also, as will be discussed in the next chapter, the disparities of unmatched image regions due to partial occlusion and uniform intensities have been estimated.

Given these correspondence maps, new views can be generated very efficiently. Figure 3.5 shows synthesized views from different positions along the baseline. The distance between adjacent views is half the baseline. The second and fourth image from the top are the left and right original image. The first, third, and fifth image from the top are synthesized views corresponding to viewpoints to the left of, in between, and to the right of the original viewpoints respectively. The holes corresponding to previously invisible points are

[4] Laveau and Faugeras [1994] report the same problem for their forward-mapping algorithm.

[5] This is the width-to-height ratio of the original images used by Intille and Bobick.

Fig. 3.4. The left and right image of the *kids* pair, and the disparity maps d_{12} and d_{21}. The disparities are encoded with gray-levels: dark represents far, light represents close.

shown in black. As expected, the center view has many fewer holes than the two extreme views, since in the center view most scene points are visible from at least one of the original views.

In Figure 3.6, the holes have been filled by mirroring the intensities of the adjacent scanlines. As can be observed in the figure, filling the holes introduces some noticeable artifacts. The outline of the filled hole is sometimes visible, in particular at locations where the stereo algorithm did not recover a depth discontinuity correctly. In other cases, the synthesized texture is not consistent with the surrounding texture, in particular where strong lines are present in the image (e.g., the tiling of the ground). The latter problem could be avoided using a texture synthesis method that matches the frequency and phase information of the surrounding texture, such as the one by Hirani and Totsuka [1996].

Other artifacts are caused by wrongly estimated disparities. One such problem is apparent in the bottom left quarter of the images, where the repeating pattern of the tiles on the ground causes severe matching errors. (This can also be noticed in Figure 3.4.) The stereo algorithm also fails to recover the correct structure of the arms of the man in the background. Other noticeable artifacts occur along the outline of the child in the foreground, in particular in the bottom image. It can be seen that the correct recovery of occlusion boundaries is critical.

The second experiment demonstrates that realistic views can be synthesized even from poor stereo data. Figure 3.7 shows the *birch* image pair, and Figure 3.8 shows the disparity maps d_{12} and d_{21}. Figure 3.9 shows a synthesized center view for the *birch* image pair. Although the disparity maps contain many errors, the synthesized view looks fairly realistic. (It would be impossible, however, to construct an even remotely accurate 3D scene model from these disparity maps.)

It is easier to evaluate the performance of the method when the synthesized views are displayed in an animated movie sequence. A movie creates a quite striking impression of depth, even if it contains noticeable errors. A movie of the *birch* image pair with a virtual viewpoint moving smoothly between the two original views is especially impressive: although the quality of the underlying disparity map is not very good, the movie communicates a high amount of scene structure. This clearly demonstrates the potential of view synthesis from stereo data for tele-reality applications.

Most of the visual artifacts created by our current implementation are caused by incorrect stereo data. The strongest artifacts are usually caused by occlusion boundaries that are recovered incorrectly (especially in "extrapolated" views). Mismatched points due to uniform intensities, on the other hand, usually do not cause problems.

Fig. 3.5. Synthesized views for the *kids* image pair from different positions along the baseline. The second and fourth row contain the original images. The holes are shown in black.

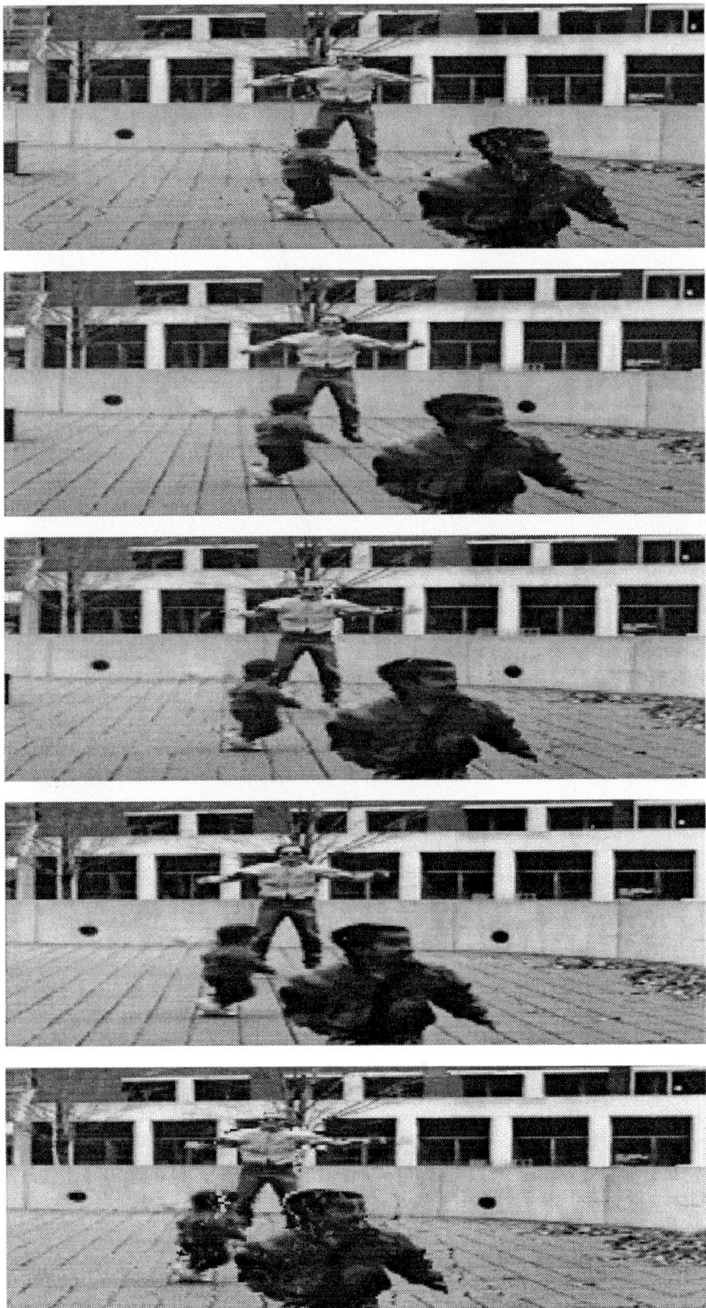

Fig. 3.6. Synthesized views for the *kids* image pair. The figure is identical to the previous one, except that the holes (in the first, third, and fifth images) have been filled by mirroring the intensities of the adjacent scanlines.

Fig. 3.7. The left and right image of the *birch* pair.

Fig. 3.8. The disparity maps d_{12} and d_{21} for the *birch* pair. The disparities are encoded with gray-levels: dark represents far, light represents close.

Fig. 3.9. A synthesized center view for the *birch* image pair.

3.4 Image-based scene representations

As mentioned in the introduction, the problem of synthesizing new views from a stereo pair can be seen as part of a larger framework, in which a scene is represented by a graph consisting of images and correspondence maps. Similar image-based scene representations have recently been proposed by several authors [Chen and Williams, 1993; Laveau and Faugeras, 1994; Fuchs *et al.*, 1994; Szeliski, 1994; Kanade *et al.*, 1995; McMillan and Bishop, 1995b; Kang and Szeliski, 1997]. Each vertex in such a graph corresponds to a view from a physical location in the scene: either a single image, or a mosaic composed from several images [Irani *et al.*, 1995; McMillan and Bishop, 1995b; Sawhney and Ayer, 1996; Szeliski and Kang, 1995]. The edges in the graph represent the correspondences between adjacent views in the form of dense disparity maps, computed by a stereo matching algorithm.

This graph constitutes a local view-based representation of the scene geometry, and new views can be generated efficiently from two nearby existing views using the techniques discussed above. Such an image-based representation avoids the problems associated with global models, but it requires dealing with regions of unknown depth or even of unknown texture caused by occlusion in the scene. If the sampling of reference images is reasonably dense, however, the instabilities of the image-based method have a relatively small effect, since we only need to deal with small changes in viewpoint.

Using only a small number of local images for view synthesis has the advantage that we only need to know the relative configurations between adjacent views, which do not need to be globally consistent. For example, images could be acquired with a hand-held camera and labeled with rough global coordinates. Then, for each pair of adjacent images, the epipolar geometry could be recovered by self-calibration. Compared to methods that try to combine image data from a wide range of viewing configurations, another advantage of using a small set of images is that common assumptions (such as Lambertian surfaces) are less commonly violated.

3.5 Summary

In this chapter we have presented a new method for synthesizing new views from a stereo pair. The method is based on three-view rectification, i.e., reprojecting the images onto a plane parallel to the tri-focal plane. In the rectified geometry, pixel displacements in the synthetic view are linear in disparity, which allows fast generation of new views by warping the existing images. Visibility can be resolved automatically using ordered forward mapping, but special care needs to be taken to avoid sampling gaps. We have also outlined possible ways of filling holes in the synthetic views which are unavoidable due to the limited information present in the reference views. Finally, we have presented experiments demonstrating the viability of the method.

4. Re-evaluating Stereo

In the previous chapter we presented a method for efficiently generating new views from two existing images. The method requires a stereo correspondence map relating the two rectified images. In this chapter we discuss the requirements imposed on stereo algorithms whose output is to be used for view synthesis.

In Section 4.1 we examine the requirements imposed by traditional applications of stereo. We then compare these requirements with the ones imposed by view synthesis in Section 4.2. We show that the achievable accuracy of stereo is sufficient for synthesizing nearby views in Section 4.3, and discuss the different criteria of *correct* and *realistic* views in Section 4.4. In Section 4.5 we show that regions of uniform intensity present less of a problem for view synthesis than for other applications of stereo. Finally, we present ways of dealing with partial occlusion in Section 4.6, and close with a summary in Section 4.7.

4.1 Traditional applications of stereo

Grimson has argued that the requirements on a stereo algorithm should be considered in light of the needs of the task that uses its output [Grimson, 1993]. He demonstrates that exact 3D distance measurements can only be achieved with very accurately calibrated cameras, and argues that stereo might be more useful for tasks other than 3D reconstruction (for example, figure-ground separation). Our new application, view synthesis, imposes yet another set of requirements on stereo. We will discuss the requirements for several different applications of stereo. We will see that limited accuracy (as well as other well-known limitations of stereo) is not as problematic when stereo is used for view synthesis.

Traditional applications of stereo include the following:

- Computation of elevation maps from aerial images
- Obstacle detection for robot navigation
- Reconstruction of 3D objects
- Recognition of 3D objects
- Visual servoing and hand-eye coordination

We will consider each of these applications in turn, and discuss their specific requirements on input, output, accuracy, and speed.

4.1.1 Automated cartography

Stereo algorithms can be used to automate the computation of digital elevation maps from aerial images taken from a plane or from a satellite. This is a classic problem in the field of *photogrammetry*, the science of "obtaining reliable measurements from photographic images" [Moffitt and Mikhail, 1980; Slama, 1980; Wolf, 1983]. Using *metric* cameras practically free of distortion, an accurate global frame is first established by matching a number of ground control points with known coordinates. Topographic maps containing elevation information can then be constructed by matching corresponding points across two images. Traditionally, matching points are established manually using specialized equipment that enables the operator to take measurements while stereoscopically fusing the two images.

The matching process can be automated using stereo algorithms. Commercial systems can compute highly accurate elevation maps (on the order of a few meters), due to precisely calibrated cameras and long baselines [ISTAR, 1993]. The correspondence problem is not too difficult in this case since aerial images are typically highly textured and rarely contain occlusion. The desired output is a dense and accurate displacement map. Real time performance is not required, and the stereo matching process is typically guided by human interaction.

4.1.2 Robot navigation

A stereo algorithm to be used for robot navigation must operate in real time. A dense depth map is usually not required, as the knowledge of the distance to a sparse set of feature points is often sufficient.

In the context of navigation of autonomous robots and unmanned planetary rovers, stereo has been proposed for obstacle detection [Horswill, 1992; Matthies, 1992]. The idea is to detect objects that extend from the ground plane ahead of the robot, and to adjust the steering angle such that a collision with these objects is avoided. To perform this task, a rough localization of close objects is sufficient, which can be achieved in a variety of ways. One possibility is to use a disparity filter tuned to a certain distance to detect close obstacles [Coombs *et al.*, 1992]. As a dense depth representation is unnecessary, it is sufficient to estimate the distance to a sparse set of features, e.g., intensity edges that can be matched reliably.

It is also possible to use an area-based stereo method, but to restrict the estimation of disparities to a sparse set of sample points arranged on a regular grid. This approach has been taken by Robert *et al.* [1995], who show that navigation decisions can be made even in a weakly-calibrated system (i.e., without metric calibration), by comparing the relative heights of the feature points over the ground plane.

An easy method for obstacle detection for indoor robot navigation is to globally transform the images using a homography that explicitly aligns the (flat) ground plane. Objects that extend from the ground plane can then be detected by directly comparing the transformed images (e.g., by differencing).

4.1.3 3D Reconstruction

The most natural output to expect from a stereo algorithm is an accurate three-dimensional description of the observed scene, since this is what our own visual system seems to provide. It is dangerous, however, to try to evaluate a stereo algorithm in isolation (i.e., independent of the proposed application). One is often tempted to judge the quality of a stereo algorithm by observing, say, a gray-level encoding of the computed disparity map, and to check whether it "looks good." The fact that humans feel competent to judge the quality of a disparity map by simply comparing it with a *single* input image clearly demonstrates that our 3D perception is aided by monocular cues, which stereo algorithms generally do not have at their disposal.

Still, stereo algorithms have been implemented that perform reasonably well according to the "looks good" criterion (given that the input images have a certain amount of local texture). For example, the system by Cochran and Medioni [1992] is fairly successful in recovering local surface structure such as depth discontinuities and creases. The detection of depth discontinuities is aided by the heuristic that object boundaries usually coincide with strong intensity gradients (see also Section 5.6).

It is possible to build explicit 3D models of observed objects from stereo data, but usually only in restricted environments (or with human assistance). Computing elevation maps from aerial images as described in Section 4.1.1 is a good example. In this case, the accuracy is sufficient due to a highly calibrated setup, and matching is facilitated by textured scenes and smoothly varying disparities. Another example is the automatic modeling of objects with relatively simple geometries (e.g., piecewise-planar surfaces). Such stereo-based modeling systems are described by Koch [1995] and by Debevec *et al.* [1996]. In the system by Koch, planar surface patches are found using a segmentation of surface normals estimated from the disparity map. The recovered object is modeled using a texture-mapped 3D triangulation. Koch uses a whole sequence of stereo images and combines the different depth measurements into a single model using a Kalman filter. The system by Debevec *et al.* is a hybrid geometry- and image-based approach for modeling and rendering architectural scenes from a sparse set of images. Using a photogrammetric modeling interface, a human operator first constructs a polyhedral model of the scene. A model-based stereo algorithm then computes the deviation of the real scene from the model.

To recover scene structure with high accuracy (and without human assistance), it is generally necessary to use the information from a whole sequence of images. This approach is usually referred to as recovering *structure from motion*; an example is the factorization method by Tomasi and Kanade [1992]. Methods such as the one by Tomasi and Kanade require the tracking of points throughout the whole sequence, which is usually only possible for image locations with large local intensity variation, i.e., a sparse set of *features*. The geometry of other points needs to be interpolated, e.g., using a 3D triangulation of the feature points. Applications of automatic object modeling that require dense, accurate 3D descriptions (such as virtual reality and telepresence), thus usually resort to other techniques, for example using *range* images [Shum *et al.*, 1995].

In summary, it is difficult to compute accurate three-dimensional descriptions of general objects observed by a stereo rig. The achievable accuracy is limited by the small baseline required for reliable matching. This can be readily observed if the recovered object is rendered from a different angle, as is often done in the "results" section of stereo papers.

4.1.4 3D Recognition

Stereo can be used for recognition by extracting the three-dimensional coordinates and orientation of (typically sparse) features, which are then compared to a database of objects.

Since it is hard to maintain the precise calibration required for accurate 3D measurements [Grimson, 1993], it has also been proposed to only reconstruct the observed objects up to an affine or projective transform, and to base the recognition algorithm on affine or projective invariants (see Section 4.1.6 below).

Another possibility is to use stereo vision to compute a $2\frac{1}{2}$D sketch of a scene [Marr, 1982], i.e., surface depth and orientation, and use this information to recognize 3D objects by the structure of their visible surfaces [Mayhew and Frisby, 1991].

The requirements on a stereo algorithm used for recognition are thus the following: the input can be a general scene, the output can be sparse (features) or dense (surfaces). Global calibration is not always necessary, but the disparities of the features need to be computed with high accuracy. Real-time performance is usually not an issue.

4.1.5 Visual servoing

If two cameras are mounted on a robot head that supports panning, tilting, and verging motions, stereo vision can be used to actively fixate on a moving object [Clark and Ferrier, 1992]. This is important in *active vision*, where the emphasis is on the reactive behavior to visual input, rather than on the (off-line) processing of a pair of static images. Real-time performance is critical in this context. Coombs and Brown [1993] describe such an active vision system, which is capable of holding gaze fixed upon a moving object. As in some obstacle-detection applications, stereo is used here as a *disparity filter* to localize objects at the *horopter*, i.e., the distance of fixation. The purpose of fixation is two-fold: it serves to separate the target from its surroundings, and it counteracts motion-blur by keeping the target's location in the image fixed.

4.1.6 Full vs. weak calibration

The role of calibration in stereo deserves separate attention. While many stereo vision tasks have traditionally relied on a fully (metrically) calibrated setup, recent work has investigated the extent to which the dependence on full calibration can be lessened. Among the first papers pursuing this idea are the ones by Koenderink and van Doorn [1991], Faugeras [1992], and Hartley *et al.* [1992]. The basic observation for stereo is that *weak calibration*, i.e., knowing only the epipolar geometry, is sufficient for the matching process, and that full metric calibration is not necessary. Furthermore, weak calibration can be achieved from the two images alone, by establishing a number of corresponding points between them.

It is possible to compute this calibration from five pairs of corresponding points, but it involves the iterative solution of five simultaneous third-order equations. This has been known by photogrammetrists for quite a while [Thompson, 1959; Slama, 1980]. A linear algorithm using eight pairs of points was proposed by Longuet-Higgins [1981]. For a robust solution, however, it is best to utilize as many point correspondences as possible.

Recall from the introduction that the epipolar geometry can be characterized concisely with the *fundamental matrix* $\mathbf{F}$, a 3×3 matrix relating a point $\mathbf{p}$ (in homogeneous coordinates) in one image with its corresponding epipolar line $\mathbf{e}$ in the other image via the equation

$$\mathbf{F}\mathbf{p} = \mathbf{e}.$$

A robust system that automatically extracts many corresponding points from a given input pair and computes the fundamental matrix from them has been made available by Zhang *et al.* [1995].

Weakly calibrated stereo and affine and projective structure from motion has been shown to have applications in reconstruction, recognition, navigation, and view synthesis [Shashua and Navab, 1994; Zeller and Faugeras, 1994; Robert *et al.*, 1995; Laveau and Faugeras, 1994]. Depending on the context, the three-dimensional scene structure is often reconstructed up to an unknown affine or projective transformation, and a scale factor. If necessary, the number of free parameters in the transformation can then be recovered by utilizing additional knowledge about the observed scene. This can be done, for example, by identifying parallel or orthogonal lines on houses or other man-made objects. To establish the overall scale, it is necessary to use a scene feature with known dimension [Faugeras *et al.*, 1995].

4.1.7 Comparison of requirements

Table 4.1 summarizes the comparisons of the five applications of stereo discussed above: cartography, navigation, 3D reconstruction, recognition, and visual servoing. It can be seen that 3D reconstruction is among the hardest of the traditional applications of stereo: the input is unconstrained, and the output has to comply with the most requirements. We now turn to the requirements for view synthesis, which are listed in the last column of the table.

Table 4.1. A comparison of requirements for different stereo applications

	Cartography	Navigation	Reconstruction	Recognition	Visual servoing	View synthesis
Input:						
constrained	yes[a]	no	no	no	yes[b]	no
always textured	yes	yes[c]	no	no	no	no
occlusion present	no[d]	yes	yes	yes	yes	yes
Requirements:						
dense output	yes	no	yes	(no)[e]	no	yes
handle occlusion	no	no	yes	no	no	yes
full calibration	yes	no[f]	yes	no	yes	no[g]
accurate depth	yes	no	yes	yes	yes	no[h]
correct geometry	yes	yes	yes	yes	yes	no[i]
real time	no	yes	no	no	yes	no

[a] Aerial images.
[b] Usually in a laboratory setting.
[c] Except for indoor navigation.
[d] Except for occlusion caused by tall buildings or bridges.
[e] Depends on the approach.
[f] Except to allow projection of steering directions into image.
[g] Except for rough estimation of reference view parameters.
[h] See Section 4.3.
[i] See Section 4.5.

4.2 Stereo for view synthesis

Compared to the applications discussed above, the requirements for view synthesis are most similar to the requirements for reconstruction. The similarities include that we need a dense disparity map with an accurate description of depth discontinuities and occluded areas. As we discuss below, it will even be necessary to estimate the depth of partially occluded areas to maximally utilize the available intensity information in synthesizing new views. (In reconstruction, such areas are ignored.)

In Section 4.1.3, however, we saw that general 3D reconstruction is the most difficult task for stereo, and that 3D modeling is usually done using more reliable sources, such as range images. Why should stereo be any better suited for the task of view synthesis? We answer this question in the remainder of this chapter, and show that stereo is indeed very well suited for view synthesis. The two main reasons for this revolve around the required accuracy in depth, and the difference between correct geometry and correct view.

4.3 Accuracy

There is a well known trade-off between ease of matching and accuracy of reconstruction: the smaller the *baseline* (i.e., the distance between the two viewpoints), the easier it is to establish correspondences across the two images. A small baseline, however, severely limits the achievable depth resolution, as the finite resolution of digital images causes discrete discernible depth levels whose spacing increases with distance.

Figure 4.1 shows a geometric construction of the non-uniform spacing of discrete depth levels for two parallel cameras with focal length f and a spatial resolution of δ. Usually $\delta = 1$ pixel, but sub-pixel disparity estimation might yield $\delta = 0.1$ pixel. Given a baseline of length b, we can derive from similar triangles the following relationship between the distance Z and the spacing of depth intervals ΔZ:

$$\Delta Z = \frac{\delta}{fb} Z(Z + \Delta Z). \tag{4.1}$$

Since ΔZ is small compared to Z, we have

$$\Delta Z \approx \frac{\delta}{fb} Z^2. \tag{4.2}$$

Thus, the spacing is roughly proportional to the square of the distance.

To give a concrete example, suppose we have two CCD cameras with a sensor width of 640 pixels, and a horizontal field of view of 50°. The focal length is

$$f = \frac{640 \text{ pixels}/2}{\tan(50°/2)} = 686 \text{ pixels}.$$

Given a resolution of $\delta = 1$ pixel, and a baseline of $b = 50mm$, the depth resolution at a distance of $Z = 0.5\,m$ is

$$\Delta Z \approx \frac{\delta}{fb} Z^2 = 7.3mm,$$

while at a distance of $Z = 5\,m$ it is only

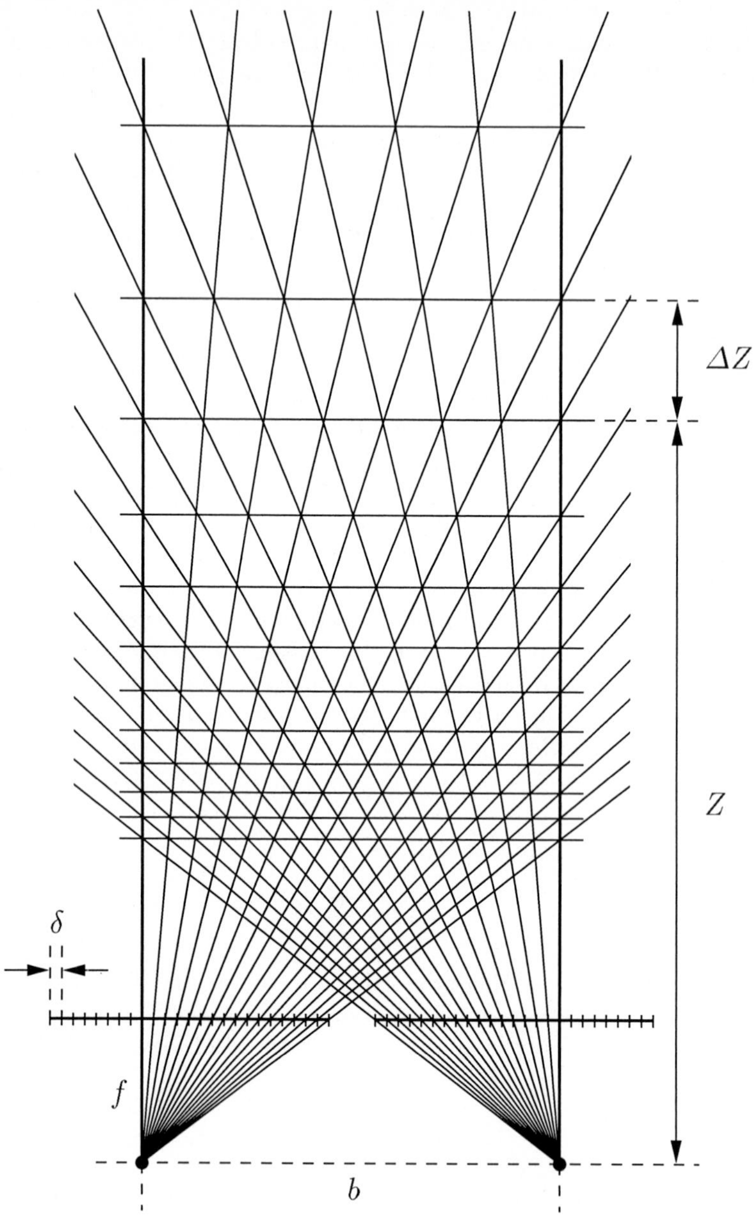

Fig. 4.1. The non-uniform spacing of discrete depth levels. Two parallel cameras with spatial resolution δ yield a depth resolution at discrete depth levels whose spacing ΔZ increases with distance Z.

$$\Delta Z \approx 0.73\,m.$$

Thus, the depth resolution at this distance would not be adequate at all for 3D reconstruction. Neither would it be adequate if we wanted to synthesize the view from a very different viewing direction, for example, from above the observed scene.

In our proposed framework of many reference views, however, we only need to synthesize views that are reasonably close to the reference views. More precisely, we require the distance between the new viewpoint and the reference viewpoints to be of a magnitude similar to the length of the baseline. For those viewpoints, the accuracy provided by a disparity map is not only adequate, but also well-matched across the depth range (i.e., neither too high nor too low). Remember that the view synthesis technique from the previous chapter uses three-view rectification to keep the virtual image plane coplanar with the existing image planes, and that the pixel motion from the old to the new views is proportional to the motion between the two original views (i.e., the disparity). Thus, errors in the computed disparities are uniformly amplified for all possible disparities, depending only on the magnitude of the offset vector to the new view. Since disparities are never explicitly converted into depth, the error associated with depth does not affect the synthesized view.

Thus, the disparities provide a compact, uniform, view-based encoding of the scene geometry, which is ideally suited for the task of view synthesis. In contrast, a uniform global encoding of the scene, such as a voxel representation,[1] would be ill-matched for view synthesis, as points far away would be represented with too much detail, while the resolution might not be adequate for close points. Even worse, the overrepresentation of far objects can actually impede fast rendering. This can only be avoided using a (more complicated) hierarchical representation, in which the scene geometry is stored at multiple levels of resolution.

4.4 Correct vs. realistic views

The second reason why stereo is better suited for view synthesis than for reconstruction has to do with the desired output. In reconstruction, the desired output is a 3D description of the observed scene. In view synthesis, the desired output are realistic-looking images of the scene as it would appear from novel viewpoints. This criterion has both a "hard" and a "soft" interpretation. The former requires the synthetic image to be *correct*, i.e., equivalent to the view that a real camera at this position would provide. The latter reflects the goal of view synthesis: to provide a human observer with a

[1] A *voxel* is the three-dimensional equivalent of a pixel: a small uniform volume element in 3-space, encoding color information.

convincing three-dimensional impression. According to this "soft" criterion, the synthetic view does not need to be correct, but rather *realistic*.

Even if we want the *correct* view, view synthesis is easier than 3D reconstruction. This is true in terms of accuracy, as was discussed in the previous section. In addition, there are common scenarios in which the correct view can be synthesized even if the underlying geometry is wrong or unknown. This is true in particular for image regions of uniform intensities, which are discussed in the next section.

In practice, however, it will hardly ever be possible to synthesize the correct view, because most real scenes contain occlusion. A new viewpoint will, more often than not, contain partially occluded areas of unknown depth and totally occluded (previously invisible) areas of unknown intensities. Thus, we will have to fall back on the "soft" criterion, i.e., trying to create a realistic impression.

To provide a convincing impression, it is necessary to estimate depth and to synthesize texture in areas with insufficient information. Ideally, these estimates should result in minimal visual artifacts, so that the synthetic views look realistic and also convey a consistent three-dimensional impression. This would satisfy the "soft" criterion, even though the views might neither be correct, nor represent the correct geometry. Obviously, it is harder to evaluate the success of a view synthesis method according to this *subjective* criterion. Instead of measuring the similarity between the synthetic view and a real reference view, we have to evaluate the impression on a human observer. A thorough evaluation would need to rely on methods from experimental psychology, which is beyond the scope of this volume. Instead, we have to try to judge the quality of the synthesized images as objectively as possible. An excellent way of testing for three-dimensional coherence is to watch a "movie" of views from a trajectory of closely-spaced viewpoints. It is much easier to spot visual artifacts and 3D incoherencies in an animated sequence, than in a single image. We can not tolerate flaws that are unnoticeable only in still images, however, since most applications of view synthesis do present animated sequences of views to the observer.

4.5 Areas of uniform intensities

View synthesis (as opposed to many other applications of stereo) requires a dense depth map that assigns depth to every pixel. During the mapping step, we can utilize information neither about certainties of depth estimates nor about unmatched points, since every pixel in the image needs to be mapped to a new position. This has two consequences: we want the stereo algorithm to pick canonical solutions that create minimal artifacts where there are multiple or ambiguous depth interpretations, and we have to make extra assumptions about the disparities of unmatched points. We first address ambiguous depth interpretations.

Whenever a local area in one image matches multiple areas in the other image (along the corresponding epipolar line), the matching problem is ambiguous. This is usually caused either by an area of locally constant intensity, or by a repetitive pattern, such as a brick wall or a patterned wallpaper.[2] Mismatches due to repetitive intensity patterns are hard to avoid, since, locally, matches have high certainty. Often a third view (from another camera) would be necessary to disambiguate the matches [Okutomi and Kanade, 1993]. Thus, repetitive patterns are problematic for view synthesis, since the synthetic view can reveal matching errors to the observer.

The situation is different for areas of uniform intensities. Ambiguous depth interpretations caused by areas of uniform intensities have been a traditional problem for stereo methods that compute dense disparity maps. The key observation for view synthesis is that these regions yield the same views largely independent of the underlying depth interpretation. In contrast to the case of repetitive intensity patterns, more views provided by extra cameras usually do not contribute any new information about uniform areas, and would not substantially decrease the ambiguity of the geometry in these regions either. Intuitively, this illustrates that the correct view of these areas can often be synthesized even though the underlying geometry may be unknown (and unknowable from visual data). Even if the correct view can not be guaranteed, it is possible to create a *plausible* view corresponding to a canonical depth interpretation.

4.5.1 Geometric constraints

To make these ideas more precise, let us consider the scenario shown in Figure 4.2. Two cameras **L** and **R** observe a textured scene containing a region of uniform intensity. The figure shows a cross section of the scene taken along an epipolar plane. The textured parts of the scene (to the left and the right of the uniform patch) can be matched unambiguously, and thus their geometry is known. Similarly, the positions of the endpoints of the uniform line are known, too. The geometry of the interior of the uniform line is unknown, however, since any point on this line matches any other point equally well. Note that while the shape of the uniform surface is unknown, it must lie within the shaded area in Figure 4.2 due to visibility constraints. If we further assume a continuous surface connecting the two endpoints that is completely visible from both **L** and **R** (i.e., there is no occlusion), the shape is constrained to lie within the central, darkly shaded region.

To aid the discussion below, we define several terms: A camera's *visibility cone* is the angular region anchored at the camera and subtended by the uniform region. The two half planes separated by the line through the two endpoints of the uniform region are the *protruding* half plane and *receding* half plane. The protruding half plane is the one containing the two cameras.

[2] Wallpapers with a regular pattern often fool the human visual system as well.

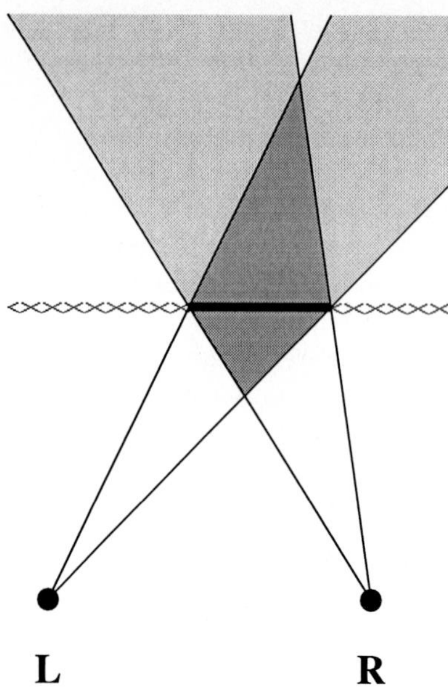

Fig. 4.2. An area of uniform intensity: The figure shows a top-down view of two cameras observing a textured scene (crisscrossed line) containing a region of uniform intensity (solid line). The geometry is constrained by the combined shaded regions in the general case, and by the darkly shaded region if no occlusion is allowed.

We can now define the *strong* and *weak shape constraint regions*. The *strong shape constraint region* is simply the intersection of the two cameras' visibility cones. The *weak shape constraint region* has a *protruding* and a *receding part*: its protruding part is the intersection of the two visibility cones (in the protruding half plane), while its receding part is the union of the two visibility cones (in the receding half plane).

According to these definitions, the darkly shaded area in Figure 4.2 is the strong shape constraint region, and the combined darkly and lightly shaded areas are the weak shape constraint region. The uniform surface has to lie within the weak shape constraint region in general, and within the strong shape constraint region under the assumption of complete visibility.

Uniform (or nearly-uniform) intensity regions abound in real images, in particular in images of indoor scenes and of artificial objects. Under the right (though perhaps unlikely) conditions of lighting and *albedo* (i.e., surface color and reflectiveness), almost any shape can appear uniform. This is true even under the assumption of Lambertian surfaces[3] which is commonly employed by intensity-based stereo algorithms. Examples of different geometries (be-

[3] Recall that a *Lambertian* surface is a perfectly matte surface whose brightness depends only on the angle of incident light and not on the angle of observation.

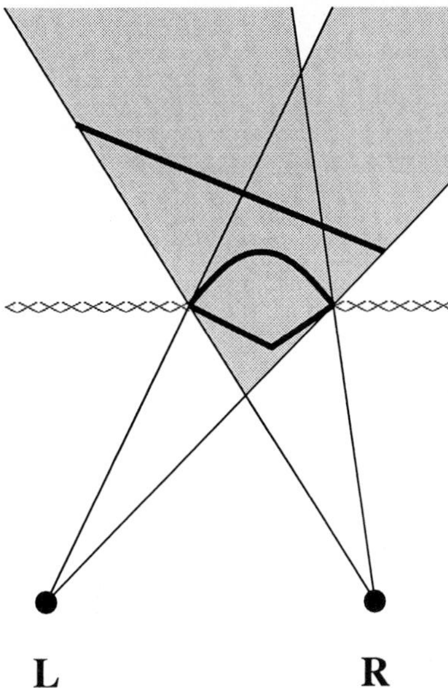

Fig. 4.3. Ambiguous geometries due to uniform intensities. The figure shows a straight, a curved, and a piecewise straight surface, all of which could give rise to a uniform intensity area. Note that even under a Lambertian surface model, any shape – although this is unlikely – could physically result in uniform intensities (given a perhaps non-uniform albedo).

sides the straight line connecting the endpoints) that could result in a uniform image are shown in Figure 4.3.

4.5.2 Interpolated views

Now, let us consider synthesizing a new view from a viewpoint in the same epipolar plane. Figure 4.4 depicts this situation for a synthetic viewpoint **S** in between the two reference views. It can be seen that any continuous, non-occluded surface yielding uniform views from **L** and **R** will also appear uniform from the new viewpoint **S** (assuming Lambertian surfaces). This is the case since the viewing cone from the synthetic view completely contains the strong shape constraint region. Thus, the new view does not impose any additional constraints on the geometry.

The situation is different if occlusion is allowed, since the new view could uncover previously occluded scene points (shown hatched in the figure). If this is the case, and the newly visible points have different intensities, the new view can not be predicted. Geometrically, the newly visible points lie within the receding part of the viewing cone from **S**, but not within the weak shape constraint region. Note that this situation is rather unlikely to occur, since it corresponds to observing a remote surface through a narrow gap.

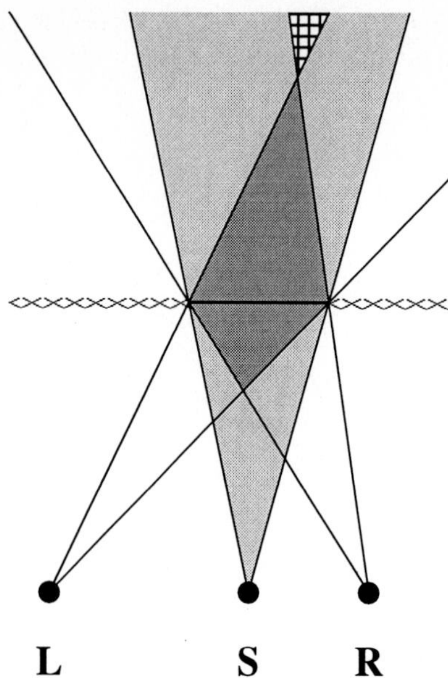

Fig. 4.4. An *intermediate* view (in between the reference views) does not constrain the unknown geometry of a uniform region, and can usually be synthesized, unless the new view uncovers previously invisible scene points (shown hatched).

Usually, the true surface will lie within the weak shape constraint region, and will appear uniform from the new viewpoint.

The observation that intermediate views of uniform areas can usually be synthesized without any knowledge of the underlying geometry is in agreement with similar results by Seitz and Dyer, who consider the problem of *view interpolation* under affine [Seitz and Dyer, 1995] and perspective [Seitz and Dyer, 1996a] projection. They propose a view interpolation algorithm that matches and shifts uniform patches of intensity as a whole (based on the dynamic-programming stereo method by Ohta and Kanade [1985]). Seitz and Dyer come to the conclusion that pure interpolation of views yields physically valid views if the images are first rectified. They also argue that, under the additional assumption of *monotonicity*, view interpolation is a well-posed problem (as opposed to 3D reconstruction). The monotonicity constraint is the basic assumption made by dynamic-programming stereo methods, and requires that the relative ordering of points along epipolar lines is preserved in all views.

Seitz and Dyer derive a *complete visibility constraint* from the monotonicity constraint, i.e., they require that all points need to remain visible in all intermediate views (which excludes any occlusion). They conclude that complete visibility is required for view synthesis. However, this conclusion is overly restrictive. As discussed above, complete visibility (across all views) is certainly a sufficient condition for the synthesis of correct views (which, geometrically, requires the surface to lie within the strong shape constraint region). It is not a necessary condition, however, as there are many more geometries (within the weak shape constraint region) that can yield the correct (uniform) image. It is not necessary to exclude occlusion, which is quite common in natural scenes. In fact, the unknown geometry could consist of multiple occluding surfaces.

In summary, most surface geometries that appear uniform from **L** and **R** will also appear uniform from an intermediate view **S**. It is not necessary to exclude occlusion (i.e., to require complete visibility), but it is harder to characterize precisely the set of surfaces that will appear uniform once occlusion is allowed.

In order to render the uniform area from a different viewpoint, we need an (arbitrary) depth interpretation for the inside of the region. The easiest such interpretation is the straight line connecting the two endpoints of known depth, which we call the *canonical depth interpretation*. Note that even when the correct view can not be predicted (i.e., if there are newly visible scene points), this depth interpretation results in a *plausible* view, because the observer (usually) has no way of predicting the appearance of the newly visible points either.

4.5.3 Extrapolated views

We now consider the case of a new view outside the original baseline, but still on the line through the two reference viewpoints (see Figure 4.5). That is, we want to synthesize an *extrapolated* view (as opposed to an interpolated one). In this case, the correct view can only be synthesized for some geometries, even if the surface is completely visible from both reference views. The reason is that if the uniform surface extends towards the front, it could occlude some of the textured background in the new view, which would be impossible to predict. For example, this happens if the surface extends into the region shown in black in Figure 4.5. The new view now constrains the geometry, as its viewing cone no longer completely contains the strong shape constraint region.

A new viewpoint outside the original baseline can also uncover previously occluded scene points. This is only possible if occlusion is present and the surface extends into a previously invisible region, for example, the area shown hatched in Figure 4.5. Since the intensity of the newly visible points is unknown, the new view can not be predicted. As in the previous section, the geometric interpretation is that the receding part of the viewing cone from the new viewpoint is not completely contained in the weak shape constraint region.

Both of the above problems make the synthesis of extrapolated views more difficult than the synthesis of interpolated views. The first problem (the constraint in the protruding part of the plane) implies that the synthetic view

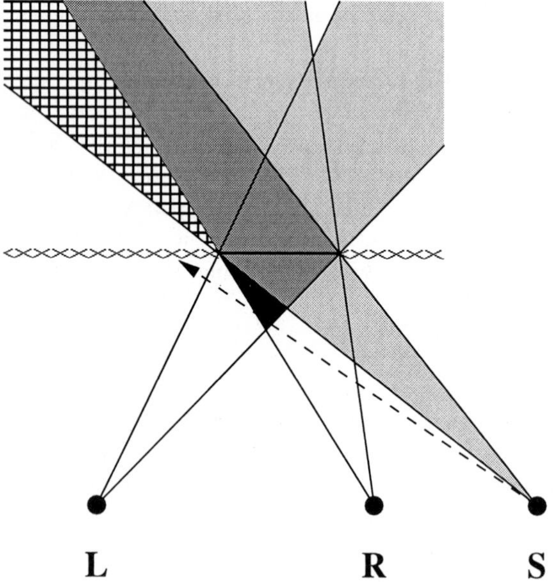

Fig. 4.5. An *extrapolated* view (outside the original baseline) constrains the geometry of a uniform region, and can only be synthesized correctly if the true surface does not extend into the black and hatched areas. (If the surface does extend into the black area, unpredictable occlusion can occur along the line of sight shown dashed.) A plausible view can always be synthesized, however, by assuming the canonical depth interpretation along the straight line connecting the endpoints of the uniform region.

can no longer be guaranteed to be correct, even if we assume a continuous surface completely visible from the original views. This was not the case for interpolated views. In addition, the second problem (that of newly visible points in the receding part of the plane), is more likely to occur, as it can be caused by any occlusion boundary. In interpolated views, on the other hand, it requires the presence of a remote surface visible through a narrow gap. As before, however, a plausible view can be synthesized by assuming the canonical depth interpretation along the straight line connecting the two points of known depth.

4.5.4 General views and the aperture problem

Recall that we have parameterized the position of the new viewpoint with the coordinates (X_S, Y_S), while the two reference views have the coordinates $(0,0)$ and $(1,0)$. So far we have investigated interpolated views (with $0 < X_S < 1$), and extrapolated views (with $X_S < 0$ or $X_S > 1$). In both cases we had $Y_S = 0$. We now consider the case where $Y_S \neq 0$.

Such views from a point *not* on the original baseline are affected by the *aperture problem*, i.e., the fact that the local displacements can only be recovered in the direction of the intensity gradient. In the context of stereo, the aperture problem has the consequence that vertical intensity edges can be matched unambiguously (unless they are part of a repetitive pattern), while horizontal intensity edges are impossible to match at a local level, because each match looks (locally) equally good. In fact, if we only consider a single (horizontal) epipolar line, a horizontal intensity edge appears uniform along this line. Thus, for new viewpoints on the original baseline, the discussion from the previous two sections extends to horizontal intensity edges. As before, the image of such edges will be correct in the new view independent of the underlying depth interpretation. We can conclude (in agreement with Seitz and Dyer [1995; 1996a]) that the aperture problem is nonexistent and that the view synthesis problem is *well-posed* in this case.

The situation is different for a new view with $Y_S \neq 0$. This case corresponds to observing the scene from a viewpoint either above or below the original viewpoints. A horizontal intensity edge in the original views will now have a different shape and position in the new view as a direct consequence of its estimated depth. This makes the synthesis of a correct view much harder.

The main difference from the previous case is that uncertainties in depth estimation and view synthesis no longer "cancel each other out". These uncertainties correspond to an intensity gradient whose component in the direction of the epipolar line is zero. Before, the epipolar lines for depth estimation and view synthesis were identical. Now, their direction differs: the epipolar lines between the two reference views are horizontal, while the epipolar lines between each reference view and the synthetic view are not.

It is still possible to avoid most visual artifacts by assigning a canonical depth interpretation, but this interpretation must now be consistent across scanlines. In the case of a uniform region within a textured area, this can be achieved by interpolating the disparities from the boundaries. The problem is harder, however, for areas where the intensity gradients have mostly vertical components (i.e., in the presence of horizontal stripes). In this case, the canonical depth interpretation needs to be consistent over a larger area.

4.5.5 Assigning canonical depth interpretations

The above discussion has shown that uniform patches usually do not create visual artifacts in the new view as long as their boundaries are matched correctly. We now discuss how the canonical depth assignments of the interior of uniform regions can be achieved by interpolating the disparities of the boundaries. The explicit assignment of disparities to the interior of uniform regions is necessary since dense disparity maps are required by the image warping step.

There are several possibilities for how the interpolation can be performed. One possibility is to use dynamic-programming stereo methods, which efficiently interpolate across uniform areas on each scanline by relying on the monotonicity constraint [Ohta and Kanade, 1985; Cox *et al.*, 1992a; Intille and Bobick, 1994; Birchfield and Tomasi, 1998a]. This is the approach taken by Seitz and Dyer [1995; 1996a]. The disadvantages are that the monotonicity constraint limits the allowable scene geometry, and that inter-scanline consistency is harder to enforce in a dynamic-programming method.

A second possibility is to use iterative stereo methods, which gradually distribute matches of high certainty (such as the boundaries) into ambiguous areas (i.e., the interior of uniform regions). Examples are the diffusion-based methods that are discussed in Chapter 6.

Finally, a third possibility is to compute explicit certainties for all matches, and to assign a “don’t know” status to all points whose certainty is below a given threshold. The resulting holes in the computed disparity map can then be filled, for example using thin-plate spline interpolation [Grimson, 1981], or by simply interpolating the values along each scanline. Filling holes due to matches of low certainty can then be combined with filling holes due to partial occlusion (which is discussed in Section 4.6). This is the approach that has been taken for the results presented in this volume.

In Chapter 5 we discuss a stereo method that incorporates the computation of certainties into the matching process.

4.5.6 Does adding more cameras help?

For unrestricted scenes, there can always be viewpoints for which incorrect views will be generated, even if the underlying disparity map is a canonical interpretation of an ambiguity. In general, this is true for any viewpoint from which an additional (real) camera could be used to disambiguate the possible depth interpretation. In other words, if an error in the computed disparities could be detected with an additional camera, then the view from this point can reveal the error. As mentioned in the beginning of this section, this includes not only ambiguities due to uniform regions, but also repetitive intensity patterns.

Multiple-camera stereo has been proposed to deal with precisely these ambiguities [Ito and Ishii, 1986; Pietikäinen and Harwood, 1986; Bolles *et al.*, 1987; Ayache and Lustman, 1991]. In this volume, however, we focus on the two-camera case. The reason is that adding more cameras makes a simultaneous global rectification for all views impossible (since a rectification plane parallel to all baselines does not exist in general). Thus, a more complicated image warping procedure would be required to allow the fusion of more than two reference images into the combined new view. An exception is the case of multiple-baseline stereo [Okutomi and Kanade, 1993], where all camera centers lie on a straight line. In this case, global rectification is still possible, and the stereo matching process is very similar to the two-view case.

To summarize, for view synthesis it is often not necessary to resolve ambiguities that arise during the stereo matching process. In many situations, assuming the canonical depth interpretation yields either the correct view, or a plausible view, which, while being incorrect, represents a consistent geometry and contains no apparent errors. That is, even though adding an extra camera would yield a different depth map (and different synthetic views), this is not necessary to convey a convincing three-dimensional structure. A similar argument can be made for the problem of filling holes in the final synthesized images, which was discussed in Section 3.2.5. The number and sizes of holes (corresponding to previously invisible scene points) can be decreased by adding extra cameras. If there are fewer holes, less "guessing" of textures is required, which increases the accuracy of the synthesized view. However, there is a trade-off involved, since adding extra cameras can require a more complicated calibration procedure, and precludes the use of the fast view synthesis method presented in the previous chapter. Unless the quality of the synthetic view could be improved substantially, adding extra cameras is thus not economical.

4.6 Partial occlusion

Besides regions of uniform intensity, we also have to deal with *partially occluded* regions that are visible from only one camera. Figure 4.6 shows an example of such a case. Note that we have intensity information but no depth information for the points that are visible only from one camera. To be able to generate new views of these half-occluded points, we have to make assumptions about their depth. A different possibility is to ignore these points completely. This approach has been taken by Ott *et al.* [1993] in their proposed

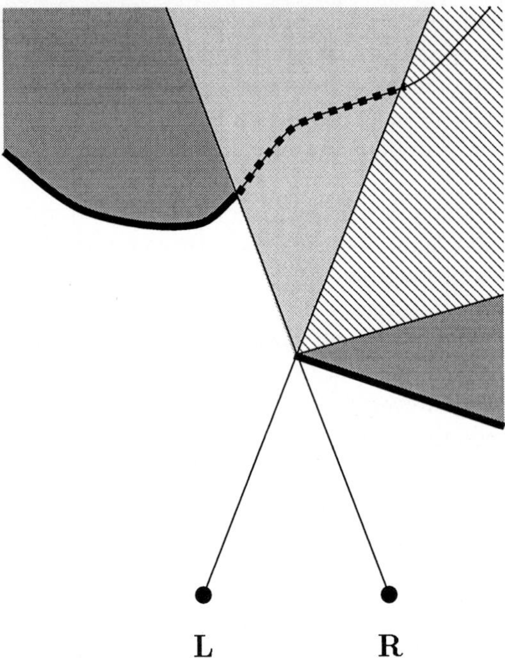

Fig. 4.6. An example of partial occlusion. The illustration shows a top-down view of two cameras **L** and **R** observing a scene in which a wedge-shaped object in the foreground partially occludes a curved background. The lightly-shaded region is only visible from the left camera, while the striped region is completely occluded. The surfaces with known intensity and geometry are marked with a solid line. The partially occluded surface, whose texture is known but whose geometry is unknown, is marked with a dashed line.

application of view synthesis for creating a center view for teleconferencing. Ignoring the partially occluded points in the image warping step results in more holes in the final image, which eventually need to be filled. We maintain that better results can usually be achieved by utilizing the intensity information provided by the partially occluded regions, instead of discarding it. To do this, we must assign explicit depth to these points.

Just as with filling holes in the final image, assigning depth has to rely on heuristics, as there are an infinite number of possible depth interpretations. Any surface spanning the lightly shaded region in Figure 4.6 could result in the observed intensities. Given the known depth of points **P** and **Q** bounding the partially occluded region, however, there are a number of reasonable generic assumptions: (**a**) interpolating the depth values between the points of known depth, (**b**) assuming constant depth, or (**c**) assuming constant depth gradient. These choices are illustrated in Figure 4.7.

Assuming interpolated depth values (**a**) is almost certainly the wrong interpretation, since it relies on an unlikely viewing position of the right camera.

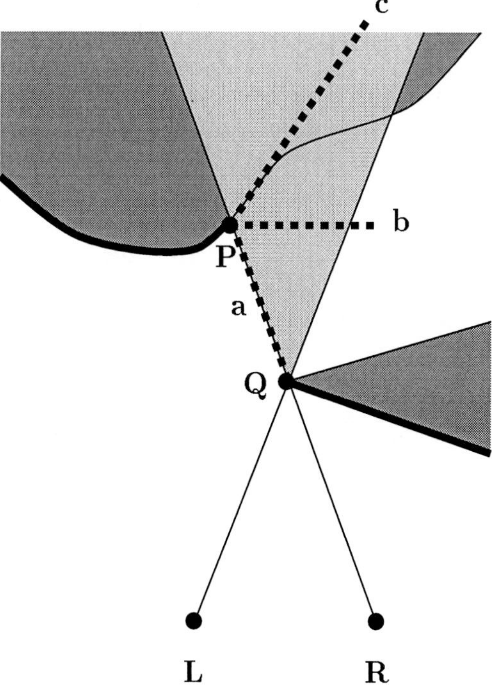

Fig. 4.7. Some possible depth interpretations under partial occlusion. Using the known depth of the boundaries **P** and **Q** of the partially occluded region, three possible depth hypotheses (among the infinitely many) include (**a**) interpolating depth; (**b**) assuming constant depth; and (**c**) assuming constant depth gradient.

That is, if (**a**) would be the correct depth interpretation, then the right camera would be looking straight along a surface. Thus, the camera would not be in a *general position* with respect to the scene, and a slight perturbation of the camera position would yield a different geometric configuration. On a related note, Nakayama and Shimojo [1990; 1992] have argued that the human visual system interprets many underconstrained visual scenarios by assuming a general viewpoint as well. Thus, we will discard choice (**a**) from consideration. (This is different from the case of uniform regions, where the canonical depth interpretation does require an interpolation of depth values.)

Assuming a general viewpoint, the most likely cause for a partially visible area is the occlusion of a surface by a (different) object at a closer distance. The depth estimate of the partially occluded region should therefore *not* depend on the depth of the near boundary of the region (i.e., point **Q** in the figure), but only on the depth of the far boundary (i.e., point **P**). This motivates the choices (**b**) and (**c**).

Assuming a constant slope of the background (**c**) seems like a good idea. A continuous surface orientation at point **P** would also be implied by the assumption of a general viewpoint. In practice, however, it is difficult to reliably estimate the depth gradient from a discrete noisy disparity map. The easiest and most stable solution turns out to be the constant-depth hypothesis (**b**). In our experiments we found that this strategy usually produces good results. Also, since the half-occluded regions are fairly narrow in most cases, the difference between constant-slope and constant-depth assumptions are usually small.

From the above discussion we can conclude that it is crucial that the stereo algorithm detects and correctly labels partially occluded points, rather than assigning random disparities in these areas. Recall that the view synthesis algorithm requires symmetric disparity maps d_{12} and d_{21}. An easy way of detecting occluded regions is to compute the two disparity maps separately, and then perform a consistency check. Points whose disparities disagree are labeled occluded. This "two-pass" approach to dealing with occlusion, using two symmetrical matching processes (left-to-right and right-to-left) and cross-checking after matching is used in our current implementation.

One can argue that it would be preferable to use a concurrent stereo matching process that computes consistent symmetric disparities while also detecting occluded regions. Stereo algorithms based on dynamic programming are examples of such processes [Belhumeur and Mumford, 1992; Cox *et al.*, 1992a; Geiger *et al.*, 1992; Intille and Bobick, 1994], but they suffer from a number of inherent problems. First, stereo methods based on dynamic programming require assigning a cost to unmatched pixels. Choosing the right cost is difficult, even if it is based on an *a priori* assumption about the likelihood of occlusion in the scene, as is done in some approaches. The second problem is that these approaches do not yield an easy way of enforcing interscanline consistency. Finally, dynamic-programming algorithms rely on the ordering constraint (or *monotonicity*), which is usually not satisfied in real scenes.

There are also other ways to detect occluded areas, or other areas that are unlikely to be matched correctly. A method based on binary matching that explicitly computes the probability of a false match is described by Huttenlocher and Jaquith [1995].

As discussed in Section 2.2.9, several promising stereo algorithms have been proposed recently that make progress towards the goals outlined above. In particular, the algorithm by Birchfield and Tomasi [1998a] is designed to recover depth discontinuities precisely, although at the price of an increased sensitivity to noise, and of diminished accuracy of the recovered scene depth. The methods by Szeliski and Golland [1998] and Baker *et al.* [1998] construct layered representations of a scene, including estimates for disparity, true color, and opacity at each pixel. Such representations are ideal for view-synthesis applications, because they allow the assignment of depth hypotheses to be integrated into the matching process.

4.7 Summary

In summary, a stereo algorithm whose output is to be used for view synthesis has to satisfy many of the requirements demanded by the task of 3D reconstruction. While it can be argued that stereo is not particularly well suited for 3D reconstruction, we have seen that this is not the case for view synthesis. The parallels between the two tasks include that the stereo algorithm must be able to perform in general, unconstrained environments containing both textured and textureless objects, and occlusion. Further, a dense disparity map with high spatial accuracy is required as output. It is particularly important that object boundaries (i.e., depth discontinuities) and partially occluded areas are accurately localized.

The two main problems for 3D reconstruction from stereo data, limited accuracy and unknown geometry in textureless areas, do not apply to the application of view synthesis, however.

The depth resolution achievable from stereo is often inadequate for accurate 3D modeling. It is sufficient, however, for the synthesis of views from nearby viewpoints, as the depths of points at greater distances need to be known with less precision. In other words, the disparity maps constitute a representation of the scene geometry well-suited for the task of synthesizing nearby views, as the achievable accuracy for remapping a point (in image coordinates) is independent of the point's depth.

Textureless areas (whose geometries are unknown) are another source of trouble for 3D reconstruction methods. In view synthesis, however, a plausible (and in many cases correct) view can be synthesized by assuming a canonical depth interpretation. This interpretation can be achieved by interpolating the depth of featureless areas from their boundaries.

Finally, for performing accurate 3D measurements, full (and exact) calibration is required, which is difficult to achieve and to maintain. View synthesis, on the other hand, can proceed from pairwise rectified stereo pairs, which can be achieved by weak calibration (without knowledge of the external camera parameters). In order to specify a synthetic viewpoint, a rough knowledge of the reference view parameters can be sufficient.

5. Gradient-Based Stereo

This chapter begins the second major part of this volume: the discussion of actual stereo algorithms. So far we have discussed how new views can be synthesized and what requirements view synthesis imposes on stereo algorithms. Given this background, we are now ready to examine several different stereo methods, and to evaluate their performance in the context of view synthesis.

The topic of this chapter is a stereo method whose similarity measure is based on comparing intensity gradients. In Chapter 6 we discuss different stereo methods that operate by iteratively diffusing support for different disparity hypotheses.

The method presented in this chapter is a continuation of previous work, which was originally motivated by the need for a robust matching technique for the computation of visual correspondence [Scharstein, 1994b]. As we will discuss in more detail below, the advantages of the method include that it is insensitive to absolute intensity differences between images (it can thus tolerate cameras with different bias), and that it allows easy integration of the concept of *confidence* (or *certainty*) into the matching process. The latter property makes the method very well suited for view synthesis applications: the fact that the certainty of a computed match can be evaluated easily is useful for assigning canonical depth interpretations in areas of uniform intensities (as was discussed in Section 4.5).

The diffusion-based methods of the next chapter, on the other hand, are motivated by the problem of boundary blurring, since poorly localized boundaries can yield strong artifacts in synthesized views.

To put the different stereo methods of this and the next chapter into context, recall the framework from Section 2.2.1, which categorizes stereo algorithms according to the following tasks:

1. Preprocessing (optional)
2. Computation of a local matching cost
3. Aggregation of spatial support
4. Selecting the best match
5. Sub-pixel disparity estimation (optional)

The main emphasis of the method in this chapter is on the matching cost. In particular, we will discuss a way of measuring the *evidence* for or against matches under a given displacement. The emphasis in the following chapter, in contrast, will be on the aggregation of support.

We start by discussing the notions of similarity and confidence in Section 5.1, and the difference between *point-oriented* and *displacement-oriented* control strategies in Section 5.2. We introduce our new gradient-based evidence measure in Section 5.3, and discuss the accumulation of the measure in Section 5.4. In Section 5.5 we present experimental results, both for the computation of stereo and of general motion. We then discuss in Section 5.6 the detection of half-occluded regions and other post-processing steps necessary for the application of view synthesis. We discuss efficiency issues in Section 5.7, and close with a discussion in Section 5.8 and a summary in Section 5.9.

5.1 Similarity and confidence

Comparing locations in two images involves a *matching criterion*: a measure of goodness of a proposed match. A key observation is that most methods for computing correspondences have *two* underlying criteria:

- a *similarity* criterion that reflects how well two locations in the two images resemble each other;
- a *confidence* criterion that reflects the likelihood that a match is correct.

Existing methods often treat these two criteria separately. The method presented here uses a single measure, which – given a certain displacement – gives a (strong) positive response where points match with (high) confidence, a negative response where there is a clear mismatch, and zero response in regions where there is neither evidence for a match nor evidence against a match. The measure is based on comparing the *gradient fields* of the images.

There are several reasons why combining the criteria of similarity and certainty is a good idea. By introducing a confidence value early in the matching process, both similarity and confidence influence the aggregation of support for a match. This causes the aggregation to proceed in a non-uniform way, as matches with higher confidence receive more weight. Thus, when it comes to selecting the best match, matches with high certainty have already influenced neighboring areas. In addition, the certainty of each selected match is preserved, and areas where no clear match has been achieved can be detected later. This allows the detection of both unmatched areas due to partial occlusion (i.e., areas visible from only one camera), and of low-confidence areas due to regions of uniform intensity. As was discussed in the previous chapter, both properties are critical for the application of view synthesis.

The gradient-based approach has the following additional advantages, each of which will be discussed in more detail below.

- The evidence measure, which is only based on the local gradients, can be computed quickly and in parallel.

- For a given displacement, the measure can be accumulated by simply averaging over a certain area. The average value represents evidence for or against a match. This enables the use of a *displacement-oriented control strategy*, which is the topic of the next section.
- Finding maxima in the accumulated measure is a stable way of computing correspondences without smoothing across motion boundaries.
- Dominant displacements can be detected by accumulating the measure over large regions. This can be used to automatically select interesting displacement ranges, and also as attention cues in the context of active vision.

5.2 Displacement-oriented stereo

A stereo algorithm can proceed according to a *point-oriented* or a *displacement-oriented* control strategy. Informally, the point-oriented strategy is "For each location in one image, find the displacement that aligns this location with the best matching location in the other image," while the displacement-oriented control strategy is "Given a certain displacement, find all the locations that match well." This can be characterized more precisely by examining the loop structure of a stereo algorithm, as discussed below.

Conceptually, a stereo algorithm contains two nested loops, "for all points" and "for all disparities," which can be nested in two different ways. The outer loop of a *point-oriented* algorithm is "for all points." For each point in one image, the point is then compared ("for all disparities") with points in the other image to select the best match. Each comparison involves the aggregation of a similarity measure over a certain neighborhood (using a third loop, "for each location in the neighborhood of the point"). Thus, the total number of operations is $O(Ndw^2)$, where N is the number of points, d is the number of disparity levels, and w is the size of the (typically square) neighborhood of aggregation. The number of pixels N usually ranges from 70,000 to 300,000; the number of disparity levels d is usually between 10 and 100. The window size w is typically between 5 and 15.

In a *displacement-oriented* algorithm, the nesting of the loops is reversed. The outer loop is now "for each disparity." For each fixed disparity (i.e., a fixed translational offset between the two images), the similarity measure is then computed ("for all points") and subsequently aggregated ("for all neighborhoods of all points"). Finally, the best match across all disparities is selected for each point.

Obviously, simply switching the order of the loops does not affect the complexity at all, which is still $O(Ndw^2)$ for the naive implementation of the displacement-oriented algorithm outlined above. However, the aggregation step at each disparity level (which corresponds to a convolution with a finite kernel of size $w \times w$) can usually be performed faster. If this kernel is *separable*[1] – as is the case for a Gaussian kernel, for example – the convolution can be performed in $O(Nw)$ instead of $O(Nw^2)$ time. For a *constant* kernel (i.e., a box filter), the convolution can be performed with a constant number of operations per pixel, so that the time further decreases to $O(N)$. It is possible to approximate non-constant kernels such as the Gaussian by a sequence of box-filter operations [Wells, 1986]. In practice, the total running time of the displacement-oriented algorithm is therefore only $O(Nd)$.

A drawback of the displacement-oriented algorithm is that its space requirements are higher, since it is necessary to store the current best match for all points, instead of only for one point. If the procedure for picking the best match is more complex than a simple minimization and needs to examine all match values, the space requirements for the displacement-oriented algorithm are $O(Nd)$, as compared to $O(N + d)$ for the point-oriented algorithm.

Recall from Section 2.2.1 that stereo algorithms can be divided into two groups, according to whether the computation of matching cost and the spatial aggregation can be separated or not. Some matching costs (for example, correlation) are defined over a fixed support region, and thus combine cost computation and aggregation into one step. In such cases, the displacement-oriented control strategy offers no advantages over the point-oriented control strategy. The point-oriented strategy is also the right choice if the disparity estimation of a sparse subset of points is sufficient for the application. This approach has been taken in the context of rover navigation [Robert *et al.*, 1995].

If a dense disparity map needs to be computed, however, it is usually better to use a displacement-oriented algorithm. This includes the application of view synthesis. Besides the faster performance, a displacement-oriented algorithm is also more easily parallelizable. (In the next chapter we will discuss a highly parallel aggregation method based on iterative diffusion.) Thus, a measure for which cost computation and aggregation can be performed in separate steps is preferable.

5.3 The evidence measure

We will now describe the gradient-based evidence measure in detail. The particular measure we introduce has proven to work quite well, and is an example of a measure that can be used in a displacement-oriented control strategy. In the following, we will treat an image as a continuous intensity function $I(x, y)$; we will discuss dealing with discrete images in Section 5.3.3.

[1] A two-dimensional convolution kernel is *separable* if it can be expressed as the convolution of two one-dimensional kernels.

5.3.1 Comparing two gradient vectors

As mentioned in Section 5.1, the method combines the notions of similarity and confidence (or distinctiveness) into a single measure of *evidence* for or against a match at a certain location under a certain displacement. The basic idea is to compare the two intensity gradients at this location. In particular, if $\mathbf{g}_L$ and $\mathbf{g}_R$ are the two gradient vectors to be compared, we use the average gradient magnitude

$$\overline{m} = (|\mathbf{g}_L| + |\mathbf{g}_R|)/2 \tag{5.1}$$

to represent confidence, and the (negated) magnitude of the difference of the two gradients

$$-d = -|\mathbf{g}_L - \mathbf{g}_R| \tag{5.2}$$

to represent similarity. We define the *evidence* for a match to be the weighted sum of these two terms:

$$\begin{aligned} e &= \overline{m} - \alpha\, d \qquad (5.3) \\ &= \frac{|\mathbf{g}_L| + |\mathbf{g}_R|}{2} - \alpha\, |\mathbf{g}_L - \mathbf{g}_R|. \end{aligned}$$

To achieve a symmetric range $[-m, m]$ of values for e when comparing two vectors of equal length m, we choose a weight parameter of $\alpha = 1$. (Evidence $e = m$ if the two vectors have the same direction, and $e = -m$ if the two vectors have opposite directions.) See Figure 5.1 for an illustration of the values of e for different pairs of gradient vectors.

If both gradients are zero, there is neither local evidence for nor against a match, and consequently $e = 0$. Note that the measure ignores the original intensities, although one can argue that comparing the intensity values directly can provide additional information (in particular, evidence *against* a match, in case the intensities are very different). In practice, however, comparing absolute intensity values is not very stable, since individual cameras often differ by global additive and multiplicative intensity factors (i.e., bias and gain).[2]

The evidence value e can also be zero for two non-zero gradient vectors, for example, in the case of two vectors of equal length subtending an angle of 60°. Intuitively, this reflects the situation where the directions of the gradients are too different to consider it a match, but not different enough to count it as a mismatch. Of course, the right value for this "angle of zero evidence" might depend on the application, in particular on how much rotation is possible in the motion between two images. By choosing a higher weight α for the

---

[2] Other approaches for dealing with global intensity changes include filtering the images [O'Gorman and Sanderson, 1987], using non-parametric measures [Zabih, 1994], and utilizing explicit models of image brightness [Gennert, 1988; Fuh and Maragos, 1991; Negahdaripour and Yu, 1993].

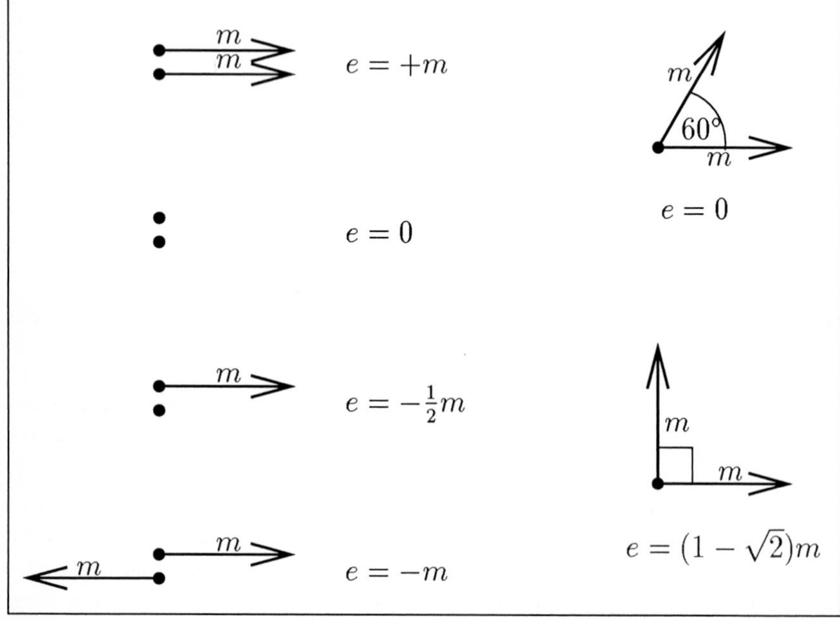

Fig. 5.1. The evidence measure e for different pairs of gradient vectors. The illustration shows the value of the evidence measure $e = \overline{m} - d$ for different pairs of gradient vectors of length m (represented by an arrow) and of length 0 (represented by a dot).

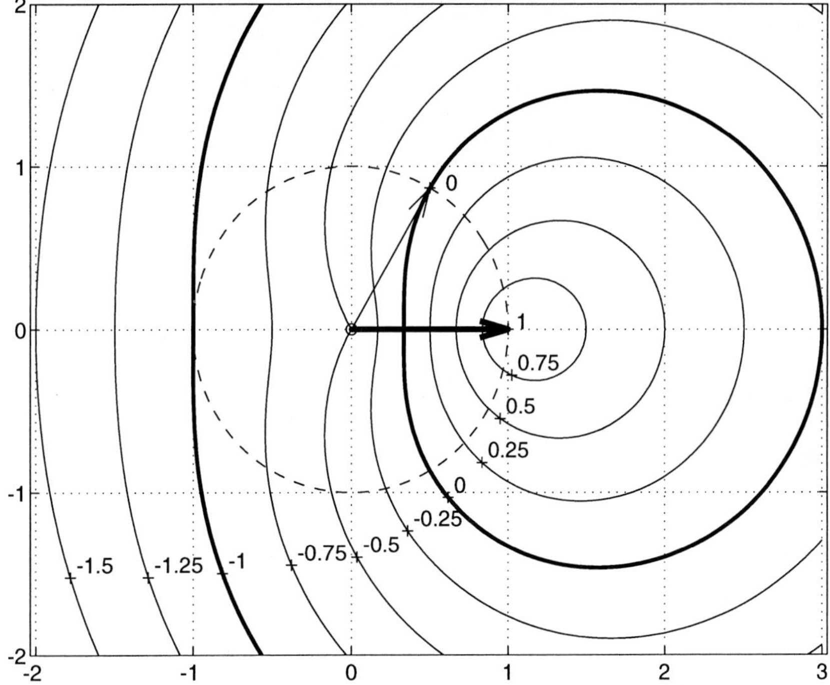

Fig. 5.2. Contour lines of the evidence measure e for a match with the unit vector $(1,0)$. The unit vector at angle 60° is shown as an example; note that its endpoint lies on the $e = 0$ curve.

gradient difference, one can reduce the angle for which $e = 0$. Our experiments have indicated, however, that changing the weight is not critical, and that $\alpha = 1$ is a reasonable general choice.

Figure 5.2 shows a contour plot of e for comparing any vector (x, y) to the unit vector $(1,0)$. The contour lines are the locations of the endpoints of all vectors that yield the same value e.

5.3.2 Comparing gradient fields

We now extend the measure to entire images. Let $I_L(x, y)$, $I_R(x, y)$ be the two images, and let ∇I_L, ∇I_R be their gradient vector fields. That is,

$$\nabla I_L = \begin{bmatrix} \frac{\partial I_L}{\partial x} \\ \frac{\partial I_L}{\partial y} \end{bmatrix}, \quad \nabla I_R = \begin{bmatrix} \frac{\partial I_R}{\partial x} \\ \frac{\partial I_R}{\partial y} \end{bmatrix}. \tag{5.4}$$

For a given displacement $\delta = (\delta_x, \delta_y)$, the *evidence* E_δ for a match at (x, y) under this displacement is

$$E_\delta(x,y) = \frac{|\nabla I_L(x,y)| + |\nabla I_R(x+\delta_x, y+\delta_y)|}{2} \qquad (5.5)$$
$$- \alpha\, |\nabla I_L(x,y) - \nabla I_R(x+\delta_x, y+\delta_y)|.$$

As before, we will use a weight $\alpha = 1$ unless noted otherwise.

Note that we have specified the displacement as a general vector, with both x and y components. In the context of stereo on rectified images, it is sufficient to only consider a scalar (horizontal) disparity $d = \delta_x$. The evidence measure can also be used in a broader context to compute general image motion. For example, the two images could be taken sequentially by a single camera observing a dynamic environment (and possibly moving itself). In this case, a two-dimensional displacement range needs to be considered (see Section 5.5.3).

Yet a different possibility in the context of stereo is not to explicitly rectify the images, but to fold rectification and disparity into one instead. That is, the displacement function δ could be a continuous transformation acting on the original images that keeps the epipolar lines aligned.

5.3.3 Computing gradients of discrete images

In order to apply the method to discrete images, we need to approximate the derivatives by finite differences:

$$\frac{\partial I}{\partial x}(x,y) \approx \Delta_x I(x,y) = I[x+1,y] - I[x,y], \qquad (5.6)$$

$$\frac{\partial I}{\partial y}(x,y) \approx \Delta_y I(x,y) = I[x,y+1] - I[x,y]. \qquad (5.7)$$

These equations can be characterized by simply specifying the convolution kernels

$$\Delta_x = \begin{bmatrix} -1 & 1 \end{bmatrix}, \quad \Delta_y = \begin{bmatrix} 1 \\ -1 \end{bmatrix}. \qquad (5.8)$$

The above kernels estimate the gradients at locations *between* the pixels. To avoid this positional offset of 1/2 pixel, symmetric kernels can be used, which are derived by convolving the differencing kernel with an averaging kernel:

$$\begin{bmatrix} -1 & 0 & 1 \end{bmatrix} = \begin{bmatrix} -1 & 1 \end{bmatrix} \otimes \begin{bmatrix} 1 & 1 \end{bmatrix}, \quad \begin{bmatrix} 1 \\ 0 \\ -1 \end{bmatrix} = \begin{bmatrix} 1 \\ -1 \end{bmatrix} \otimes \begin{bmatrix} 1 \\ 1 \end{bmatrix} \qquad (5.9)$$

(where $\otimes$ denotes the *convolution operator*).

In practice, it is more stable to use square kernels that average not only in the direction of the gradient, but also in the direction orthogonal to it. This yields the well know *Sobel operator*:

$$\begin{bmatrix} -1 & 0 & 1 \\ -2 & 0 & 2 \\ -1 & 0 & 1 \end{bmatrix} = \begin{bmatrix} -1 & 1 \\ -1 & 1 \end{bmatrix} \otimes \begin{bmatrix} 1 & 1 \\ 1 & 1 \end{bmatrix}, \quad \begin{bmatrix} 1 & 2 & 1 \\ 0 & 0 & 0 \\ -1 & -2 & -1 \end{bmatrix} = \begin{bmatrix} 1 & 1 \\ -1 & -1 \end{bmatrix} \otimes \begin{bmatrix} 1 & 1 \\ 1 & 1 \end{bmatrix}.$$

A different set of gradient operators has been proposed by Simoncelli [1994] in a paper on the design of multi-dimensional derivative filters. Simoncelli argues that the estimation of gradients by simple differencing can give highly inaccurate results, and proposes an alternate set of small derivative kernels with sizes ranging from 2×2 to 5×5. These kernels are *separable* into two one-dimensional kernels: a symmetric prefilter kernel p_k, and an anti-symmetric derivative kernel d_k. The key idea underlying the design is that the prefilter and the derivative filter are *matched*, which means that the derivative filter should be a good approximation of the derivative of the prefilter. The filter pairs of size 3 and size 5 are

$$\begin{aligned} p_3 &= [\ 0.2242\ 0.5516\ 0.2242\ ], \\ d_3 &= [\ -0.4553\ 0.0\ 0.4553\ ], \end{aligned}$$

$$\begin{aligned} p_5 &= [\ 0.0357\ 0.2489\ 0.4308\ 0.2489\ 0.0357\ ], \\ d_5 &= [\ 0.1077\ -0.2827\ 0.0\ 0.2827\ 0.1077\ ]. \end{aligned}$$

The horizontal gradient is computed by convolution with the vertical prefilter and the horizontal derivative filter, while the vertical gradient is computed by convolution with the horizontal prefilter and the vertical derivative filter.

In our implementation we have experimented with both the simple 3×1 kernels from Equation (5.9), and Simoncelli's filters of size 3 and 5. We found no noticeable difference in performance, except that Simoncelli's filters perform a higher degree of smoothing (in particular the 5×5 filter), which results in loss of detail. This demonstrates that our method is robust, and insensitive to the particular choice of gradient computation. A small amount of smoothing is often necessary to compensate for quantization error and noise, however, and we have used a Gaussian filter with $\sigma = 0.5$ pixels in conjunction with the 3×1 kernels from Equation (5.9) for the experimental results reported here.

In computing the displacement fields, we only consider displacements $\delta = (\delta_x, \delta_y)$ whose components are multiples of whole pixels. If sub-pixel accuracy is required, it is possible to compute E_δ for non-integer displacements by interpolating the gradients. An alternative is to increase the resolution by interpolating the images before the gradients are computed.

For a given displacement, E_δ can be computed very fast, since only a few floating point operations and a single square root is needed at each pixel. The square root is necessary to compute the magnitude of the gradient differences. The two magnitudes of gradients $|\nabla I_L|$ and $|\nabla I_R|$, which do not depend on the displacement δ, only need to be computed once. The local nature of the computations makes the method ideally suited for a parallel implementation. In Section 5.7 we will discuss performance issues in more detail.

5.4 Accumulating the measure

Recall that area-based stereo methods involve the aggregation of a similarity measure over local neighborhoods. The reason is that the amount of local information at each point is insufficient to solve the underconstrained matching problem, in particular in the presence of noise. That is, if we were to maximize E_δ (across all δ) for each point in isolation, we would be left with a noisy and inconsistent displacement field.

To avoid these instabilities, we aggregate E_δ for each δ, using the displacement-oriented control strategy discussed in Section 5.2. The underlying assumption validating the aggregation step is that, almost everywhere, nearby points have similar displacements. This assumption is made by most stereo and motion methods that compute a dense displacement field (i.e., a dense depth map, or a dense motion field). It is based on the observation that most natural scenes are composed of solid objects with continuous surfaces. A slight change in viewpoint will usually yield very similar visual motions of neighboring points, except if the points belong to two different objects (i.e., lie on different sides of an occlusion boundary). Since discontinuities in the visual motion (or disparity) field caused by occlusion boundaries violate the "smooth motion" assumption, occlusion boundaries present the biggest problem for aggregation-based algorithms. This is the topic of the next chapter.

In this chapter we will use a uniform aggregation procedure, for each displacement δ independently (i.e., we will not aggregate across neighboring displacements). This corresponds to the assumption that the visual motion of neighboring points can be described locally by pure translation, or, in other words, that the surface geometry can be approximated by small fronto-parallel patches. The assumption is reasonable for small neighborhoods, in which the effects of surface slant and of perspective foreshortening are small. For the computation of general motion, this also restricts the allowable rotational component of the visual motion between corresponding image patches (although the gradient measure itself tolerates a certain amount of local rotation as was discussed above).

Some point-oriented motion methods utilize the assumption of a smooth motion field *after* computing initial matches by smoothing the displacement field, often employing some confidence measure associated with each match to constrain the smoothing process [Horn and Schunck, 1981; Anandan, 1989]. The problem is that this tends to smooth over motion discontinuities, which contain important information about the scene geometry.

In contrast, our displacement-oriented method uses the assumption of a smooth motion field *while* finding the matches. The idea is that if a certain displacement δ aligns two matching objects, E_δ will have a strong positive response at the location of the match. By aggregating E_δ over a certain area (i.e., computing the average or smoothing with a Gaussian filter), dominant motions can be detected. Only the correct displacement E_δ will yield support for a match over a larger area, thereby creating a maximum among all δ under consideration.

Note that our method does not smooth over motion boundaries, since it is not assumed that *all* close pixels have the same disparity. A point on a motion boundary will give rise to a positive response for two different displacements, corresponding to the two different motions. Depending on the amount of support for each of the two candidate displacements, however, it is possible that the point be "co-opted" into the wrong displacement. Instead of smoothing over the disparity values, this has the effect of *boundary blurring*. (A more detailed discussion of this phenomenon can be found in Section 6.2.) Ideally, the local response at the point could help in deciding between the two candidate displacements. If the two neighboring regions with different displacements also have different amounts of texture, however, the more strongly textured region will tend to dominate the estimated motion of the less textured region.

To accumulate E_δ, a simple convolution can be performed for each displacement δ. A box filter (i.e., averaging over a rectangular window) can be performed most quickly, but in our implementation we found that a convolution with a Gaussian kernel produces superior results. Using a Gaussian filter for accumulation, the influence of neighboring points decreases gradually with their distance. Another advantage is rotational symmetry. In practice, we use an approximation of a true Gaussian kernel by a sequence of three or four box-filter operations, as proposed by Wells [1986].

Since our measure represents *evidence* (instead of just similarity), the aggregated measure yields a meaningful way of comparing matches of larger areas, such as a quarter of an image or even an entire image. By accumulating E_δ over very large areas, it is possible to find an initial set of interesting displacements. Most displacements will only align a small subset of features, yielding a negative value for the accumulated E_δ. Only the displacements that align larger parts of the image will yield an above-average response, which can serve to select an initial set of displacements for which the matching with smaller windows is undertaken. In the next section we present experiments that demonstrate this discriminating property of the accumulated evidence measure. To speed up the initial selection of interesting displacements, a scale-space approach could be used. Peaks in the accumulated E_δ as a function of δ can also serve as attention cues for active vision systems.

5.5 Experiments

In this section we undertake several experiments to support the ideas presented so far. The first experiments demonstrate the ideas discussed in the previous section. We will then use the evidence measure to compute the disparities of a rectified stereo pair (with a 1D search). Finally, we will test the suitability of the measure for computing general image motion (using a

2D search). We will also demonstrate how the magnitude of the maximal response can be used as a confidence measure, which is important in the context of view synthesis.

5.5.1 Observing E_δ for interesting displacements

An interesting experiment is to observe a gray-level rendering of E_δ for different displacements δ. As test data we use a stereo pair from the *street* image sequence depicting a woman crossing a street, which is shown in Figure 5.3. The *street* images were provided by Wilfried Enkelmann, Fraunhofer Institut für Informations- und Datenverarbeitung IITB, Karlsruhe, Germany. This image pair is a challenging example because it contains large regions with little texture, and the absolute intensities are quite different between the two images.

To illustrate the power of using maxima in the accumulated measure E_δ as attention cues, we have selected the displacements that yield the strongest response (maximal $\sum E_\delta$) in each of the four quadrants of the image. Figure 5.4 shows plots of E_δ for the resulting four displacements δ. Gray corresponds to a value of zero, light to positive values, and dark to negative values. Note that these displacements align the dominant features in each quadrant, and also that the measure is insensitive to the brightness difference between the original images.

Figure 5.5 shows a surface plot of the cumulative response $\sum E_\delta$ over the entire image for a large range of displacements ($\delta_x = -40 \ldots 50$, and $\delta_y = -20 \ldots 20$). For comparison, Figure 5.6 shows a surface plot of the (negated) root-mean-square differences of the entire image under the different offsets. While both measures peak at roughly the same displacement of $\delta = (0, 0)$, the evidence measure is clearly more discriminatory.

5.5.2 Stereo: 1D search range

We now show disparity maps computed by a stereo matcher that uses the evidence measure to select matches. We use rectified images with purely horizontal displacements. After precomputing the gradients and gradient magnitudes, we compute E_δ for a range of different δ. The measure is then accumulated by smoothing each E_δ with a Gaussian filter G_σ:

$$\hat{E}_\delta = G_\sigma \otimes E_\delta. \tag{5.10}$$

In the experiments reported here, we use $\sigma = 2$. The disparity $D(x, y)$ at each point (x, y) is taken to be the displacement that maximizes the accumulated measure:

$$D = \arg\max_\delta \hat{E}_\delta. \tag{5.11}$$

In the first experiment, we use the *tree* image pair shown in Figure 5.7. These are two images from the Stanford *tree* sequence (provided by Harlyn

Fig. 5.3. The left and right images of the *street* pair used as test data for the gradient-based stereo method. The image pair is challenging in that it contains large untextured areas and global intensity differences due to different camera characteristics.

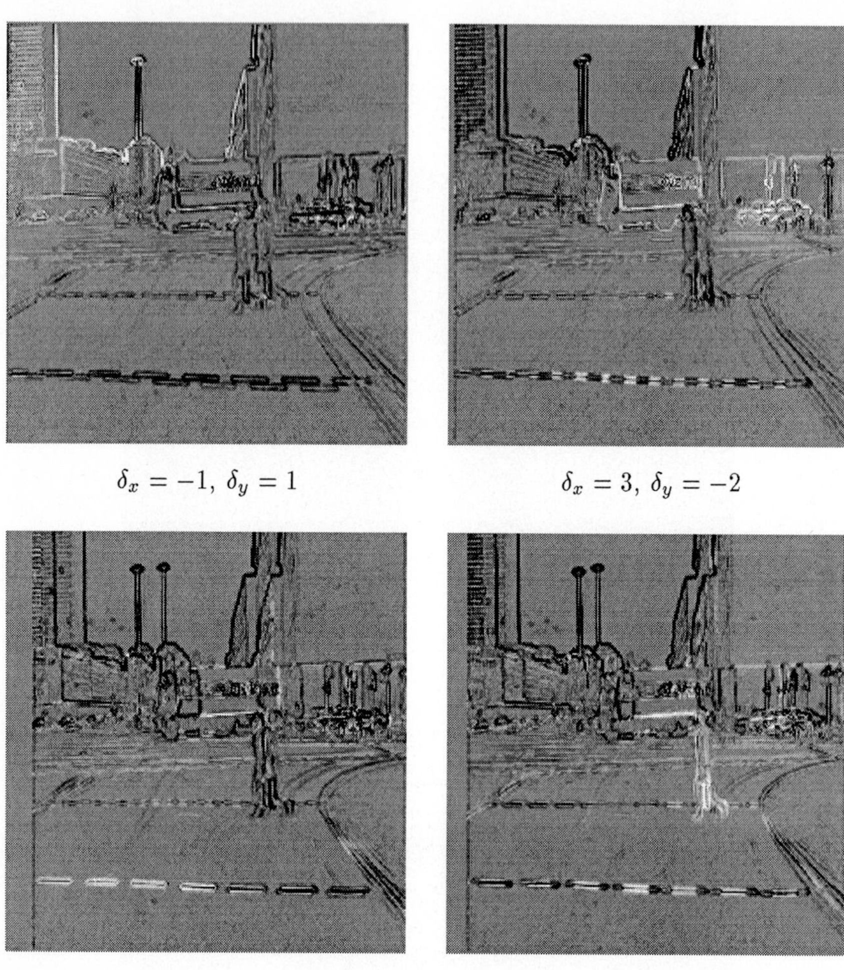

$\delta_x = -1,\ \delta_y = 1$ $\delta_x = 3,\ \delta_y = -2$

$\delta_x = 15,\ \delta_y = -1$ $\delta_x = 11,\ \delta_y = -2$

Fig. 5.4. Gray-level plots of E_δ for maximizing displacements. The four plots correspond to the displacements δ that maximize $\sum E_\delta$ in each of the four quadrants. Gray corresponds to a value of zero, light to positive values, and dark to negative values. Thus, light image regions indicate image features in alignment, while dark regions indicate mismatches. Most image regions are gray, indicating that there is neither evidence for nor against a match.

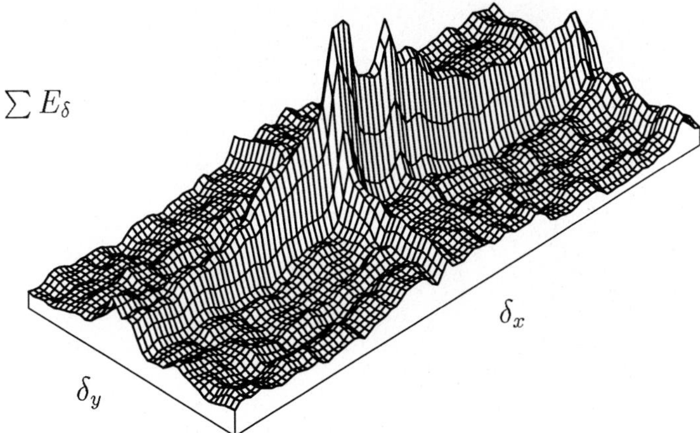

Fig. 5.5. Surface plot of the cumulative response $\sum E_\delta$ over the entire image for a displacement range of $\delta_x = -40 \dots 50$, and $\delta_y = -20 \dots 20$. The strongest peak is located at roughly $\delta = (0, 0)$. Note that the distinct ridge of high responses corresponds to purely horizontal displacements, which keep the epipolar lines aligned.

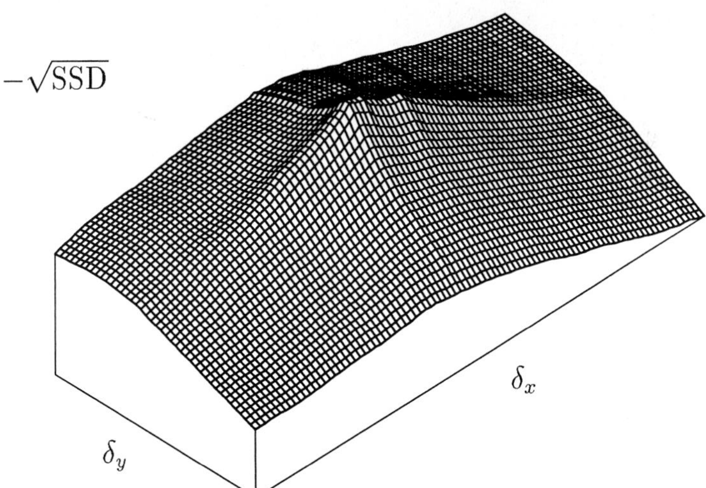

Fig. 5.6. Surface plot of the negated root-mean-square difference over the entire image for the same displacement range as in Figure 5.5. The sum of squared differences is clearly less discriminatory than the cumulative response $\sum E_\delta$.

Fig. 5.7. The left and right images of the *tree* pair.

Fig. 5.8. Disparities for the *tree* image pair. Gray levels correspond to disparities: lighter is closer, darker is farther away.

Baker and Bob Bolles at SRI), which was taken sequentially with a camera mounted on a horizontal motion stage. We use images 18 and 24 as right and left images respectively. The images depict an outdoor scene and are highly textured, and thus well suited for an area-based method.

Figure 5.8 shows a gray-level plot of the computed disparities. Lighter shades of gray correspond to closer points, darker shades correspond to points farther away. The considered disparity range is $\delta_x = 0 \ldots 12$.

In the next experiment we show how confidence can be incorporated into the matcher. We use the *street* image pair from Figure 5.3 above. The image pair has been rectified manually, so that the search range can again be restricted to displacements with $\delta_y = 0$. The confidence information is important for dealing with images containing untextured areas, which can lead to matching ambiguities. An advantage of the evidence measure is that the *value* M of the achieved maximum is related to the gradient magnitude at that point, and thus represents the confidence that the match is correct. Formally,

$$M = \max_{\delta} \hat{E}_{\delta}. \tag{5.12}$$

Unreliable matches can be suppressed by setting a threshold for the actual achieved maximum at each point. Figure 5.9 shows two gray-level plots of the computed disparities. The first image shows all computed disparities. Note the erroneous matches in untextured areas (e.g., the sky), and in areas

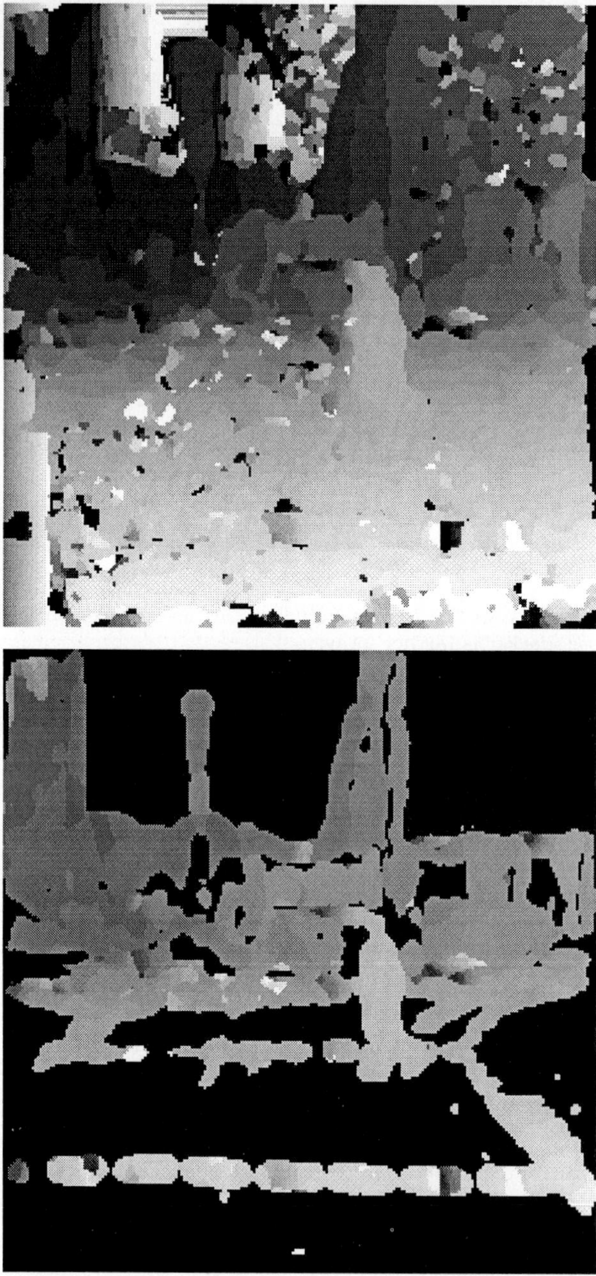

Fig. 5.9. Disparities for the *street* image pair. Gray levels correspond to disparities: lighter is closer, darker is farther away. In the bottom image, uncertain matches are displayed in black.

that can not be matched (e.g., the lower left corner). The second image shows only the disparities at locations for which $M > 2$ (i.e., the points with high confidence), while all other (unreliable) matches are displayed in black. The considered range of disparities is $\delta_x = -3 \ldots 21$. As opposed to feature-based matchers, which try to decide beforehand which locations to match, our method allows the selection of reliable points after the matching process.[3]

5.5.3 General motion: 2D search range

To test the method on general motion, we use frames 1 and 5 from the *cat* image sequence (provided by John Woodfill). The images are shown in Figure 5.10. The sequence depicts a cat walking on a lawn in front of some bushes. The camera follows the cat, so that the visual motion of the cat is almost only caused by its (non-rigid) change of shape, whereas the background moves by more than 10 pixels to the left. As the displacements are no longer constrained to occur along epipolar lines, we now have to consider a two-dimensional displacement range. Here, the considered ranges are $\delta_x = -15 \ldots 4$, $\delta_y = -2 \ldots 1$. Accumulation is done as before with a Gaussian filter G_σ with $\sigma = 2$.

Figure 5.11 shows the x-components of the displacements that maximize the accumulated measure. Like the *tree* images, the *cat* images are well textured, so we do not display the confidence information here.

5.6 Computing disparity maps for view synthesis

Recall from Chapters 3 and 4 that we need two symmetric disparity maps d_{12} and d_{21} for our view synthesis method. Furthermore, these disparity maps should satisfy the following requirements:

1. The occlusion boundaries need to be recovered accurately;
2. Partially occluded points need to be detected, and a disparity estimate needs to be computed for them (see Section 4.6);
3. Uncertain disparity estimates (in areas of uniform intensities) need to be replaced with a canonical depth interpretation (see Section 4.5).

We have implemented several extensions to our gradient-based method to deal with these requirements. We start by computing two disparity maps (left-to-right and right-to-left) independently using the method described above, and then perform several post-processing steps, which are explained in detail below. Figure 5.12 illustrates the post-processing of the disparity maps for the right image of the *kids* image pair.

[3] A confidence value can also be derived for other similarity measures (such as SSD) by examining the distribution of values for all disparities at each pixel [Matthies *et al.*, 1989].

Fig. 5.10. The *cat* image pair. The two images are frames 1 and 5 from a sequence of images containing camera motion as well as independent object motion.

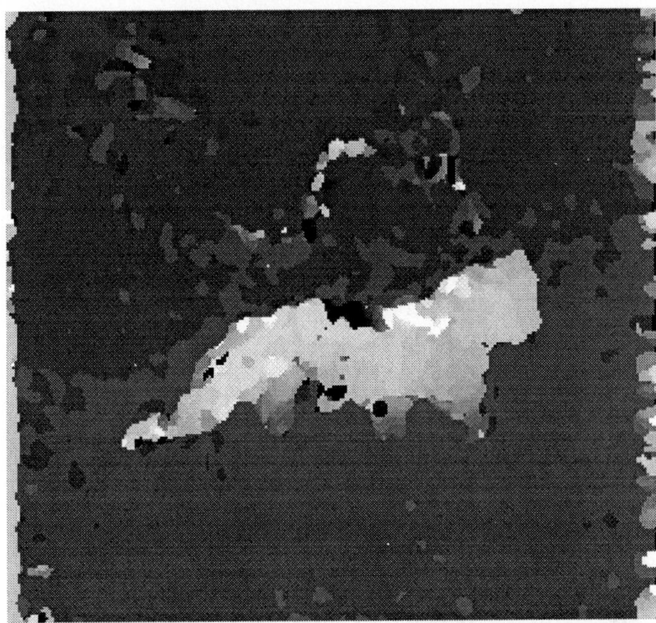

Fig. 5.11. Horizontal components of the maximizing displacements for the *cat* images. Dark shades correspond to motions to the left, light shades correspond to motions to the right.

5.6.1 Occlusion boundaries

In synthesized views, incorrectly recovered object boundaries can cause noticeable artifacts. Object boundaries typically correspond to coinciding intensity discontinuities and depth discontinuities. Our basic gradient-based method has the disadvantage that intensity discontinuities are not considered during the estimation of depth. (The same is true for any stereo method that uses a uniform aggregation process.) In particular, strongly textured objects in front of a fairly uniform background are often found too large, since the influence of matches with high certainty (within the object) extends past the objects' boundaries. Similarly, uniform objects in front of a textured background tend to be found too small.

To counteract this undesirable effect, we adjust the depth discontinuities in the computed disparity maps. We first compute intensity edges with the edge detector by Canny [1986], using the following parameters: $\sigma = 1$ for smoothing, $lo = 6$, and $hi = 10$. We then adjust depth discontinuities that are at most 4 pixels away from an edge such that they coincide with the edge. The first three images from the top in Figure 5.12 illustrate this process.

Although this post-processing step performs reasonably well in practice, it would be preferable to use a stereo method that recovers the location of

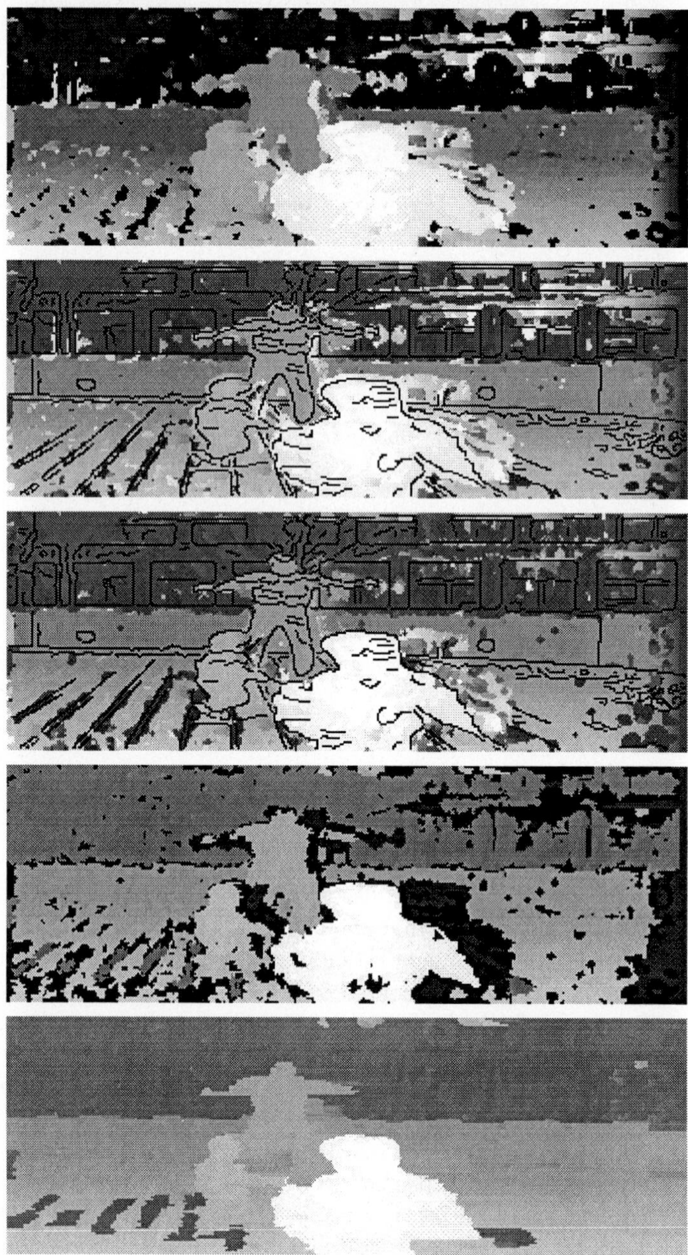

Fig. 5.12. Post-processing of the computed disparities for the right image of the *kids* pair. The figure shows from top to bottom the original disparities, the original disparities with edges overlaid, the adjusted disparities with edges overlaid, the disparities with partially occluded points detected, and the final extrapolated disparities.

depth discontinuities correctly in the first place. This is the motivation for the method presented in the next chapter.

5.6.2 Detecting partially occluded points and uniform regions

After the depth discontinuities have been adjusted, we detect partially occluded points by *cross-checking*. That is, we perform a consistency check between the two disparity maps, and mark every point whose left-to-right and right-to-left disparities disagree by more than a fixed amount t. That is, we mark all points (i, j) for which

$$|d_{12}(i,j) + d_{21}(i + d_{12}(i,j), j)| \geq t. \tag{5.13}$$

(Recall that d_{12} and d_{21} have different signs.) The allowable disparity difference t should be chosen proportional to the disparity range of the image pair. We use a value of $t = 3$ for the images in Figure 5.12, which have a disparity range of 4–48.

To deal with regions of uniform intensities, we also mark all points with insufficient confidence in the correctness of the match. Referring to Equation (5.12), we mark those points (i, j) for which

$$M(i,j) \leq 0. \tag{5.14}$$

Note that it is difficult to distinguish between partial occlusion and uncertain matches after the disparities have been computed, because partially occluded points often also match with low certainty, while uniform regions usually also result in disagreeing matches. We therefore use a single "unmatched" status for both cases. The fourth image in Figure 5.12 shows these unmatched points in black.

5.6.3 Extrapolating the disparities

We use the constant-depth hypothesis described in Section 4.6 to fill the unmatched regions in both disparity maps. In particular, we process each scanline and assign to all unmatched pixels the disparity of the adjacent *background* pixel. Note that this means that the holes in d_{12} are filled from the left, while the holes in d_{21} are filled from the right. (The unmatched pixels at the border of each image need to be filled from the other side, since they only have one neighboring disparity value.) The result of this disparity extrapolation process is shown in the bottom image in Figure 5.12.

5.7 Efficiency

As stated before, the computation of E_δ can be carried out very quickly, using precomputed gradients. In addition, the computation is easily parallelizable. A sequential implementation on a SPARCstation 5 takes 1.2 seconds to compute E_δ for a 512×512 pixel image.

Depending on the hardware, additional speed can be gained by approximating the Euclidean norm L_2, which involves the computation of a square root, by simpler norms such as the L_1 or the L_∞ norm.

These norms are not rotationally invariant; their relative error with respect to the Euclidean norm depends on the orientation of the vector. One can visualize this by comparing the unit circles of the different norms, which are a diamond, a circle, and a square for L_1, L_2, and L_∞, respectively. A much better approximation to the circle is given by an octagon, and the corresponding norm is only slightly more complicated. It can be expressed as a weighted sum of the L_1 and the L_∞ norm:

$$L_{\text{oct}} = \beta(\alpha L_1 + (1-\alpha)L_\infty). \tag{5.15}$$

A weight $\alpha = \sqrt{2} - 1$ yields a regular octagon; together with the optimal scaling factor $\beta = 2/(1+\sqrt{4-\sqrt{8}})$ the relative error $(L_2 - L_{\text{oct}})/L_2$ always remains below 4%. Thus, the best weighted sum is given by

$$L_{\text{oct}} = f_1 L_1 + f_\infty L_\infty, \tag{5.16}$$

with

$$\begin{aligned} f_1 &= (\sqrt{2}-1)\frac{2}{1+\sqrt{4-\sqrt{8}}} \approx 0.3978, \\ f_\infty &= (2-\sqrt{2})\frac{2}{1+\sqrt{4-\sqrt{8}}} \approx 0.5626. \end{aligned} \tag{5.17}$$

Using L_{oct} instead of the Euclidean norm in the computation of E_δ can yield a speedup of 30%, depending on the hardware. This can be particularly interesting for highly parallel architectures where single processors have only limited arithmetic capabilities.

Experiments indicate that the results of the matching process are usually not affected by this change, and depend mainly on the qualitative "shape" of the evidence function e. This is further indication of the robustness of our method.

5.8 Discussion and possible extensions

A problem with the measure discussed here is that partially aligned intensity edges yield a positive response, which can make it hard to find the component of the displacement that is parallel to these edges. For example, in Figure 5.9 one can observe errors in the computed disparities of the street marks in the foreground of the scene. This is due to the so-called *aperture problem*, which states that, locally, only the component of displacement in the direction of the intensity gradient can be recovered. Thus, edges that are aligned with the epipolar lines present a problem for all stereo algorithms, since their disparity can not be estimated locally.

An important observation is that derivatives of all orders can contribute to evidence *against* a match, while evidence *for* a match is harder to capture. That is, different absolute intensities as well as different gradients are indicators for a mismatch, while (purely local) identical intensities are not evidence for a match, and identical gradients only tell us about a match in the direction of the gradient. Other information needs to be taken into account to avoid these *false positives.* For example, in a calibrated stereo system in which the epipolar lines coincide with the scanlines, only the gradient in the x direction should be counted as evidence for a match (but the gradient in the y direction can still tell us about mismatches).

As mentioned earlier, an obvious extension to the current method would be to incorporate it into a scale-space approach, and thereby make the evidence measure sensitive to a larger pool of displacements. Multiple scales can also be used in accumulating E_δ, to allow for varying levels of detail of image features.

5.9 Summary

In this chapter we have presented a simple yet powerful method to perform point-to-point matching between two images. The method uses an *evidence measure* that is based on the gradient fields of the images and that combines the notions of *similarity* between two locations, and *confidence* for a correct match. The computation of the measure is simple and highly parallelizable. Furthermore, the method is robust with respect to the computation of the intensity gradients, the choice of the weight parameter α, and approximations to the Euclidean norm.

For a given displacement, the measure can be accumulated over a larger area, to collect evidence for or against a match at this location. Using a *displacement-oriented* control strategy that accumulates evidence for a range of different displacements, dominant motions can be detected, which can serve as attention cues in an active vision system.

Finding maxima in the accumulated measure is a stable way of computing correspondences without smoothing across motion boundaries. The method works well both on highly textured images and on images containing regions of uniform intensities, and can be used for a variety of applications, including stereo vision, motion segmentation, object tracking, and active vision.

6. Stereo Using Diffusion

The topic of this chapter is diffusion-based stereo. The methods presented here are motivated by the problem of *boundary blurring* inherent in most area-based approaches. As we have seen, poorly localized boundaries can yield strong visual artifacts in synthesized views. Thus, the correct recovery of object boundaries by the stereo algorithm is critical.

Boundary blurring in area-based stereo is caused by the presence of multiple points at different depths in the supporting area around a point. That is, the underlying assumption that all points in the supporting area have the same displacement is violated. This can be caused by perspective foreshortening, by partially occluded points, and if the supporting region spans a depth boundary. Thus, the estimated disparities of points close to object boundaries are often wrong.

The central problem is to find the optimal size and shape of the support region. If the region is too small, a wrong match might be found due to ambiguities and noise. If the region is too big, it can no longer be matched as a whole. Ideally, we would like the support region to be as large as possible without crossing object boundaries. To find the boundaries, however, we would need to run a stereo algorithm first.

Jones and Malik [1992a] have proposed an iterative solution to this "recursive" problem. An initial run of a stereo algorithm yields estimates of the location of depth boundaries, which are then used to control the size of support regions in subsequent runs.

Kanade and Okutomi have addressed the problem of choosing the right support region with *adaptive windows* [Okutomi and Kanade, 1992; Kanade and Okutomi, 1994]. At each point, a rectangular window is grown to an optimal size based on an estimate of disparity uncertainty in the current window. A greedy algorithm (gradient descent) is used to select the best of the four possible directions to grow the window at each step.

A different way of implementing variable support regions is proposed by Boykov *et al.* [1997]: using a maximum likelihood argument, the plausible matches at each disparity level are grouped into connected components. The disparity at each pixel is then selected to be the one with the largest connected component of support.

The approach taken in this chapter avoids the problem of explicitly selecting the optimal size and shape of the support region. Instead of using fixed windows, we aggregate support using *non-uniform* and *non-linear diffusion*.

Recall from Section 2.2.1 that area-based stereo algorithms typically perform four tasks: computing a local matching cost, aggregating support spatially, finding the best disparity, and computing a sub-pixel disparity estimate. This framework allows us to compare different approaches that have been taken for each task in isolation, without being distracted by how the other tasks are being solved. In the previous chapter, we focussed on a new matching cost; in this chapter, we focus mainly on the second task: aggregating support. We discuss various kinds of local diffusion, including a membrane model and a Bayesian model, and contrast them with existing approaches, such as SSD and adaptive windows.

The other three tasks, although important, are not the central issue of this chapter. Unless noted otherwise, we use squared intensity differences as a matching cost, and, after the aggregation step, simply select the best disparity locally at each pixel. In the cases where we compute sub-pixel disparity estimates, we fit a parabola to the three cost values centered around the best disparity. It is important to keep in mind that the algorithms presented here are independent of these choices and apply also to more sophisticated matching costs and disparity selection strategies.

We start by introducing the concept of *disparity space*, which is used by all our diffusion algorithms. We then review the traditional SSD algorithm, and discuss the need for spatially-adaptive support regions. In Sections 6.3 and 6.4 we introduce aggregation by diffusion, and discuss a non-uniform diffusion process using *local stopping.* We then develop a Bayesian model of stereo using explicit disparity distributions, and a novel iterative support aggregation algorithm based on this model in Section 6.5. We present a comparative experimental evaluation of our algorithms in Section 6.6, and close with a discussion of the results.

6.1 Disparity space

As was discussed in Section 5.2, the control strategy of a stereo algorithm can be *point-oriented* or *displacement-oriented.* For a square, fixed-size support region, a point-oriented algorithm would compare a square window in one image with several windows on the corresponding scanline.[1] This is illustrated in Figure 6.1 (**a**). The same computation can be performed more efficiently by a displacement-oriented algorithm in a 3D data volume that we call *disparity space* (Figure 6.1 (**b**)): for each displacement, the matching cost can be aggregated at all points by convolution with the window. The best match can then be selected in each vertical *disparity column.*

[1] Throughout this chapter we assume rectified images.

(a)

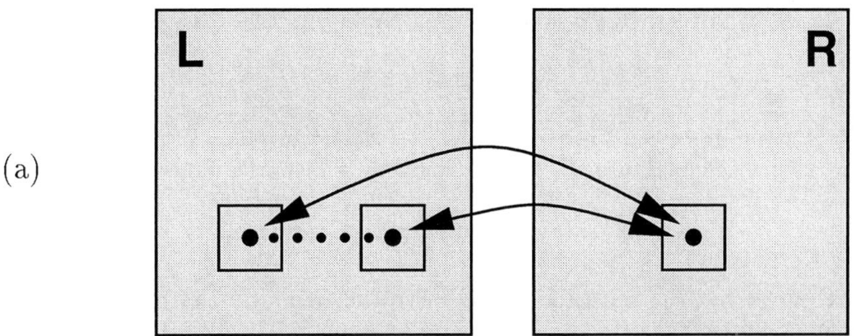

(b)

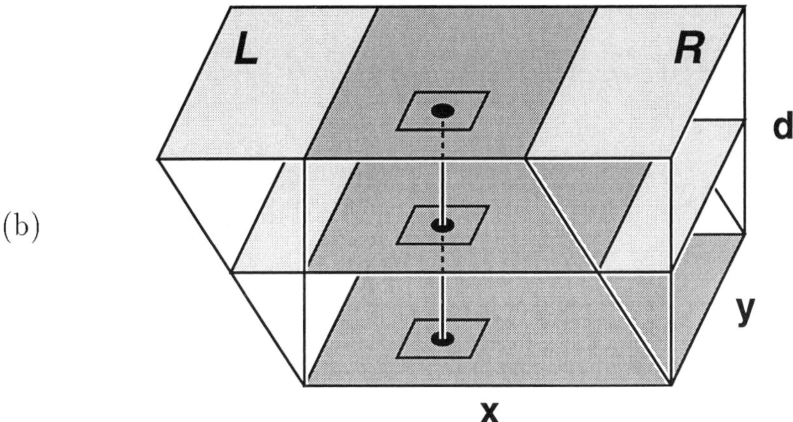

Fig. 6.1. Comparing windows in disparity space. **(a)** A point-oriented stereo algorithm compares a window in one image with several windows in the other image. **(b)** The same computation in disparity space. After convolving each layer with a square window, the best match is selected in a vertical *disparity column*.

Formally, we define the initial (not yet aggregated) disparity space E_0 as

$$E_0(x, y, d) = \rho(I_L(x + d, y) - I_R(x, y)), \tag{6.1}$$

where I_L, I_R, are the intensity functions of the left and right images respectively, and ρ measures the similarity between two intensities, e.g.,

$$\rho(l - r) = (l - r)^2. \tag{6.2}$$

This formulation uses I_R as the *reference image.* After aggregating support into a final space $E(x, y, d)$, we can compute a disparity function

$$d(x, y) = \arg\min_{d \in D} E(x, y, d) \tag{6.3}$$

that represents the matches as offsets to the points in the right image. In practice, we will use the discrete disparity space $E(i, j, d) = E(x_i, y_j, d)$ and

$$d_{i,j} = d(x_i, y_j). \tag{6.4}$$

E is a skewed version of the symmetric disparity space $\hat{E}$ [Marr and Poggio, 1976],

$$\hat{E}(x_R, x_L, y) = \rho(I_R(x_R, y) - I_L(x_L, y)), \tag{6.5}$$

which is not biased towards either eye. In a symmetric setting, however, it is more difficult to enforce uniqueness for each pixel and to define the final disparity map. (See Section 6.7 for a discussion.) Figure 6.2 illustrates the shape of slices through E and $\hat{E}$ for a given y and a limited disparity range $D = [d_{\min}, d_{\max}]$.

6.2 The SSD algorithm and boundary blurring

The standard sum-of-squared-differences algorithm (SSD) uses square windows to aggregate the evidence at each disparity. As mentioned before, choosing the right window size involves a trade-off between a noisy disparity map and blurring of depth boundaries. We will illustrate this using two synthetic image pairs. Both pairs have the same disparity pattern (see Figure 6.3): a central square floating in front of a background with constant disparity. Figure 6.3 (c) includes the occlusion information: the area displayed in white can not be matched due to occlusion, and thus algorithms will assign arbitrary disparities in this region.

Figure 6.4 shows the two synthetic image pairs based on this disparity pattern. The first pair, *ramp*, is similar to the image pair in Figure 5 in the paper by Kanade and Okutomi [1994], which we will use as a benchmark for our results. The image pair is based on a linear intensity ramp in the direction of the baseline; Gaussian noise has been added to each image independently.

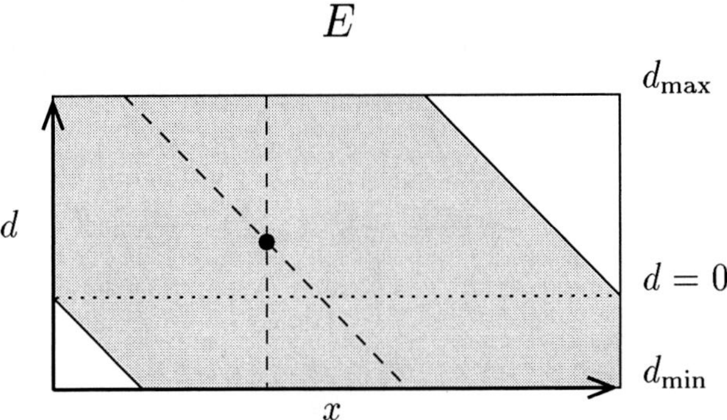

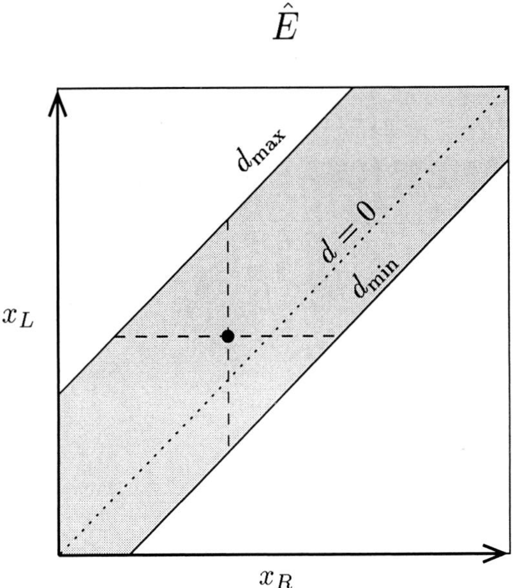

Fig. 6.2. Slices through (skewed) disparity space E and symmetric disparity space $\hat{E}$ for a fixed y. The lines of sight are shown as dashed lines for a given point in disparity space. The vertical dashed line corresponds to the right line of sight in both representations.

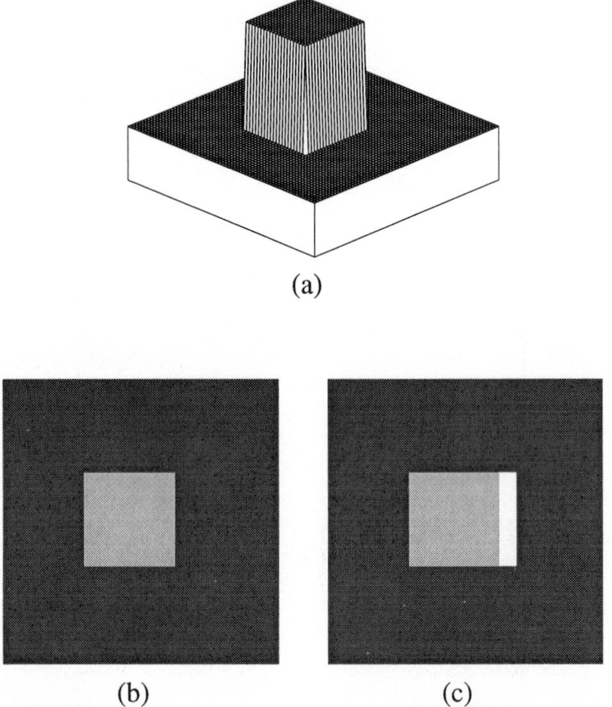

Fig. 6.3. The disparity pattern for the *ramp* and *rds* pairs: (a) isometric plot; (b) gray-level encoding; (c) gray-level encoding with occlusion information.

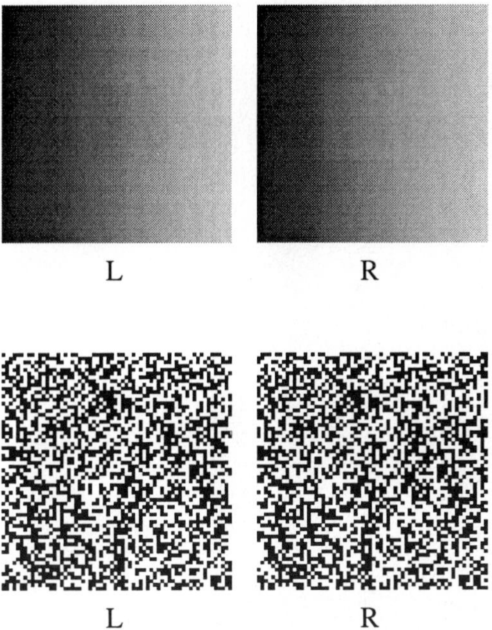

Fig. 6.4. Synthetic stereo pairs *ramp* (top) and *rds* (bottom). The left and right images of both pairs differ in that a central square region is offset horizontally.

The second image pair, *rds*, is based on a binary random dot pattern using two gray levels with equal probability. No noise has been added to this image pair.

The two image pairs are quite different. The *ramp* pair has no local texture variation and constant gradients everywhere, except for the boundaries of the central square. The two images can only be matched by comparing absolute intensities, and any algorithm based on band-pass filtered intensities or gradients will fail (as will the human visual system). The *rds* pair, on the other hand, has strong local texture variation, but is highly ambiguous since pixels not in correspondence still have a 50% chance of matching.

Figure 6.5 shows the performance of the simple SSD algorithm on these two image pairs using two different window sizes, $w = 3$ and $w = 7$. As can be seen, the bigger window size yields a disparity map with less noise, but results in an overall blurring of the features. (The "bumpiness" in the recovered disparities is due to sub-pixel disparity estimation, which is done by fitting a parabola to the three SSD values centered around the best match.) The effect on the two image pairs is quite different: in the ramp pair, the disparities are smoothed across the boundaries, while in the *rds* pair only the *outlines* of the square are blurred, i.e., the corners are rounded, while the two disparity levels of foreground and background are clearly recovered.

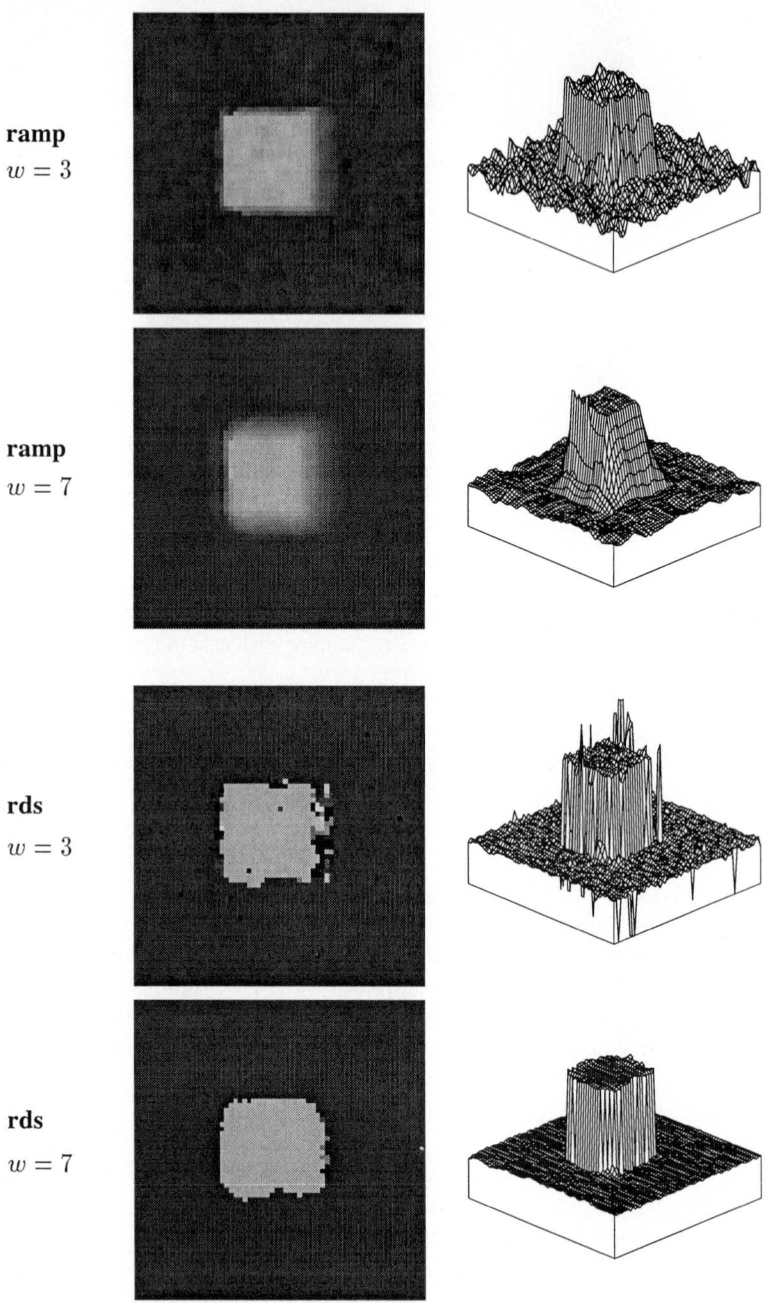

Fig. 6.5. Performance of the SSD algorithm using square windows with sizes $w = 3$ and $w = 7$ on the *ramp* and *rds* image pairs.

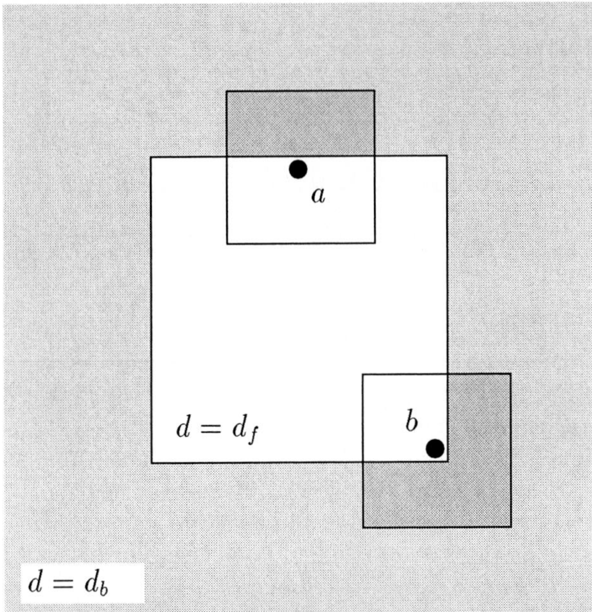

Fig. 6.6. Support for the two disparities d_f and d_b of foreground and background for two points a and b close to the boundary of the central square.

The latter effect, smoothing of object boundaries, is more common in real image pairs than the smoothing of disparities. The smoothing of disparities we observed in the *ramp* pair is a direct result of the ramp intensity pattern and the small local variations in intensity.

Let us briefly discuss the reasons for boundary blurring by considering the support for two points a and b inside the central square, but close to its boundary (see Figure 6.6). Both points receive partial support for the two disparities d_f and d_b of foreground and background respectively, and little support for other disparities. Point a, lying next to one of the sides of the square, receives slightly more support from the inside of the square, and is thus correctly found to be at disparity d_f. Point b, lying in the corner, however, receives more support for d_b, since almost 3/4 of its support region covers the background, and thus is erroneously found to be at disparity d_b. The overall effect is that corners get rounded since points close to corners are "co-opted" into the wrong disparity. Straight object boundaries are not affected. Note also that no smoothing of the disparity values takes place.

6.3 Aggregating support by diffusion

Instead of using a fixed window, support can also be aggregated with a weighted support function such as a Gaussian. A convolution with a Gaussian can be implemented using local iterative diffusion [Szeliski and Hinton, 1985] defined by the equation

$$\frac{\partial E}{\partial t} = \nabla^2 E. \tag{6.6}$$

In a discrete system, this yields the update rule

$$E(i,j,d) \leftarrow (1-4\lambda)E(i,j,d) + \lambda \sum_{(k,l)\in\mathcal{N}_4} E(i+k,j+l,d), \tag{6.7}$$

where $\mathcal{N}_4 = \{(-1,0),(1,0),(0,-1),(0,1)\}$ is the local neighborhood containing the four direct neighbors, and λ controls the speed of the diffusion. A value of $\lambda < 0.25$ is needed to ensure convergence; we use $\lambda = 0.15$ for the experiments reported in this chapter.

Aggregation using a finite number of simple diffusion steps yields results fairly similar to using square windows. Advantages include the rotational symmetry of the support kernel and the fact that points further away have gradually less influence. The problem of boundary blurring still exists, however.

6.3.1 The membrane model

A problem with simple diffusion is that the size of the support region increases with the number of iterations. In other words, while the diffusion would eventually converge to a uniform support covering the whole image, we are interested in an intermediate time step in which the diffusion has only progressed to a certain degree. We can change this behavior by adding a term to the diffusion equation that measures the amount each current value has diverged from its original value, yielding the *membrane equation* [Terzopoulos, 1986; Szeliski and Hinton, 1985].

$$\frac{\partial E}{\partial t} = \nabla^2 E + \beta(E_0 - E). \tag{6.8}$$

In the discrete implementation we use

$$E(i,j,d) \leftarrow [1-\lambda(\beta+4)]E(i,j,d) + \lambda \left[\beta E_0(i,j,d) + \sum_{(k,l)\in\mathcal{N}_4} E(i+k,j+l,d)\right]. \tag{6.9}$$

Unless noted otherwise, we use the parameters $\lambda = 0.15$ and $\beta = 0.5$ in the experimental results shown in this chapter. The β-term ensures that the diffusion converges to a stable solution not too far from the original values.

Figure 6.7 shows the results of applying our diffusion process to the *rds* image pair. The amount of support at each discrete disparity level is shown before diffusion (E_0), after one iteration, and after 10 iterations. Light regions

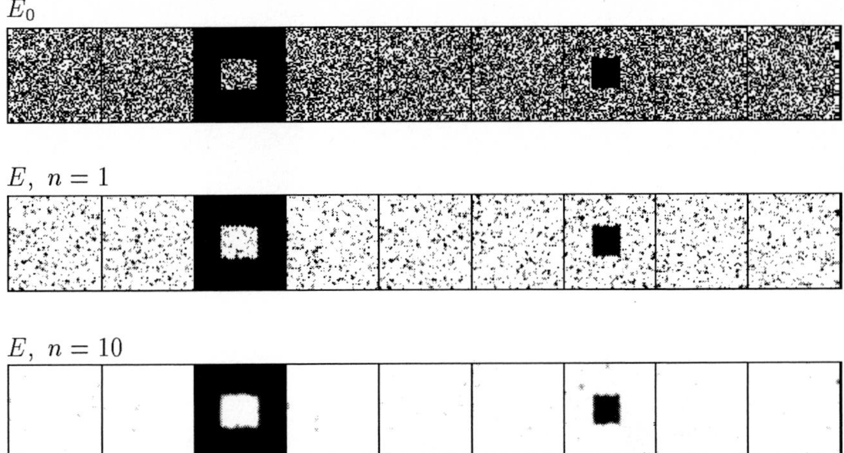

Fig. 6.7. Sections through the disparity space of the *rds* image pair during diffusion using the membrane model. The initial disparity space E_0 is displayed at the top. The diffused disparity space E is shown after one iteration (middle) and after 10 iterations (bottom). Light regions correspond to little support, dark regions indicate strong support.

correspond to little support, dark regions indicate strong support. Figure 6.8 shows the results for accumulating support using the membrane model for the *ramp* and *rds* pairs. The number of diffusion iterations is $n = 10$ (the results are almost identical at $n = 5$).

Using the membrane model alleviates the contour blurring problem to some extent, since the β-term "ties" the center of each support region to its original value. For very noisy images, however, β needs to be chosen quite small to produce enough smoothing for stable matching, making the process more similar to regular diffusion.

6.3.2 Support function for the membrane model

Analyzing the shape of the support function for the membrane model yields additional intuition. A solution for the support function can be derived using Fourier analysis as follows. The support function (i.e., *impulse response* or *kernel*) for the membrane model (6.8) is a function that can be convolved with the original input data E_0 to yield the final value of E. This function can be computed by setting E_0 to a unit impulse $E(i,j) = \delta(i)\delta(j)$, and setting the right-hand side of Equation (6.8) to 0.

For the discrete case, this involves solving the coupled set of equations

$$\beta\left(\delta(i)\delta(j) - f(i,j)\right) + \sum_{(k,l)\in\mathcal{N}_4} \left(f(i+k,j+l) - f(i,j)\right) = 0 \qquad (6.10)$$

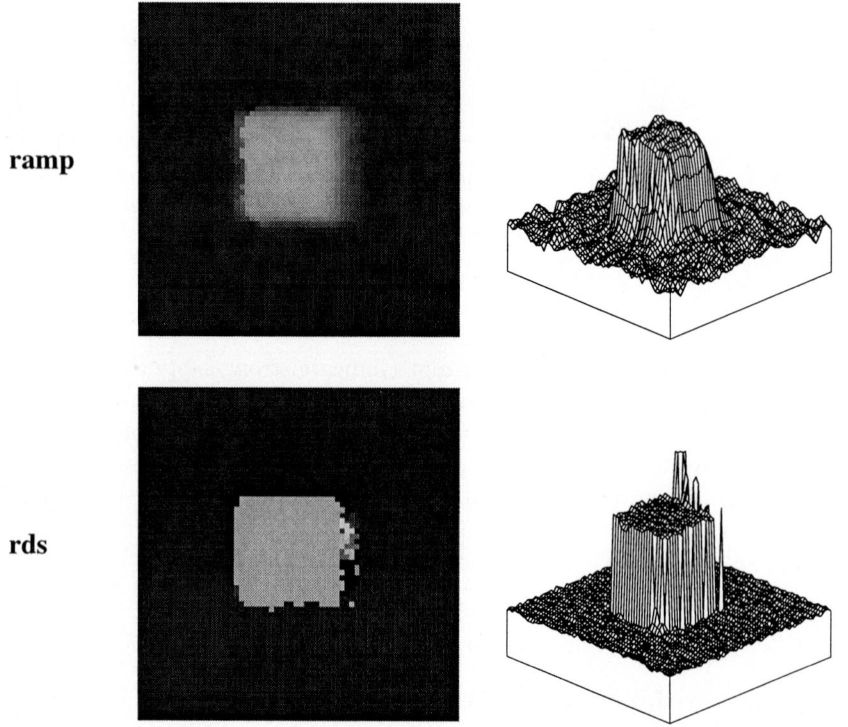

Fig. 6.8. Performance of the membrane model on the *ramp* and *rds* image pairs (gray level images and isometric plots).

(the support function is the same for all disparity levels d). Re-writing these in the Fourier domain, we obtain

$$\beta(1 - F(\omega_x, \omega_y)) + \sum_{(k,l)\in\mathcal{N}_4} \left(F(\omega_x, \omega_y)e^{j(k\omega_x + l\omega_y)} - F(\omega_x, \omega_y)\right) = 0 \quad (6.11)$$

or

$$F(\omega_x, \omega_y) = \frac{\beta}{\beta + 4 - 2\cos\omega_x - 2\cos\omega_y}. \quad (6.12)$$

While the inverse transform of $F(\omega_x, \omega_y)$ has no closed-form solution, it can be computed numerically. Figure 6.9 shows plots of the support function. It can be seen that the kernel is cone-shaped, as opposed to the rounded shape of a Gaussian kernel. This matches our intuition of assigning more weight to the center pixel. However, both regular diffusion and the membrane model yield identical, rotationally symmetric support regions at every location. We now turn to non-uniform diffusion methods to achieve adaptive support.

6.4 Diffusion with local stopping

The first non-uniform diffusion strategy for preventing both corner co-opting and diffusion to uniformity is to locally stop the diffusion process depending on the distribution of values in each disparity column. To do this, we associate a measure of *certainty* $C(i,j)$ with each location. Intuitively, this measure should reflect how "clear" a minimum there is among the values $E(i,j,d)$ for all d. Given such a measure C, we can aggregate support using *non-uniform diffusion*:

> For each (i,j), compute certainties C and C' before and after a single iteration of diffusion. If $C(i,j) > C'(i,j)$, do not diffuse, i.e., restore the old values $E(i,j,d)$ for all d.

The idea is that diffusion takes place only at locations of ambiguous matches. Also, certainties never decrease, thus guaranteeing convergence.

We have experimented with several different certainty measures. The two measures that worked best are the *winner margin* and the *entropy*. The winner margin C_m is the normalized difference between the minimum and the second minimum in a disparity column:

$$C_m(i,j) = \frac{E_{\min 2} - E_{\min}}{\sum_d E(i,j,d)}, \quad (6.13)$$

with

$$E_{\min} = \min_d E(i,j,d), \quad E_{\min 2} = \min_{d, E(i,j,d) \neq E_{min}} E(i,j,d). \quad (6.14)$$

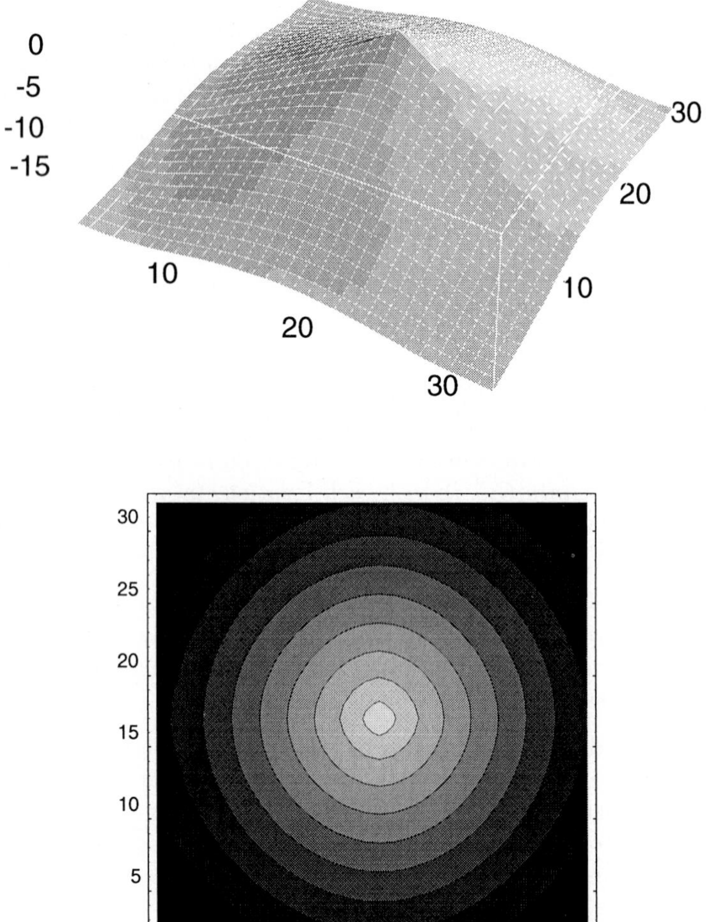

Fig. 6.9. Shape of the membrane support function for $\beta = 0.7$: 3D plot (top) and contour plot (bottom).

The second measure C_e is the negative entropy of the probability distribution in the disparity column. We convert to probabilities by taking the inverse exponent and normalizing[2]:

$$C_e(i,j) = -\sum_d p(d)\log p(d), \qquad \text{with} \qquad p(d) = \frac{e^{-E(i,j,d)}}{\sum_{d'} e^{-E(i,j,d')}}. \tag{6.15}$$

Figure 6.10 shows disparity maps for the *ramp* pair computed with four kinds of diffusion and increasing iterations. The first row shows regular diffusion, the second and third row show diffusion with local stopping based on C_m and C_e. The fourth row shows diffusion using the membrane model for comparison. It is clearly visible that regular diffusion keeps blurring the features as the number of iterations increases, while the other three diffusion processes converge quickly to a stable solution. Which of the three performs best is hard to tell by looking at the disparity maps. In Section 6.6 we analyze their respective performance based on errors in the computed disparities.

6.5 A Bayesian model of stereo matching

In this section, we develop a Bayesian model for stereo matching that includes both a measurement model corresponding to the matching criterion and a prior Markov Random Field model corresponding to the aggregation function. Our model uses robust (non-Gaussian) statistics to handle gross errors and discontinuities in the surface. We also develop a novel approximation algorithm that results in a non-linear diffusion process, and show how this produces better results than standard diffusion.

As before, stereo reconstruction is specified as the estimation of a discrete disparity field $d_{i,j} = d(x_i, y_j)$ given two input images $I_L(x,y)$ and $I_R(x,y)$. Using a Bayesian framework, we first specify a model of image formation, and then derive estimation algorithms from this model.

6.5.1 The prior model

The Bayesian model of stereo image formation consists of two parts. The first part, a *prior model* for the disparity surface, uses a traditional Markov Random Field (MRF) to encode preferences for smooth surfaces [Geman and Geman, 1984]. This model is specified as a Gibbs distribution p_P, the exponential of a potential function E_P:

$$p_P(\mathbf{d}) = \frac{1}{Z_P}\exp\left(-E_P(\mathbf{d})\right), \tag{6.16}$$

where $\mathbf{d}$ is the vector of all disparities $d_{i,j}$ and Z_P is a normalizing factor. The potential function itself is the sum of clique potentials

[2] We will develop the idea of converting to probabilities further in the next section.

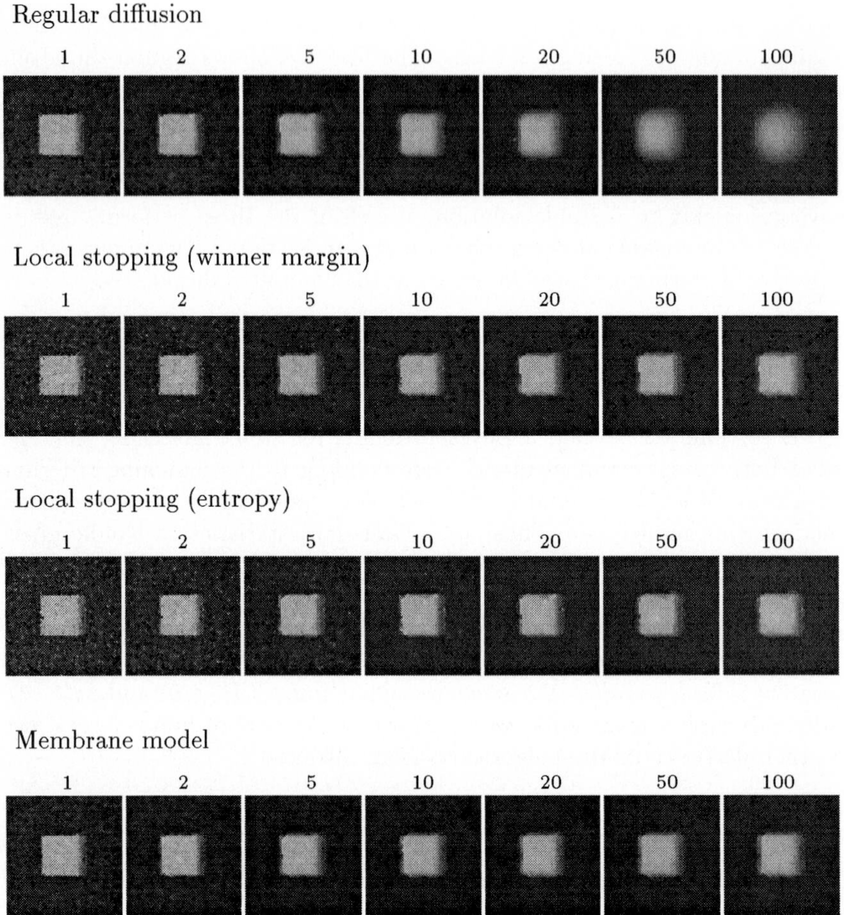

Fig. 6.10. Disparities of the *ramp* image pair based on diffusion with local stopping compared to regular diffusion and the membrane model. The number of iteration ranges from 1 to 100.

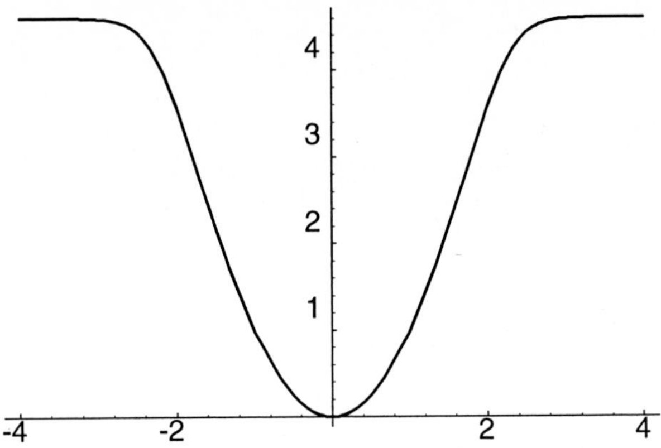

Fig. 6.11. Shape of the robust penalty function ρ_P for $\epsilon = 0.01$ and $\sigma = 1$

$$E_P(\mathbf{d}) = \sum_{c \in C} E_c(\mathbf{d}) \tag{6.17}$$

which only involve neighboring sites in the field. Here, we study only first-order fields, where

$$E_P(\mathbf{d}) = \sum_{i,j} \rho_P(d_{i+1,j} - d_{i,j}) + \rho_P(d_{i,j+1} - d_{i,j}) \tag{6.18}$$

(see [Terzopoulos, 1986; Szeliski, 1989] for generalizations to higher order fields).

When $\rho(x)$ is a quadratic, $\rho(x) = x^2$, the field is a Gauss-MRF, and corresponds in a probabilistic sense to a first-order regularized (*membrane*) surface model [Terzopoulos, 1986; Szeliski, 1989]. When $\rho(x)$ is a unit impulse, $\rho(x) = 1 - \delta(x)$, it corresponds to a MRF that favors fronto-parallel surfaces [Geman and Geman, 1984; Marroquin *et al.*, 1987]. In between these two extremes are functions derived from *robust statistics* [Huber, 1981], which behave much like surface models with discontinuities [Blake and Zisserman, 1987; Geiger and Girosi, 1991; Black and Rangarajan, 1994; Black and Rangarajan, 1996]. A wide variety of robust penalty functions are possible. Here, we use a contaminated Gaussian model,

$$\rho_P(x) = -\log\left((1 - \epsilon_P)\exp(-x^2/2\sigma_P^2) + \epsilon_P\right). \tag{6.19}$$

Figure 6.11 shows the shape of this function for $\epsilon = 0.01$ and $\sigma = 1$.

6.5.2 The measurement model

The second part of our Bayesian model is the *data* or *measurement model* which accounts for differences in intensities between left and right images. This model assumes independent, identically distributed measurement errors,

$$p_M(I_L, I_R|\mathbf{d}) = \prod_{i,j} p_M(I_L(x_i + d_{i,j}, y_j) - I_R(x_i, y_j)). \tag{6.20}$$

This distribution does not fully specify the distributions of I_L and I_R, only the distribution of their intensity differences at matching pixels.[3] As mentioned before, traditional stereo matching methods use either a squared intensity error metric (Gaussian noise), $\rho_M(x) = \log p_M(x) = x^2$, or an exact binary matching criterion (e.g., for random-dot stereograms or binary features such as edges or the sign of the Laplacian), $\rho_M(x) = 1 - \delta(x)$. We again use a contaminated Gaussian model,

$$\rho_M(x) = -\log\left((1 - \epsilon_M)\exp(-x^2/2\sigma_M^2) + \epsilon_M\right), \tag{6.21}$$

to model both Gaussian noise and possible outliers due to occlusions or non-modeled photometric effects such as specularities.

The posterior distribution $p(\mathbf{d}|I_L, I_R)$ can be derived from the prior and measurement models using Bayes' rule,

$$p(\mathbf{d}|I_L, I_R) \propto p_P(\mathbf{d}) p_M(I_L, I_R|\mathbf{d}). \tag{6.22}$$

As is often the case, it is more convenient to study the negative log probability distribution

$$\begin{aligned} E(\mathbf{d}) &= -\log p(\mathbf{d}|I_L, I_R) \\ &= \sum_{i,j} \rho_P(d_{i+1,j} - d_{i,j}) + \rho_P(d_{i,j+1} - d_{i,j}) \\ &\quad + \sum_{i,j} \rho_M(I_L(x_i + d_{i,j}, y_j) - I_R(x_i, y_j)). \end{aligned} \tag{6.23}$$

While $p(\mathbf{d}|I_L, I_R)$ specifies a complete distribution, usually only a single optimal estimate of $d(x, y)$ is desired (but see [Szeliski, 1989] for why modeling of uncertainties may be useful). The most commonly studied estimate is the peak of the distribution, or *Maximum A Posteriori* (MAP) estimate, which is equivalent to minimizing the energy given in Equation (6.23). Alternate estimates include quantities such as the mean of the distribution [Marroquin *et al.*, 1987].

A variety of techniques have been developed for minimizing Equation (6.23). Two of the most popular are the Gibbs Sampler [Geman and Geman, 1984; Marroquin *et al.*, 1987] and mean field theory [Geiger and Girosi, 1991]. The Gibbs Sampler randomly chooses values for each $d_{i,j}$ site according to the local distribution determined by the current guesses for a site's neighbors [Geman and Geman, 1984; Szeliski and Hinton, 1985;

[3] Our formulation easily admits fractional disparities, since $I_L(x, y)$ and $I_R(x, y)$ are viewed as continuous functions. Sub-pixel disparities can be used to improve the accuracy of stereo reconstructions [Matthies *et al.*, 1989].

Barnard, 1989]. This process will in theory converge to a statistically optimal sample, given enough time. Mean field theory updates an estimate of the *mean* value of $d_{i,j}$ at each site using a deterministic update rule derived from the original probability distribution [Geman and Geman, 1984]. It is not guaranteed to find an optimal estimate, but in practice it often finds a good solution, similar to one available through continuation methods [Blake and Zisserman, 1987].

6.5.3 Explicit local distribution model

The Gibbs Sampler and its variants can produce good solutions, but at the cost of long computation times. Mean field techniques, on the other hand, are not very good at modeling ambiguous estimates, such as multiple potential matches at each pixel. Instead of using either of these two traditional approaches, we will develop a novel estimation algorithm based on modeling the probability distribution of $d_{i,j}$ at each site. To do this, we associate a scalar value between 0 and 1 with each possible discrete value of d at each pixel (i, j), and require that

$$\sum_d p(i,j,d) = 1. \tag{6.24}$$

Our representation is therefore the same as that used by diffusion-based algorithms, i.e., we explicitly model all possible disparities at each pixel, rather than modeling a single estimated disparity as in traditional Gibbs Sampler or mean-field approaches [Barnard, 1989].

To initialize our algorithm, we calculate the probability distribution for each pixel (i, j) based on the intensity errors between matching pixels, i.e.,

$$p_0(i,j,d) \propto \exp\left(-E_0(i,j,d)\right), \tag{6.25}$$

where

$$E_0(i,j,d) = \rho_M(I_L(x_i + d, y_j) - I_R(x_i, y_j)) \tag{6.26}$$

is the matching cost of pixel (i, j) at disparity d.

To derive the update formula, we start with a basic observation about Markov Random Fields: if the joint probability distribution of all interacting neighbors is known, the local probability distribution of a site is completely determined. To compute this distribution, we take the part of the potential energy (Equation (6.23)) which involves (i, j), i.e.,

$$\tilde{E}(d_{i,j}|\{d_{i+k,j+l}\}) = E_0(i,j,d) + \sum_{(k,l)\in\mathcal{N}_4} \rho_P(d_{i+k,j+l} - d_{i,j}), \tag{6.27}$$

and turn this into a probability distribution

$$\tilde{p}(d_{i,j}|\{d_{i+k,j+l}\}) = p_0(i,j,d) \prod_{(k,l)\in\mathcal{N}_4} \exp\left(-\rho_P(d_{i+k,j+l} - d_{i,j})\right). \tag{6.28}$$

We then integrate out all of the neighboring disparities according to their joint probability distribution

$$p(d_{i,j}) \propto \sum_{\{d_{i+k,j+l}\}} \tilde{p}(d_{i,j}|\{d_{i+k,j+l}\})p(\{d_{i+k,j+l}\}). \tag{6.29}$$

In practice, however, it is impossible to estimate the full joint probability distribution of the neighbors, without resorting to a statistical technique such as the Gibbs Sampler.[4] Instead, we assume (sub-optimally) that the neighboring disparity columns have independent distributions

$$p(\{d_{i+k,j+l}\}) = \prod_{(k,l)\in\mathcal{N}_4} p(d_{i+k,j+l}) \tag{6.30}$$

where the $p(d_{i+k,j+l})$ are the current probability density estimates for each neighboring site $(i+k, j+l)$.

The complete update formula is therefore

$$p(d_{i,j}) \propto p_0(i,j,d) \prod_{(k,l)\in\mathcal{N}_4} \left[\sum_{d'_{i+k,j+l}} \exp\left(-\rho_P(d'_{i+k,j+l} - d_{i,j})\right) p(d'_{i+k,j+l}) \right] \tag{6.31}$$

or

$$E(i,j,d) \leftarrow E_0(i,j,d) + \sum_{(k,l)\in\mathcal{N}_4} \log \left[-\sum_{d'} \exp\left(-\rho_P(d'-d) - E(i+k, j+l, d')\right) \right]. \tag{6.32}$$

For notational and computational convenience, we will introduce a few more additional quantities. The *smoothed probability distribution*

$$\begin{aligned} p_S(i,j,d) &= \sum_{d'} e^{-\rho_P(d'-d)} p(i,j,d') \\ &= \sum_{d'} w_P(d'-d) p(i,j,d') \end{aligned} \tag{6.33}$$

is simply the current probability distribution $p(i,j,d)$ after it has been convolved *vertically* (in disparity) with the smoothing kernel

$$w_P(d) \propto e^{-\rho_P(d)}, \qquad \text{with} \qquad \sum_d w_P(d) = 1.$$

It has a corresponding *smoothed energy*

$$E_S(i,j,d) = -\log p_S(i,j,d). \tag{6.34}$$

[4] This is not true, however, of 1D processes such as Markov Random Walks.

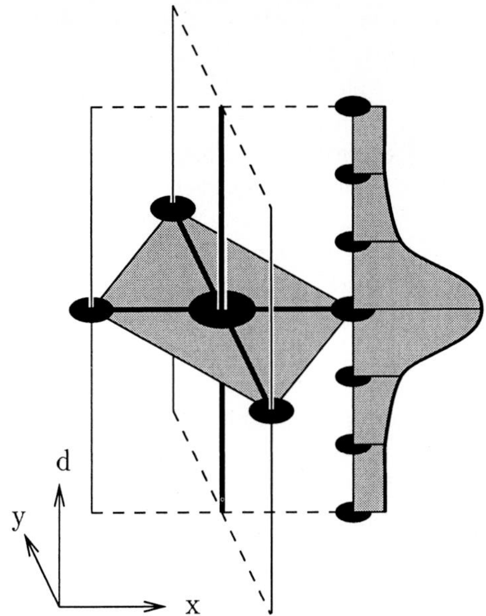

Fig. 6.12. Illustration of the four-step diffusion algorithm. At each iteration, the probabilities are smoothed vertically in each disparity column, converted to energies, diffused horizontally, and converted back to probabilities.

Finally, the update rule can be written as a pair of equations

$$E(i,j,d) \leftarrow E_0(i,j,d) + \sum_{(k,l)\in\mathcal{N}_4} E_S(i+k,j+l,d), \tag{6.35}$$

$$p(i,j,d) \leftarrow \frac{e^{-E(i,j,d)}}{\sum_{d'} e^{-E(i,j,d')}}. \tag{6.36}$$

In practice, since the values of $E(i,j,d)$ are being updated simultaneously at all pixels and disparity, we use a modified version of (6.35),

$$E(i,j,d) \leftarrow E_0(i,j,d) + \mu \left[E_S(i,j,d) + \sum_{(k,l)\in\mathcal{N}_4} E_S(i+k,j+l,d) \right], \tag{6.37}$$

i.e., we weight the neighboring values somewhat less (we use $\mu = 0.5$) and include the current estimated energy in the update rule.

If we interpret the above Equations (6.33), (6.34), (6.37), and (6.36) as a four-step algorithm for iteratively computing the best stereo matches, we see that they are a special instance of a non-linear diffusion process. This is illustrated in Figure 6.12.

The smoothing step (Equations (6.33), (6.34)) blurs the current disparity probabilities vertically along a column, thereby enabling different nearby disparities to support each other (depending on the size of σ_P). It also adds a small amount to each probability (ϵ_P), which in effect limits the largest possible value that E_S can take and thus limits the effect of disparity discontinuities.

The update step (Equations (6.37), (6.36)) is identical to a regular diffusion step with β-terms (membrane model). However, the probability renormalization step ensures that the energies represent meaningful log probabilities (in practice, it forces the smallest E to be slightly above 0). The robust form of the E_0 function also ensures that bad matches have only limited effects, thus allowing for occlusions or other non-modeled errors to occur.

For the above algorithm to work well, the various parameters $\{\sigma_P, \epsilon_P, \sigma_M, \epsilon_M\}$ must be set to appropriate values. The values for σ_M and ϵ_M should be based on the expected noise in the image sensor, i.e., σ_M should be proportional to the regular image noise, while ϵ_M should be the probability of gross errors or occlusions (say 1–10%). The choice of σ_P depends on the class of disparity surfaces which may be expected, i.e., a small σ_P favors fronto-parallel surfaces. For the experiments presented here, we set $\sigma_P = 0.1$ and $\epsilon_P = 0.01$.

Figure 6.13 shows the results of our probabilistic aggregation technique applied to the *ramp* and *rds* images. We use a different σ_M for the two image pairs: $\sigma_M = 2$ for *ramp*, and $\sigma_M = 20$ for *rds*, to compensate for the different signal strengths of the two pairs. The other parameters are the same for both image pairs: $\epsilon_M = 0.1, \sigma_P = 0.1, \epsilon_P = 0.01$. The number of diffusion iterations is $n = 10$.

6.6 Experiments

In this section we numerically evaluate the performance of the different algorithms on synthetic images. We also show results for real image data.

For our experiments we use five synthetic image pairs, based on combining three different intensity patterns *ramp*, *rds*, and *real*, and two different disparity patterns, *square* and *bars*. We have already introduced the *square* disparity pattern (Figure 6.3), and the combinations *ramp/square* and *rds/square* (Figure 6.4).

The new disparity pattern *bars* consists of two rectangular regions with two different disparities (see Figure 6.14). The narrow region in the bottom half of the image is displaced by more than twice its width, thus violating the commonly assumed monotonicity (ordering) constraint. Together with the large disparity range, this provides an extra challenge to stereo algorithms, but reflects common situations in real images. The new intensity pattern, *real*, is part of a real image depicting ground covered with grass.

Figure 6.15 shows all five synthetic image pairs, including the three new image pairs synthesized using the texture/disparity combinations *real/square*,

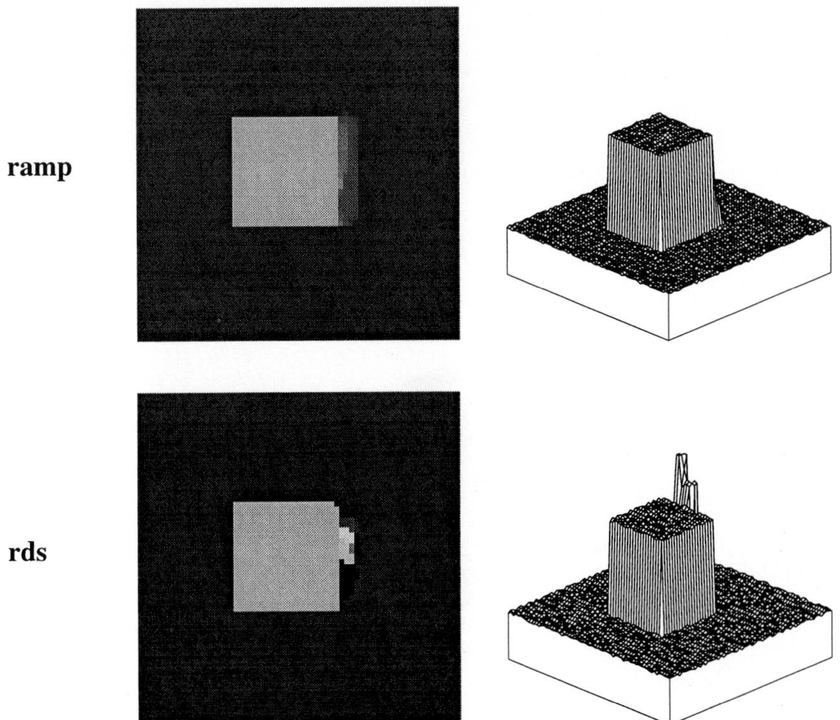

Fig. 6.13. Performance of the probabilistic model on the *ramp* and *rds* image pairs (gray-level images and isometric plots).

rds/bars, and *real/bars*. We do not use the combination *ramp/bars* since the narrow region can not be matched unambiguously, resulting in meaningless disparity error statistics.

We compared the following algorithms: SSD, diffusion using the membrane model, diffusion with local stopping, and diffusion using the probabilistic model. For each algorithm, we varied the parameters: window size (SSD), β, λ (membrane), certainty measure (local stopping), $\sigma_M, \sigma_P, \epsilon_M, \epsilon_P, \mu$ (probabilistic), and the number of iterations (all diffusion algorithms). For each parameter setting, we ran the algorithm on a test set of 40 images (the 5 image pairs with 8 different levels of additive Gaussian noise: $\sigma = 0$, 0.25, 0.5, 1, 2, 4, 8, 16). We tried more than 70 different parameter settings, resulting in about 3000 experiments. In each experiment, we compared the computed disparities with the true disparities (ignoring the occluded regions), and collected three different error statistics: mean absolute disparity error, root-mean-square (RMS) disparity error, and the "percentage of bad points", i.e., the percentage of points whose absolute disparity error is greater than 1/2.

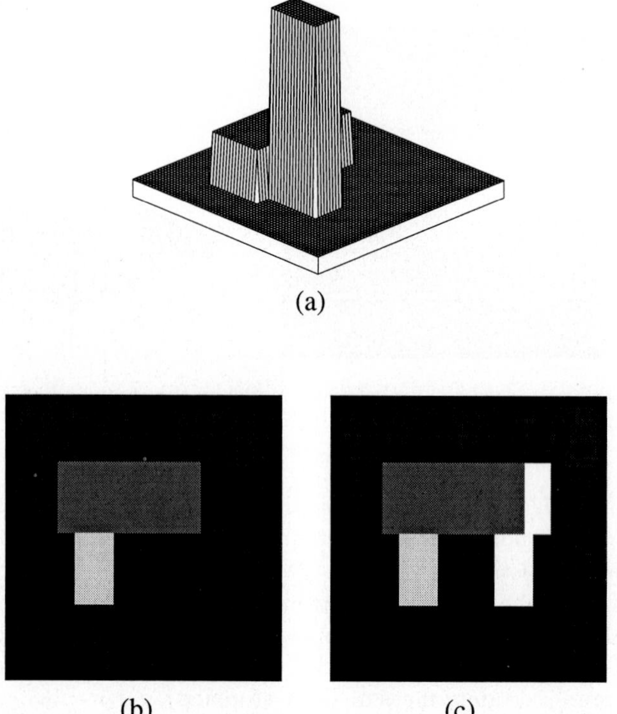

(a)

(b) (c)

Fig. 6.14. The *bars* disparity pattern, containing an ordering constraint violation: (a) isometric plot; (b) gray-level encoding; (c) gray-level encoding with occlusion information.

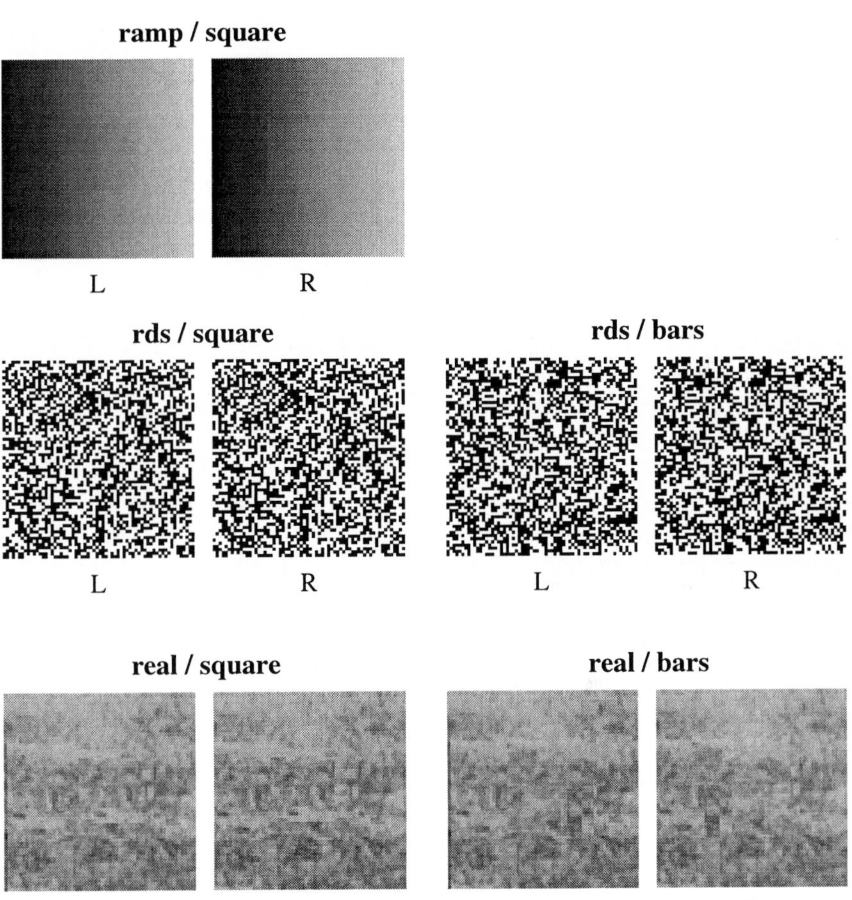

Fig. 6.15. The five synthetic image pairs.

Remember that our goal in devising the different algorithms was to recover the occlusion boundaries correctly. The percentage of bad points gives a good indication of whether the boundaries are recovered correctly, since this is where the errors are big. For similar reasons, we prefer the RMS error over the mean absolute error since it penalizes outliers more.

First we analyzed the error statistics for each method separately to gain understanding of the effect of the different parameters. Then we chose the best parameters for each method, and compared the different methods with each other. We present in detail the results of the second, comparative stage, after briefly discussing the general trends we noticed.

SSD, which we include for comparison, has only one parameter: the size of the support region. The same holds for simple diffusion, where the size of the support region is controlled by the number of iterations. Not surprisingly, the optimal size of the support region depends on the noise level. In general, higher noise levels (or, more precisely, lower signal-to-noise ratios) require larger window sizes. The best window size can also depend on the image.

The membrane model behaves similarly to regular diffusion with a fixed number of iterations. For small noise levels, a value of β between 1/3 and 1 usually yields smaller errors than regular diffusion, but not always. Also, as mentioned before, for high noise levels, β needs to be chosen quite small to produce enough smoothing for stable matching.

In analyzing regular diffusion with local stopping, we found that the certainty measure is critical. In our experiments, the winner margin C_m almost always outperformed the measure based on entropy C_e. A problem with our definition of local stopping is that an initial wrong but "certain" match can survive. There is clearly a potential for both better certainty measures and different ways of implementing local stopping.

The probabilistic model, which performed by far the best, also has the most parameters. We found, however, that many parameters have only small effects and can be set to default values, including $\epsilon_M = 0.1, \epsilon_P = 0.01$, and $\mu = 0.5$. As expected, a small σ_P worked best for our test images composed from fronto-parallel surfaces. For real images, we found that σ_P needs to be chosen slightly higher. The most important parameter is σ_M, which should reflect the strength of the image signal. We used three different values for the three different textures of our test images. Finally, the number of iterations is less critical, since the method seems to converge relatively fast to a stable solution. Higher numbers of iterations are necessary for images containing regions of uniform intensity, such as the real images discussed below.

For direct comparison of the methods, we plot the disparity error versus the noise level on all five image pairs: Figure 6.16 shows the RMS errors, and Figure 6.17 shows the percentage of bad points. We compare SSD with a window size of 5, the membrane model with $\beta = 0.5$, diffusion with local stopping based on winner margin C_m, and the probabilistic model with $\epsilon_P =$

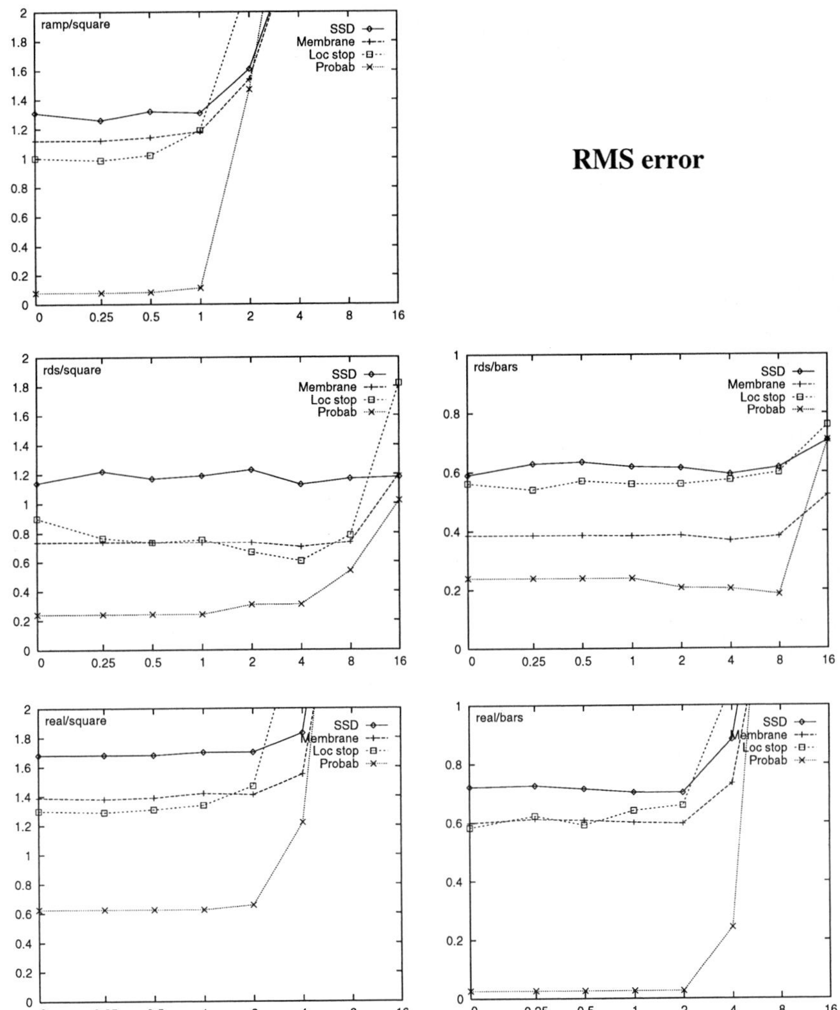

Fig. 6.16. Comparative performance of four stereo algorithms on five test image pairs. The plots show the RMS error of the computed disparities versus the standard deviation of image noise. The error at occluded points is not included.

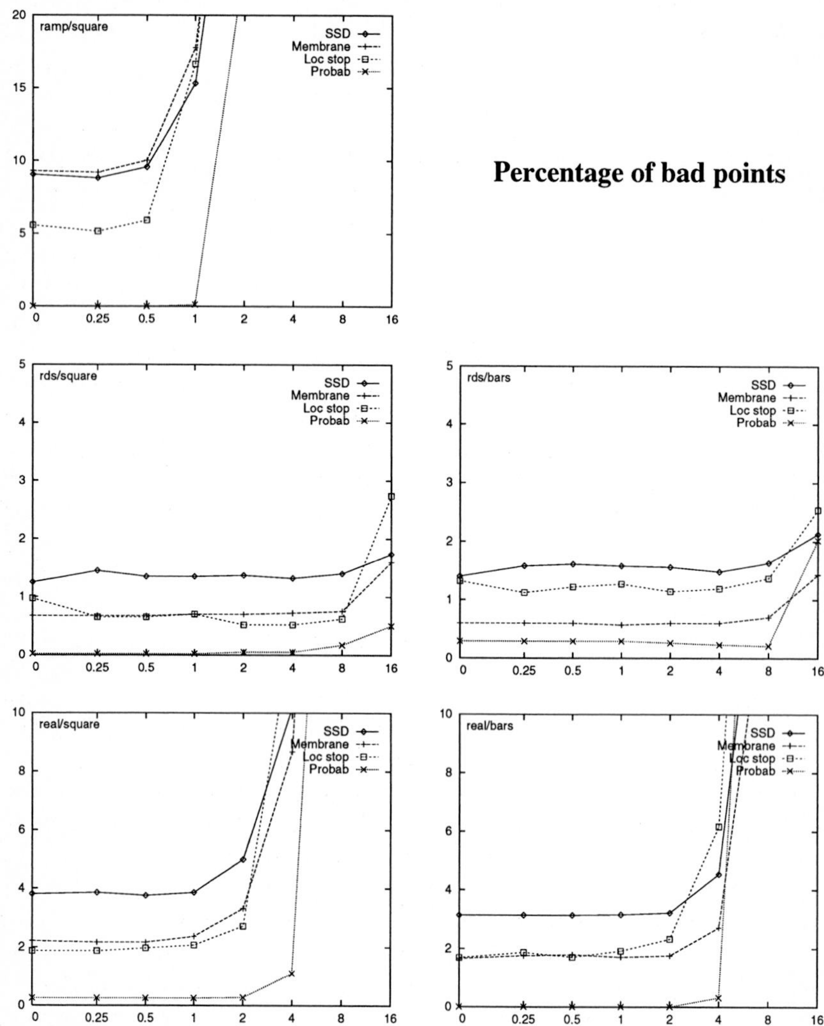

Fig. 6.17. Comparative performance of four stereo algorithms on five test image pairs. The plots show the percentage of points whose absolute disparity error is greater than 1/2, versus the standard deviation of image noise. Occluded points are not considered.

$0.01, \sigma_P = 0.1, \epsilon_M = 0.1$, and $\sigma_M = 2, 8, 20$, for *ramp*, *real*, and *rds* textures respectively. The number of iterations is 10 for all methods.

The probabilistic model clearly beats the three other methods. For small noise levels, the occlusion boundaries are recovered almost perfectly. In fact, in three of five images the percentage of bad points is 0%, i.e., the absolute RMS error is less than 1/2 everywhere. Note that the algorithm recovers the "correct" disparity pattern, even though the notion of true disparities is not well defined for ambiguous images such as random dot stereograms.

We also tested our algorithms on real images. We include results of the probabilistic method on images from the SRI's *tree* sequence and CMU's *town* sequence. We used multiple baseline stereo based on five images to initialize the disparity space with the sum of four (appropriately scaled) similarity measures [Okutomi and Kanade, 1993]. Figures 6.18 and 6.19 show the disparity maps computed by the probabilistic algorithm after 50 iterations, using the following parameters: $\sigma_P = 0.4, \epsilon_P = 0.01, \sigma_M = 5, \epsilon_M = 0.1$. Note that we use a bigger σ_P than before to account for slanted surfaces.

The running times are 220 seconds for the *tree* pair (image size: 256×233, disparity levels: 16), and 119 seconds for the *town* pair (image size: 240×256, disparity levels: 9). Thus, on average about 4.5 microseconds are spent per pixel per disparity per iteration. These times were obtained on a DEC Alpha workstation using an experimental implementation that was not optimized for speed.

6.7 Discussion and possible extensions

As we have shown, linear and non-linear diffusion algorithms are an attractive alternative to the adaptive windows introduced by Kanade and Okutomi [Kanade and Okutomi, 1994]. In its simplest form, the membrane algorithm simply requires the iterative summation of neighboring matching costs, with an additional term thrown in to prevent the support region from growing indefinitely. The increased weighting of the central pixel relative to the periphery is sufficient to counteract many of the artifacts introduced by the squared summing window used in SSD. When combined with a local stopping condition, the resulting non-linear diffusion process has an adaptive support behavior similar to the variably-sized window algorithm. The inclusion of additional non-linearities in the Bayesian diffusion algorithm improves the performance even more.

In addition to their simplicity and computational efficiency, our non-linear diffusion algorithms can also handle stereograms with more ambiguity than the adaptive window SSD algorithm. Kanade and Okutomi's algorithm is based on locally adjusting the sub-pixel disparity estimate simultaneously with growing the window size. This presupposes that the algorithm is somehow initialized in the vicinity of the true disparity. This is achieved in their synthetic image sequences using small disparities, and in their real sequences

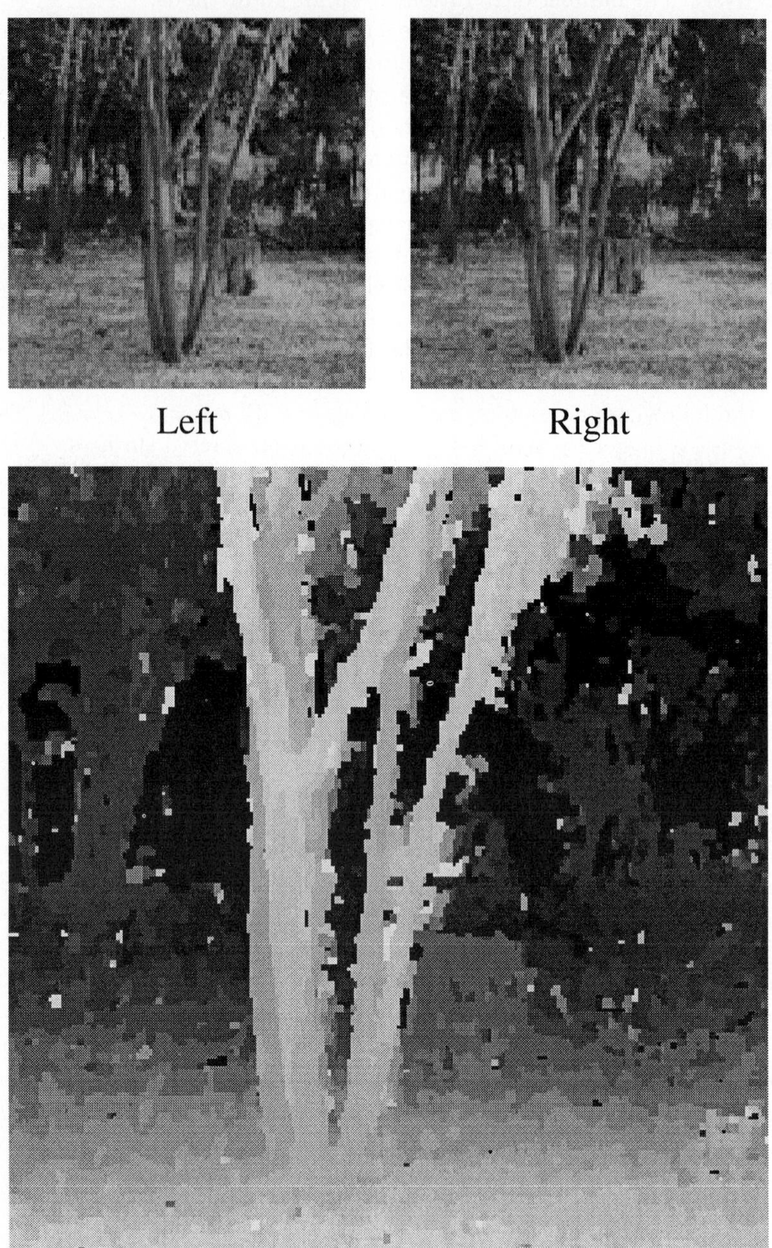

Fig. 6.18. *Tree* images (top) and disparities computed by the probabilistic algorithm (bottom).

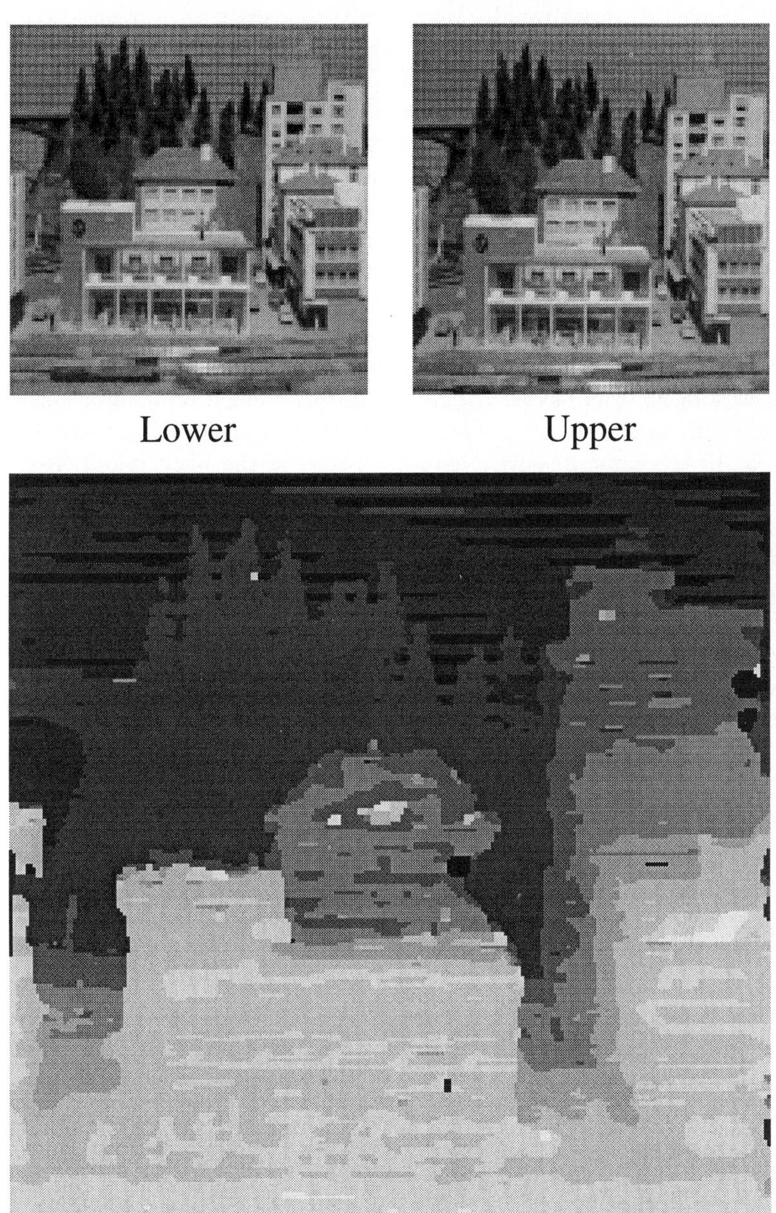

Fig. 6.19. *Town* images (top) and disparities computed by the probabilistic algorithm (bottom).

using a multi-frame version of the basic SSD algorithm [Okutomi and Kanade, 1993]. Image pairs with rapidly varying textures and many potential matches such as the random-dot stereograms used in our experiments could not be handled by their current algorithm. Of course, their basic method could potentially be extended to include a standard multiple disparity search component, but the performance of such a hybrid method is as yet unknown.

In its present form, our algorithm computes monocular rather than binocular disparity maps, i.e., the disparity map is associated with the right image. A binocular representation would remove this restriction, enabling the representation of occluded regions in both left and right images. Extending our diffusion algorithms to a binocular representation is relatively straightforward: the concept of neighbors at the same disparity is modified to define equal disparities in the *cyclopean* representation of depth, i.e., the depth seen by a camera halfway between the original two. Such a representation would also allow us to deal with occlusions more gracefully, allowing occluded pixels to float to the same disparity as other pixels in the background. However, it is unclear how to extend the Bayesian algorithm, since it requires the renormalization of disparities along each column in disparity space.

In addition to these extensions, we also plan to study better local stopping conditions based on improved certainty measures. We would also like to investigate multi-resolution versions of our diffusion algorithms to help fill in regions which have few features to match.

6.8 Summary

In this chapter we have demonstrated that diffusion-based aggregation of support is a useful alternative to both traditional area-based correlation and to more recent techniques based on adaptive window sizes. Our algorithms are simple to implement and computationally efficient, and result in better quality estimates, especially near discontinuities in the disparity surface. The addition of local stopping conditions to the basic diffusion process results in a behavior similar to that of adaptively sized windows. Furthermore, our novel non-linear diffusion algorithm derived from a Bayesian model of stereo matching results in markedly improved performance.

7. Conclusion

In this volume, we have investigated the use of stereo vision for the application of view synthesis. We conclude by summarizing the contributions made and by outlining possible extensions and directions of future research.

7.1 Contributions in view synthesis

In Chapter 3, we proposed a new method for view synthesis from real images using stereo vision. In our approach, scene geometry is implicitly represented by correspondence maps acquired by stereo vision techniques.

Using three-view rectification, we achieve a purely two-dimensional way of phrasing view synthesis under the full perspective model as rectification, warping, and derectification. In the rectified geometry, pixel displacements in the synthetic view are linear in disparity, allowing the efficient generation of new views by local image warping. Visibility is resolved automatically by using ordered forward mapping.

A prime advantage of our method of synthesizing new views from stereo data is that realistic views can be synthesized easily and quickly independent of scene complexity. A disadvantage is the limited available information about scene geometry, requiring strategies for dealing with partially occluded points of unknown geometry and totally occluded points of unknown intensity. We have proposed possible ways of dealing with both problems.

We have also outlined a framework for view synthesis, in which a scene is represented by a graph of images and correspondence maps. The basic building block in this framework is our method for synthesizing new views from a single stereo pair. This approach has the advantage that a globally consistent calibration of all reference views is not necessary, as view synthesis can proceed from pairwise rectified image pairs.

In Chapter 4, we re-evaluated the requirements on stereo algorithms in light of the new application of view synthesis. We compared view synthesis to several traditional applications of stereo, and concluded that stereo vision is better-suited for view synthesis than for applications requiring explicit 3D reconstruction.

While the correct recovery of occlusion boundaries and the detection of partially occluded regions becomes especially important for view synthesis, two major problems for 3D reconstruction do not affect view synthesis. The first problem for reconstruction is the limited depth resolution achievable from stereo. Since disparities are never explicitly converted to depths in the view synthesis process, the achievable accuracy for remapping a point is independent of its depth. Thus, disparity maps constitute an ideal representation of scene geometry for the task of synthesizing nearby views. The other main problem for 3D reconstruction are textureless areas, whose geometry can not be recovered. In view synthesis, however, a plausible (and in many cases correct) view can be synthesized by assuming a canonical depth interpretation. Finally, the difficult task of maintaining full calibration necessary for accurate 3D reconstruction is not necessary for view synthesis.

We have presented experiments demonstrating that it is possible to efficiently synthesize realistic new views even from inaccurate and incomplete depth information, thus meeting our goal of creating convincing impressions of three-dimensional structure.

7.2 Contributions in stereo

We have also presented two new stereo methods that are motivated by the requirements imposed by view synthesis.

In Chapter 5, we introduced a new gradient-based evidence measure that combines the notions of similarity and confidence. This measure allows stable matching and easy assignment of canonical depth interpretations in image regions of insufficient information.

In Chapter 6, we presented several new diffusion-based stereo algorithms motivated by the problem of boundary blurring. These algorithms are simple to implement and computationally efficient. Non-uniform diffusion using local stopping conditions results in adaptive support similar to the algorithm using variably-sized windows. The best results are achieved by a novel non-linear diffusion algorithm derived from a Bayesian model of stereo matching, which significantly outperforms traditional window-based techniques.

7.3 Extensions and future work

Most of the visual artifacts created by our current implementation are caused by incorrect stereo data. The strongest artifacts are usually caused by occlusion boundaries that are recovered incorrectly (especially in "extrapolated" views).

While the stereo algorithms presented in this volume are motivated by the application of view synthesis, they should only be considered a first step towards designing better algorithms that are specifically tailored to view synthesis. The discussion in Chapter 4 is intended to stimulate and focus such further development.

There are several possibilities for improving the stereo methods presented here. One idea is to combine the evidence measure from Chapter 5 with the diffusion-based aggregation methods from Chapter 6. A problem with the evidence measure that needs to be taken into account is that the intensity gradient across occlusion boundaries can be quite different between the two images, which can lead to substantial matching errors.

The diffusion methods themselves can also be improved. In particular, we plan to investigate new ways of implementing local stopping. One possibility is to let the diffusion of support be influenced by a concurrent anisotropic diffusion of intensities, to encourage depth boundaries to coincide with locations of strong intensity gradients (i.e., intensity edges). We are also interested in symmetric representations of disparities. One option is to use a cyclopean representation; another is to employ dynamic-programming methods for selecting the disparities. We believe that further study of the basic support and aggregation methods in stereo matching is central to developing algorithms with improved performance over a wide range of imagery.

There is also room for improving the view synthesis method presented in this volume. As mentioned in Section 3.2.7, explicit three-view rectification can not be used if the tri-focal plane intersects the observed scene. In addition, multiple resampling of the images introduces blur. Both problems could be remedied by aggregating rectification, warping, and derectification into a single transformation [Seitz and Dyer, 1996b; Seitz and Dyer, 1996a]. We would like to devise a fast local warping algorithm that could be used in conjunction with such a combined transform. This might require extending our view synthesis method to backward mapping, in order to avoid sampling gaps. How this can be done efficiently while also resolving visibility is an interesting problem. Another area with room for improvement is the task of filling holes in the synthesized view. A possible approach would be to extend existing texture synthesis algorithms developed for the application of image restoration.

Generally, our plans for future work are based on the belief that image-based scene representations have the potential to fundamentally change the fields of computer vision and computer graphics as they are known today. We believe that viewer-centered applications such as tele-reality will gain central importance in the next two decades and will require re-thinking commonly assumed paradigms in computer vision. In the context of view synthesis, we plan to further investigate stereo algorithms that are able to robustly handle depth discontinuities and occlusion. We also plan to investigate view synthesis methods that incorporate multiple images without requiring a global calibration between all images, as well as the combination of stereo with image registration and image mosaicing techniques.

Bibliography

[Adelson and Bergen, 1991] E. H. Adelson and J. R. Bergen. The plenoptic function and the elements of early vision. In M. Landy and J. Movshon, editors, *Computational Models of Visual Processing*, chapter 1. MIT Press, Cambridge, MA, 1991.

[Adelson, 1995] E. H. Adelson. Layered representations for vision and video. In *IEEE Workshop on Representations of Visual Scenes*, pages 3–9, Cambridge, MA, June 1995.

[Anandan, 1989] P. Anandan. A computational framework and an algorithm for the measurement of visual motion. *International Journal of Computer Vision*, 2(3):283–310, January 1989.

[Arnold, 1983] R. D. Arnold. Automated stereo perception. Technical Report AIM-351, Artificial Intelligence Laboratory, Stanford University, March 1983.

[Avidan and Shashua, 1997] S. Avidan and A. Shashua. Novel view synthesis in tensor space. In *IEEE Computer Society Conference on Computer Vision and Pattern Recognition (CVPR'97)*, pages 1034–1040, San Juan, Puerto Rico, June 1997. IEEE Computer Society Press.

[Avidan *et al.*, 1997] S. Avidan, T. Evgeniou, A. Shashua, and T. Poggio. Image-based view synthesis by combining trilinear tensors and learning techniques. In *ACM Symposium on Virtual Reality Software and Technology*, Lausanne, Switzerland, September 1997.

[Ayache and Lustman, 1991] N. J. Ayache and F. Lustman. Trinocular stereo vision for robotics. *IEEE Transactions on Pattern Analysis and Machine Intelligence*, 13(1):73–85, January 1991.

[Ayer and Sawhney, 1995] S. Ayer and H. S. Sawhney. Layered representation of motion video using robust maximum-likelihood estimation of mixture models and MDL encoding. In *Fifth International Conference on Computer Vision (ICCV'95)*, pages 777–784, Cambridge, MA, June 1995. IEEE Computer Society Press.

[Baker *et al.*, 1998] S. Baker, R. Szeliski, and P. Anandan. A layered approach to stereo reconstruction. In *IEEE Computer Society Conference on Computer Vision and Pattern Recognition (CVPR'98)*, pages 434–441, Santa Barbara, CA, June 1998. IEEE Computer Society Press.

[Baker, 1980] H. H. Baker. Edge based stereo correlation. In L. S. Baumann, editor, *Image Understanding Workshop*, pages 168–175. Science Applications International Corporation, April 1980.

[Ballard and Brown, 1982] D. H. Ballard and C. M. Brown. *Computer Vision.* Prentice-Hall, Englewood Cliffs, NJ, 1982.

[Barnard and Fischler, 1982] S. T. Barnard and M. A. Fischler. Computational stereo. *ACM Computing Surveys*, 14(4):553–572, December 1982.

[Barnard, 1989] S. T. Barnard. Stochastic stereo matching over scale. *International Journal of Computer Vision*, 3(1):17–32, 1989.

[Belhumeur and Mumford, 1992] P. N. Belhumeur and D. Mumford. A Bayesian treatment of the stereo correspondence problem using half-occluded regions. In *IEEE Computer Society Conference on Computer Vision and Pattern Recognition (CVPR'92)*, pages 506–512, Champaign-Urbana, IL, June 1992. IEEE Computer Society Press.

[Belhumeur, 1996] Peter N. Belhumeur. A Bayesian approach to binocular stereopsis. *International Journal of Computer Vision*, 19(3):237–260, August 1996.

[Bergen *et al.*, 1992] J. R. Bergen, P. Anandan, K. J. Hanna, and R. Hingorani. Hierarchical model-based motion estimation. In *Second European Conference on Computer Vision (ECCV'92)*, pages 237–252, Santa Margherita Ligure, Italy, May 1992. LNCS 588, Springer-Verlag.

[Beymer and Poggio, 1995] D. Beymer and T. Poggio. Face recognition from one example view. In *Fifth International Conference on Computer Vision (ICCV'95)*, pages 500–507, Cambridge, MA, June 1995. IEEE Computer Society Press.

[Beymer and Poggio, 1996] D. Beymer and T. Poggio. Image representations for visual learning. *Science*, 272:1905–1909, 1996.

[Beymer *et al.*, 1993] D. Beymer, A. Shashua, and T. Poggio. Example based image analysis and synthesis. A.I. Memo 1431, Massachusetts Institute of Technology, Cambridge, MA, November 1993.

[Birchfield and Tomasi, 1998a] S. Birchfield and C. Tomasi. Depth discontinuities by pixel-to-pixel stereo. In *Sixth International Conference on Computer Vision (ICCV'98)*, pages 1073–1080, Bombay, India, January 1998. IEEE Computer Society Press.

[Birchfield and Tomasi, 1998b] S. Birchfield and C. Tomasi. A pixel dissimilarity measure that is insensitive to image sampling. *IEEE Transactions on Pattern Analysis and Machine Intelligence*, 20(4):401–406, April 1998.

[Black and Anandan, 1993] M. J. Black and P. Anandan. A framework for the robust estimation of optical flow. In *Fourth International Conference on Computer Vision (ICCV'93)*, pages 231–236, Berlin, Germany, May 1993. IEEE Computer Society Press.

[Black and Rangarajan, 1994] M. J. Black and A. Rangarajan. The outlier process: Unifying line processes and robust statistics. In *IEEE Computer Society Conference on Computer Vision and Pattern Recognition (CVPR'94)*, pages 15–22, Seattle, WA, June 1994. IEEE Computer Society Press.

[Black and Rangarajan, 1996] M. J. Black and A. Rangarajan. On the unification of line processes, outlier rejection, and robust statistics with applications in early vision. *International Journal of Computer Vision*, 19(1):57–91, July 1996.

[Blake and Zisserman, 1987] A. Blake and A. Zisserman. *Visual Reconstruction*. MIT Press, Cambridge, MA, 1987.

[Bolles *et al.*, 1987] R. C. Bolles, H. H. Baker, and D. H. Marimont. Epipolar-plane image analysis: An approach to determining structure from motion. *International Journal of Computer Vision*, 1:7–55, 1987.

[Bolles *et al.*, 1993] R. C. Bolles, H. H. Baker, and M. J. Hannah. The JISCT stereo evaluation. In *DARPA Image Understanding Workshop*, pages 263–274, Washington, DC, April 1993.

[Boykov *et al.*, 1997] Y. Boykov, O. Veksler, and R. Zabih. Component matching for visual correspondence. In *IEEE Computer Society Conference on Computer Vision and Pattern Recognition (CVPR'97)*, pages 470–475, San Juan, Puerto Rico, June 1997. IEEE Computer Society Press.

[Boykov *et al.*, 1998] Y. Boykov, O. Veksler, and R. Zabih. Markov random fields with efficient approximations. In *IEEE Computer Society Conference on Com-*

puter Vision and Pattern Recognition (CVPR'98), pages 648–655, Santa Barbara, CA, June 1998. IEEE Computer Society Press.

[Brown, 1992] L. G. Brown. A survey of image registration techniques. *Computing Surveys*, 24(4):325–376, December 1992.

[Burt and Anandan, 1994] P. J. Burt and P. Anandan. Image stabilization by registration to a reference mosaic. In *ARPA Image Understanding Workshop*, Monterey, CA, November 1994.

[Canny, 1986] J. F. Canny. A computational approach to edge detection. *IEEE Transactions on Pattern Analysis and Machine Intelligence*, 8(6):34–43, 1986.

[Capel and Zisserman, 1998] D. Capel and A. Zisserman. Automated mosaicing with super-resolution zoom. In *IEEE Computer Society Conference on Computer Vision and Pattern Recognition (CVPR'98)*, pages 885–891, Santa Barbara, CA, June 1998. IEEE Computer Society Press.

[Chang and Zakhor, 1997] N. Chang and A. Zakhor. View generation for three-dimensional scenes from video sequences. *IEEE Transactions on Image Processing*, 6(4):584–598, April 1997.

[Chen and Medioni, 1997] Q. Chen and G. Medioni. Image synthesis from a sparse set of views. In *IEEE Visualization*, pages 277–283, 552, Phoenix, Arizona, October 1997.

[Chen and Williams, 1993] S. E. Chen and L. Williams. View interpolation for image synthesis. In *Computer Graphics (SIGGRAPH'93)*, pages 279–288, 1993.

[Chen, 1995] S. E. Chen. Quicktime VR — an image-based approach to virtual environment navigation. In *Computer Graphics (SIGGRAPH'95)*, pages 29–38, 1995.

[Clark and Ferrier, 1992] J. Clark and N. Ferrier. Attentive visual servoing. In A. Blake and A. Yuille, editors, *Active Vision*, pages 137–154. MIT Press, Cambridge, MA, 1992.

[Cochran and Medioni, 1992] S. D. Cochran and G. Medioni. 3-D surface description from binocular stereo. *IEEE Transactions on Pattern Analysis and Machine Intelligence*, 14(10):981–994, 1992.

[Coombs and Brown, 1993] D. Coombs and C. Brown. Real-time binocular smooth pursuit. *International Journal of Computer Vision*, 11(2):147–164, October 1993.

[Coombs *et al.*, 1992] D. Coombs, I. Horswill, and P. von Kaenel. Disparity filtering: Proximity detection and segmentation. In *11th SPIE Conference on Intelligent Robots and Computer Vision: Algorithms, Techniques, and Active Vision*, pages 195–206, Boston, MA, November 1992.

[Cox *et al.*, 1992a] I. J. Cox, S. Hingorani, B. M. Maggs, and S. B. Rao. Stereo without disparity gradient smoothing: A Bayesian sensor fusion solution. In *British Machine Vision Conference*, pages 337–346, Leeds, UK, September 1992.

[Cox *et al.*, 1992b] I. J. Cox, S. Hingorani, B. M. Maggs, and S. B. Rao. Stereo without regularization. Technical report, NEC Research Institute, Princeton, NJ, October 1992.

[Cox, 1994] I. J. Cox. A maximum likelihood n-camera stereo algorithm. In *IEEE Computer Society Conference on Computer Vision and Pattern Recognition (CVPR'94)*, pages 733–739, Seattle, WA, June 1994. IEEE Computer Society Press.

[Debevec *et al.*, 1996] P. E. Debevec, C. J. Taylor, and J. Malik. Modeling and rendering architecture from photographs: A hybrid geometry- and image-based approach. In *Computer Graphics (SIGGRAPH'96)*, pages 11–20, August 1996.

[Debevec, 1998] P. Debevec. Rendering synthetic objects into real scenes: Bridging traditional and image-based graphics with global illumination and high dynamic range photography. In *Computer Graphics (SIGGRAPH'98)*, pages 189–198, July 1998.

[Deriche *et al.*, 1994] R. Deriche, Z. Zhang, Q.-T. Luong, and O. Faugeras. Robust recovery of the epipolar geometry for an uncalibrated stereo rig. In *Third European Conference on Computer Vision (ECCV'94)*, volume I, pages 567–576, Stockholm, Sweden, May 1994. LNCS 800, Springer-Verlag.

[Dhond and Aggarwal, 1989] U. R. Dhond and J. K. Aggarwal. Structure from stereo—a review. *IEEE Transactions on Systems, Man, and Cybernetics*, 19(6):1489–1510, November/December 1989.

[Faugeras and Robert, 1996] O. Faugeras and L. Robert. What can two images tell us about a third one? *International Journal of Computer Vision*, 18(1):5–19, 1996.

[Faugeras *et al.*, 1995] O. Faugeras, S. Laveau, L. Robert, G. Csurka, and C. Zeller. 3-D reconstruction of urban scenes from sequences of images. In A. Gruen, O. Kuebler, and P. Agouris, editors, *Automatic Extraction of Man-Made Objects from Aerial and Space Images*, pages 145–168. Birkhäuser Verlag, Basel, Switzerland, 1995. INRIA Technical Report No. 2572.

[Faugeras, 1992] O. Faugeras. What can be seen in three dimensions with an uncalibrated stereo rig? In *Second European Conference on Computer Vision (ECCV'92)*, pages 563–578, Santa Margherita Ligure, Italy, May 1992. LNCS 588, Springer-Verlag.

[Faugeras, 1993] O. Faugeras. *Three-Dimensional Computer Vision.* MIT Press, Cambridge, MA, 1993.

[Fischler and Firschein, 1987] M. A. Fischler and O. Firschein. *Readings in Computer Vision: Issues, Problems, Principles, and Paradigms.* Morgan Kaufmann, 1987.

[Foley *et al.*, 1990] J. D. Foley, A. van Dam, S. K. Feiner, and J. F. Hughes. *Computer Graphics: Principles and Practice.* Addison-Wesley, Reading, MA, second edition, 1990.

[Fua, 1993] P. Fua. A parallel stereo algorithm that produces dense depth maps and preserves image features. *Machine Vision and Applications*, 6:35–49, 1993.

[Fua, 1997] P. Fua. From multiple stereo views to multiple 3-D surfaces. *International Journal of Computer Vision*, 24(1):19–35, August 1997.

[Fuchs *et al.*, 1994] H. Fuchs, G. Bishop, K. Arthur, L. McMillan, R. Bajcsy, S. Lee, H. Farid, and T. Kanade. Virtual space teleconferencing using a sea of cameras. In *First International Symposium on Medical Robotics and Computer Assisted Surgery*, Pittsburgh, PA, September 1994.

[Fuh and Maragos, 1991] C.-S. Fuh and P. Maragos. Motion displacement estimation using an affine model for image matching. *Optical Engineering*, 30(7):881–887, July 1991.

[Geiger and Girosi, 1991] D. Geiger and F. Girosi. Mean field theory for surface reconstruction. *IEEE Transactions on Pattern Analysis and Machine Intelligence*, 13(5):401–412, May 1991.

[Geiger *et al.*, 1992] D. Geiger, B. Ladendorf, and A. Yuille. Occlusions and binocular stereo. In *Second European Conference on Computer Vision (ECCV'92)*, pages 425–433, Santa Margherita Ligure, Italy, May 1992. LNCS 588, Springer-Verlag.

[Geman and Geman, 1984] S. Geman and D. Geman. Stochastic relaxation, Gibbs distribution, and the Bayesian restoration of images. *IEEE Transactions on Pattern Analysis and Machine Intelligence*, 6(6):721–741, November 1984. Also in [Fischler and Firschein, 1987].

[Genc and Ponce, 1998] Y. Genc and J. Ponce. Parameterized image varieties: A novel approach to the analysis and synthesis of image sequences. In *Sixth International Conference on Computer Vision (ICCV'98)*, pages 11–16, Bombay, India, January 1998. IEEE Computer Society Press.

[Gennert, 1988] M. A. Gennert. Brightness-based stereo matching. In *Second International Conference on Computer Vision (ICCV'88)*, pages 139–143, Tampa, FL, December 1988. IEEE Computer Society Press.

[Gortler *et al.*, 1996] S. J. Gortler, R. Grzeszczuk, R. Szeliski, and M. F. Cohen. The lumigraph. In *Computer Graphics (SIGGRAPH'96)*, pages 43–54, August 1996.

[Grimson, 1981] W. E. L. Grimson. *From Images to Surfaces: a Computational Study of the Human Early Visual System.* MIT Press, Cambridge, MA, 1981.

[Grimson, 1985] W. E. L. Grimson. Computational experiments with a feature based stereo algorithm. *IEEE Transactions on Pattern Analysis and Machine Intelligence*, 7(1):17–34, January 1985.

[Grimson, 1993] W. E. L. Grimson. Why stereo vision is not always about 3D reconstruction. A.I. Memo 1435, Artificial Intelligence Laboratory, Massachusetts Institute of Technology, Cambridge, MA, July 1993.

[Hanna, 1991] K. J. Hanna. Direct multi-resolution estimation of ego-motion and structure from motion. In *IEEE Workshop on Visual Motion*, pages 156–162, Princeton, NJ, October 1991.

[Hannah, 1974] M. J. Hannah. *Computer Matching of Areas in Stereo Images.* PhD thesis, Stanford University, 1974.

[Hansen *et al.*, 1994] M. Hansen, P. Anandan, K. Dana, G. van der Wal, and P. Burt. Real-time scene stabilization and mosaic construction. In *ARPA Image Understanding Workshop*, Monterey, CA, November 1994.

[Hartley *et al.*, 1992] R. Hartley, R. Gupta, and T. Chang. Stereo from uncalibrated cameras. In *IEEE Computer Society Conference on Computer Vision and Pattern Recognition (CVPR'92)*, pages 761–764, Champaign-Urbana, IL, June 1992. IEEE Computer Society Press.

[Havaldar *et al.*, 1996] P. Havaldar, M.-S. Lee, and G. Medioni. View synthesis from unregistered images. In *Graphics Interface*, pages 61–69, Toronto, Canada, May 1996.

[Havaldar *et al.*, 1997] P. Havaldar, M.-S. Lee, and G. Medioni. Synthesizing novel views from unregistered 2-D images. *Computer Graphics Forum*, 16(1):65–73, March 1997.

[Hirani and Totsuka, 1996] A. N. Hirani and T. Totsuka. Combining frequency and spatial domain information for fast interactive image noise removal. In *Computer Graphics (SIGGRAPH'96)*, pages 269–276, August 1996.

[Hlaváč *et al.*, 1996] V. Hlaváč, A. Leonardis, and T. Werner. Automatic selection of reference views for image-based scene representations. In *Fourth European Conference on Computer Vision (ECCV'96)*, volume I, pages 526–535, Cambridge, UK, April 1996. LNCS 1064, Springer-Verlag.

[Hoff and Ahuja, 1989] W. Hoff and N. Ahuja. Surfaces from stereo: Integrating feature matching, disparity estimation, and contour detection. *IEEE Transactions on Pattern Analysis and Machine Intelligence*, 11(2):121–136, February 1989.

[Horn and Schunck, 1981] B. K. P. Horn and B. G. Schunck. Determining optical flow. *Artificial Intelligence*, 17:185–203, 1981.

[Horn, 1986] B. K. P. Horn. *Robot Vision.* MIT Press, Cambridge, MA, 1986.

[Horswill, 1992] I. D. Horswill. Proximity detection using a filter tuned in three-space. In *DARPA Image Understanding Workshop*, pages 973–978, San Diego, CA, January 1992.

[Huber, 1981] P. J. Huber. *Robust Statistics*. John Wiley & Sons, New York, NY, 1981.

[Huttenlocher and Jaquith, 1995] D. P. Huttenlocher and E. W. Jaquith. Computing visual correspondence: Incorporating the probability of a false match. In *Fifth International Conference on Computer Vision (ICCV'95)*, pages 515–522, Cambridge, MA, June 1995. IEEE Computer Society Press.

[Huttenlocher, 1996] D. P. Huttenlocher. Computer vision. In A. Tucker, editor, *CRC Computer Science and Engineering Handbook*. CRC Press, December 1996.

[Intille and Bobick, 1994] S. S. Intille and A. F. Bobick. Disparity-space images and large occlusion stereo. In *Third European Conference on Computer Vision (ECCV'94)*, volume II, pages 179–186, Stockholm, Sweden, May 1994. LNCS 801, Springer-Verlag.

[Irani and Peleg, 1991] M. Irani and S. Peleg. Improving resolution by image registration. *Graphical Models and Image Processing*, 53(3):231–239, May 1991.

[Irani *et al.*, 1995] M. Irani, P. Anandan, and S. Hsu. Mosaic-based representations of video sequences and their applications. In *Fifth International Conference on Computer Vision (ICCV'95)*, pages 605–611, Cambridge, MA, June 1995. IEEE Computer Society Press.

[ISTAR, 1993] ISTAR. Commercial brochure. Sophia Antipolis, France, 1993.

[Ito and Ishii, 1986] M. Ito and A. Ishii. Three view stereo analysis. *IEEE Transactions on Pattern Analysis and Machine Intelligence*, 8(4):524–532, July 1986.

[Izquierdo and Kruse, 1998] E. Izquierdo and S. Kruse. Image analysis for 3D modeling, rendering, and virtual view generation. *Computer Vision and Image Understanding*, 71(2):231–253, August 1998.

[Jägersand, 1997] M. Jägersand. Image based view synthesis of articulated agents. In *IEEE Computer Society Conference on Computer Vision and Pattern Recognition (CVPR'97)*, pages 1047–1053, San Juan, Puerto Rico, June 1997. IEEE Computer Society Press.

[Jenkin *et al.*, 1991] M. R. M. Jenkin, A. D. Jepson, and J. K. Tsotsos. Techniques for disparity measurement. *CVGIP: Image Understanding*, 53(1):14–30, January 1991.

[Jones and Malik, 1992a] D. G. Jones and J. Malik. A computational framework for determining stereo correspondence from a set of linear spatial filters. In *Second European Conference on Computer Vision (ECCV'92)*, pages 395–410, Santa Margherita Ligure, Italy, May 1992. LNCS 588, Springer-Verlag.

[Jones and Malik, 1992b] D. G. Jones and J. Malik. Determining three-dimensional shape from orientation and spatial frequency disparities. In *Second European Conference on Computer Vision (ECCV'92)*, pages 661–669, Santa Margherita Ligure, Italy, May 1992. LNCS 588, Springer-Verlag.

[Kanade and Okutomi, 1994] T. Kanade and M. Okutomi. A stereo matching algorithm with an adaptive window: Theory and experiment. *IEEE Transactions on Pattern Analysis and Machine Intelligence*, 16(9):920–932, September 1994.

[Kanade *et al.*, 1995] T. Kanade, P. J. Narayanan, and P. W. Rander. Virtualized reality: Concepts and early results. In *IEEE Workshop on Representations of Visual Scenes*, pages 69–76, Cambridge, MA, June 1995.

[Kanade *et al.*, 1996] T. Kanade, A. Yoshida, K. Oda, H. Kano, and M. Tanaka. A stereo machine for video-rate dense depth mapping and its new applications. In *IEEE Computer Society Conference on Computer Vision and Pattern Recognition (CVPR'96)*, pages 196–202, San Francisco, CA, June 1996. IEEE Computer Society Press.

[Kanade *et al.*, 1997] T. Kanade, P. J. Narayanan, and P. W. Rander. Virtualized reality: Constructing virtual worlds from real scenes. *IEEE MultiMedia*, 4(1), January 1997.

[Kanade, 1994] T. Kanade. Development of a video-rate stereo machine. In *Image Understanding Workshop*, pages 549–557, Monterey, CA, November 1994. Morgan Kaufmann Publishers.

[Kang and Desikan, 1998] S. B. Kang and P. Desikan. Virtual navigation of complex scenes using clusters of cylindrical panoramic images. In *Graphics Interface*, pages 223–232, Vancouver, Canada, June 1998.

[Kang and Szeliski, 1996] S. B. Kang and R. Szeliski. 3-D scene data recovery using omnidirectional multibaseline stereo. In *IEEE Computer Society Conference on Computer Vision and Pattern Recognition (CVPR'96)*, pages 364–370, San Francisco, CA, June 1996. IEEE Computer Society Press.

[Kang and Szeliski, 1997] S. B. Kang and R. Szeliski. 3-D scene data recovery using omnidirectional multibaseline stereo. *International Journal of Computer Vision*, 25(2):167–183, November 1997.

[Kang *et al.*, 1995] S. B. Kang, J. Webb, L. Zitnick, and T. Kanade. A multibaseline stereo system with active illumination and real-time image acquisition. In *Fifth International Conference on Computer Vision (ICCV'95)*, pages 88–93, Cambridge, MA, June 1995. IEEE Computer Society Press.

[Kang, 1997] S. B. Kang. A survey of image-based rendering techniques. Technical Report 97/4, Digital Equipment Corporation, Cambridge Research Lab, August 1997.

[Kass, 1988] M. Kass. Linear image features in stereopsis. *International Journal of Computer Vision*, 1(4):357–368, January 1988.

[Katayama *et al.*, 1995] A. Katayama, K. Tanaka, T. Oshino, and H. Tamura. A viewpoint dependent stereoscopic display using interpolation of multi-viewpoint images. In *SPIE Stereoscopic Displays and Virtual Reality Systems II*, volume 2409, pages 11–20, February 1995.

[Koch, 1995] R. Koch. 3-D surface reconstruction from stereoscopic image sequences. In *Fifth International Conference on Computer Vision (ICCV'95)*, pages 109–114, Cambridge, MA, June 1995. IEEE Computer Society Press.

[Koenderink and van Doorn, 1991] J. J. Koenderink and A. J. van Doorn. Affine structure from motion. *Journal of the Optical Society of America A*, 8(2):377–385, 1991.

[Kokaram and Godsill, 1996] A. C. Kokaram and S. J. Godsill. A system for reconstruction of missing data in image sequences using sampled 3D AR models and MRF motion priors. In *Fourth European Conference on Computer Vision (ECCV'96)*, volume II, pages 613–624, Cambridge, UK, April 1996. LNCS 1065, Springer-Verlag.

[Kuglin and Hines, 1975] C. D. Kuglin and D. C. Hines. The phase correlation image alignment method. In *IEEE 1975 Conference on Cybernetics and Society*, pages 163–165, New York, September 1975.

[Kumar *et al.*, 1994] R. Kumar, P. Anandan, and K. Hanna. Shape recovery from multiple views: A parallax based approach. In *ARPA Image Understanding Workshop*, Monterey, CA, November 1994.

[Kumar *et al.*, 1995] R. Kumar, P. Anandan, M. Irani, J. Bergen, and K. Hanna. Representation of scenes from collections of images. In *IEEE Workshop on Representations of Visual Scenes*, pages 10–17, Cambridge, MA, June 1995.

[Kumar, 1994] R. Kumar. Direct recovery of shape from multiple views: A parallax based approach. In *12th International Conference on Pattern Recognition (ICPR'94)*, volume 1, pages 685–688, Jerusalem, Israel, October 1994.

[Lasseter and Daly, 1995] J. Lasseter and S. Daly. *Toy Story: The Art and Making of The Animated Film.* Hyperion, November 1995. See also `http://www.disney.com/ToyStory/`.

[Laveau and Faugeras, 1994] S. Laveau and O. Faugeras. 3-D scene representation as a collection of images. In *12th International Conference on Pattern Recognition (ICPR'94)*, volume 1, pages 689–691, Jerusalem, Israel, October 1994. INRIA Technical Report No. 2205.

[Lee and Medioni, 1998] M.-S. Lee and G. Medioni. Inferring segmented surface description from stereo data. In *IEEE Computer Society Conference on Computer Vision and Pattern Recognition (CVPR'98)*, pages 346–352, Santa Barbara, CA, June 1998. IEEE Computer Society Press.

[Lengyel, 1998] J. Lengyel. The convergence of graphics and vision. *IEEE Computer*, pages 46–53, July 1998.

[Levoy and Hanrahan, 1996] M. Levoy and P. Hanrahan. Light field rendering. In *Computer Graphics (SIGGRAPH'96)*, pages 31–42, August 1996.

[Longuet-Higgins, 1981] H. C. Longuet-Higgins. A computer algorithm for reconstructing a scene from two projections. *Nature*, 293:133–135, September 1981. Also in [Fischler and Firschein, 1987].

[Lucas and Kanade, 1981] B. D. Lucas and T. Kanade. An iterative image registration technique with an application in stereo vision. In *Seventh International Joint Conference on Artificial Intelligence (IJCAI-81)*, pages 674–679, Vancouver, 1981.

[Luong and Faugeras, 1996] Q.-T. Luong and O. Faugeras. The fundamental matrix: Theory, algorithms, and stability analysis. *International Journal of Computer Vision*, 17(1):43–75, January 1996.

[Mann and Picard, 1994] S. Mann and R. W. Picard. Virtual bellows: Constructing high-quality stills from video. In *First IEEE International Conference on Image Processing (ICIP'94)*, volume I, pages 363–367, Austin, TX, November 1994. IEEE Computer Society Press. MIT Media Lab Report No. 259.

[Mark *et al.*, 1997] W. Mark, L. McMillan, and G. Bishop. Post-rendering 3D warping. In *Symposium on Interactive 3D Graphics*, pages 7–16, Providence, RI, April 1997. ACM Press.

[Marr and Poggio, 1976] D. Marr and T. Poggio. Cooperative computation of stereo disparity. *Science*, 194:283–287, October 1976.

[Marr and Poggio, 1979] D. C. Marr and T. Poggio. A computational theory of human stereo vision. *Proceedings of the Royal Society of London*, B 204:301–328, 1979.

[Marr, 1982] D. Marr. *Vision*. W. H. Freeman and Company, New York, 1982.

[Marroquin *et al.*, 1987] J. Marroquin, S. Mitter, and T. Poggio. Probabilistic solution of ill-posed problems in computational vision. *Journal of the American Statistical Association*, 82(397):76–89, March 1987.

[Matthies *et al.*, 1989] L. Matthies, R. Szeliski, and T. Kanade. Kalman filter-based algorithms for estimating depth from image sequences. *International Journal of Computer Vision*, 3:209–236, 1989.

[Matthies, 1992] L. Matthies. Stereo vision for planetary rovers: Stochastic modeling to near-real time implementation. *International Journal of Computer Vision*, 8(1):71–91, 1992.

[Mayhew and Frisby, 1991] J. E. W. Mayhew and J. P. Frisby. *3D Model Recognition from Stereoscopic Cues*. MIT Press, Cambridge, MA, 1991.

[McMillan and Bishop, 1995a] L. McMillan and G. Bishop. Head-tracked stereo display using image warping. In *SPIE Stereoscopic Displays and Virtual Reality Systems II*, volume 2409, pages 21–30, February 1995.

[McMillan and Bishop, 1995b] L. McMillan and G. Bishop. Plenoptic modeling: An image-based rendering system. In *Computer Graphics (SIGGRAPH'95)*, pages 39–46, August 1995.

[McMillan, 1995a] L. McMillan. Acquiring immersive virtual environments with an uncalibrated camera. Technical Report 95-006, University of North Carolina, Chapel Hill, 1995.

[McMillan, 1995b] L. McMillan. A list-priority rendering algorithm for redisplaying projected surfaces. Technical Report 95-005, University of North Carolina, Chapel Hill, 1995.

[McMillan, 1997] L. McMillan. *An Image-based Approach to Three-Dimensional Computer Graphics.* PhD thesis, University of North Carolina at Chapel Hill, April 1997.

[Moezzi *et al.*, 1997] S. Moezzi, L.-C. Tai, and P. Gerard. Virtual view generation for 3D digital video. *IEEE MultiMedia*, 4(1):18–26, January 1997.

[Moffitt and Mikhail, 1980] F. H. Moffitt and E. M. Mikhail. *Photogrammetry.* Harper & Row, New York, third edition, 1980.

[Nakamura *et al.*, 1996] Y. Nakamura, T. Matsuura, K. Satoh, and Y. Ohta. Occlusion detectable stereo — occlusion patterns in camera matrix. In *IEEE Computer Society Conference on Computer Vision and Pattern Recognition (CVPR'96)*, pages 371–378, San Francisco, CA, June 1996. IEEE Computer Society Press.

[Nakayama and Shimojo, 1990] K. Nakayama and S. Shimojo. Da Vinci stereopsis: Depth and subjective occluding contours from unpaired image points. *Vision Research*, 30(11):1811–1825, 1990.

[Nakayama and Shimojo, 1992] K. Nakayama and S. Shimojo. Experiencing and perceiving visual surfaces. *Science*, 257:1357–1363, September 1992.

[Nalwa, 1993] V. S. Nalwa. *A Guided Tour of Computer Vision.* Addison-Wesley, 1993.

[Narayanan *et al.*, 1998] P. J. Narayanan, P. W. Rander, and T. Kanade. Constructing virtual worlds using dense stereo. In *Sixth International Conference on Computer Vision (ICCV'98)*, pages 3–10, Bombay, India, January 1998. IEEE Computer Society Press.

[Negahdaripour and Yu, 1993] S. Negahdaripour and C. H. Yu. A generalized brightness change model for computing optical flow. In *Fourth International Conference on Computer Vision (ICCV'93)*, pages 2–11, Berlin, Germany, May 1993. IEEE Computer Society Press.

[Nishihara, 1984] H. K. Nishihara. Practical real-time imaging stereo matcher. *Optical Engineering*, 23(5):536–545, September/October 1984. Also in [Fischler and Firschein, 1987].

[Nordström, 1990] N. Nordström. Biased anisotropic diffusion — a unified regularization and diffusion approach to edge detection. In *First European Conference on Computer Vision (ECCV'90)*, pages 18–27, Antibes, France, May 1990. LNCS 427, Springer-Verlag.

[O'Gorman and Sanderson, 1987] L. O'Gorman and A. C. Sanderson. A comparison of methods and computation for multi-resolution low- and band-pass transforms for image processing. *Computer Vision, Graphics, and Image Processing*, 37:386–401, 1987.

[Ohta and Kanade, 1985] Y. Ohta and T. Kanade. Stereo by intra- and interscanline search using dynamic programming. *IEEE Transactions on Pattern Analysis and Machine Intelligence*, 7(2):139–154, March 1985.

[Okutomi and Kanade, 1992] M. Okutomi and T. Kanade. A locally adaptive window for signal matching. *International Journal of Computer Vision*, 7(2):143–162, April 1992.

[Okutomi and Kanade, 1993] M. Okutomi and T. Kanade. A multiple-baseline stereo. *IEEE Transactions on Pattern Analysis and Machine Intelligence*, 15(4):353–363, 1993.

[Olsen, 1990] S. I. Olsen. Stereo correspondence by surface reconstruction. *IEEE Transactions on Pattern Analysis and Machine Intelligence*, 12(3):309–314, March 1990.

[Olson and Lockwood, 1992] T. J. Olson and R. J. Lockwood. Fixation-based filtering. In *11th SPIE Conference on Intelligent Robots and Computer Vision: Algorithms, Techniques, and Active Vision*, pages 685–695, Boston, MA, November 1992.

[Ott *et al.*, 1993] M. Ott, J. Lewis, and I. J. Cox. Teleconferencing eye contact using a virtual camera. In *INTERCHI '93*, pages 109–110, 1993.

[Peleg and Herman, 1997] S. Peleg and Joshua Herman. Panoramic mosaics by manifold projection. In *IEEE Computer Society Conference on Computer Vision and Pattern Recognition (CVPR'97)*, pages 338–343, San Juan, Puerto Rico, June 1997. IEEE Computer Society Press.

[Perona and Malik, 1990] P. Perona and J. Malik. Scale-space and edge detection using anisotropic diffusion. *IEEE Transactions on Pattern Analysis and Machine Intelligence*, 12(7):629–639, July 1990.

[Pietikäinen and Harwood, 1986] M. Pietikäinen and D. A. Harwood. Depth from three camera stereo. In *IEEE Computer Society Conference on Computer Vision and Pattern Recognition (CVPR'86)*, pages 2–8, Miami Beach, FL, June 1986. IEEE Computer Society Press.

[Pollard *et al.*, 1985] S. B. Pollard, J. E. W. Mayhew, and J. P. Frisby. PMF: A stereo correspondence algorithm using a disparity gradient limit. *Perception*, 14:449–470, 1985.

[Pratt, 1992] W. K. Pratt. *Digital Image Processing.* Wiley, New York, second edition, 1992.

[Prazdny, 1985] K. Prazdny. Detection of binocular disparities. *Biological Cybernetics*, 52(2):93–99, 1985. Also in [Fischler and Firschein, 1987].

[Press *et al.*, 1992] W. H. Press, B. P. Flannery, S. A. Teukolsky, and W. T. Vetterling. *Numerical Recipes in C: The Art of Scientific Computing.* Cambridge University Press, Cambridge, England, second edition, 1992.

[Proesmans *et al.*, 1994] M. Proesmans, L. J. VanGool, E. Pauwels, and A. Oosterlinck. Determination of optical flow and its discontinuities using non-linear diffusion. In *Third European Conference on Computer Vision (ECCV'94)*, volume II, pages 295–304, Stockholm, Sweden, May 1994. LNCS 801, Springer-Verlag.

[Quam, 1984] L. H. Quam. Hierarchical warp stereo. In *Image Understanding Workshop*, pages 149–155, New Orleans, Louisiana, December 1984. Science Applications International Corporation. Also in [Fischler and Firschein, 1987].

[Rademacher and Bishop, 1998] P. Rademacher and G. Bishop. Multiple-center-of-projection images. In *Computer Graphics (SIGGRAPH'98)*, pages 199–206, July 1998.

[Rander *et al.*, 1997] P. W. Rander, P. J. Narayanan, and T. Kanade. Virtualized reality: Constructing time-varying virtual worlds from real events. In *IEEE Visualization*, pages 277–283, 552, Phoenix, Arizona, October 1997.

[Robert and Hébert, 1994] L. Robert and M. Hébert. Deriving orientation cues from stereo images. In *Third European Conference on Computer Vision (ECCV'94)*, volume I, pages 377–388, Stockholm, Sweden, May 1994. LNCS 800, Springer-Verlag.

[Robert *et al.*, 1995] L. Robert, M. Buffa, and M. Hébert. Weakly-calibrated stereo perception for rover navigation. In *Fifth International Conference on Computer Vision (ICCV'95)*, pages 46–51, Cambridge, MA, June 1995. IEEE Computer Society Press.

[Roy and Cox, 1998] S. Roy and I. J. Cox. A maximum-flow formulation of the N-camera stereo correspondence problem. In *Sixth International Conference on Computer Vision (ICCV'98)*, pages 492–499, Bombay, India, January 1998. IEEE Computer Society Press.

[Ryan *et al.*, 1980] T. W. Ryan, R. T. Gray, and B. R. Hunt. Prediction of correlation errors in stereo-pair images. *Optical Engineering*, 19(3):312–322, May/June 1980.

[Satoh and Ohta, 1996] K. Satoh and Y. Ohta. Occlusion detectable stereo — systematic comparison of detection algorithms. In *13th International Conference on Pattern Recognition (ICPR'96)*, volume 1, Vienna, Austria, August 1996.

[Satoh *et al.*, 1996] K. Satoh, I. Kitahara, and Y. Ohta. 3D image display with motion parallax by camera matrix stereo. In *Third Intl. Conf. on Multimedia Computing and Systems (ICMCS'96)*, Hiroshima, Japan, June 1996.

[Sawhney and Ayer, 1996] H. S. Sawhney and S. Ayer. Compact representations of videos through dominant and multiple motion estimation. *IEEE Transactions on Pattern Analysis and Machine Intelligence*, 18(8):814–830, August 1996.

[Sawhney and Kumar, 1997] H. S. Sawhney and R. Kumar. True multi-image alignment and its application to mosaicing and lens distortion correction. In *IEEE Computer Society Conference on Computer Vision and Pattern Recognition (CVPR'97)*, pages 450–456, San Juan, Puerto Rico, June 1997. IEEE Computer Society Press.

[Sawhney *et al.*, 1995] H. S. Sawhney, S. Ayer, and M. Gorkani. Model-based 2D&3D dominant motion estimation for mosaicing and video representation. In *Fifth International Conference on Computer Vision (ICCV'95)*, pages 583–590, Cambridge, MA, June 1995. IEEE Computer Society Press.

[Sawhney, 1994a] H. S. Sawhney. 3D geometry from planar parallax. In *IEEE Computer Society Conference on Computer Vision and Pattern Recognition (CVPR'94)*, pages 929–934, Seattle, WA, June 1994. IEEE Computer Society Press.

[Sawhney, 1994b] H. S. Sawhney. Simplifying motion and structure analysis using planar parallax and image warping. In *12th International Conference on Pattern Recognition (ICPR'94)*, volume 1, pages 403–408, Jerusalem, Israel, October 1994.

[Scharstein and Szeliski, 1996] D. Scharstein and R. Szeliski. Stereo matching with non-linear diffusion. In *IEEE Computer Society Conference on Computer Vision and Pattern Recognition (CVPR'96)*, pages 343–350, San Francisco, CA, June 1996. IEEE Computer Society Press.

[Scharstein and Szeliski, 1998] D. Scharstein and R. Szeliski. Stereo matching with nonlinear diffusion. *International Journal of Computer Vision*, 28(2):155–174, June/July 1998.

[Scharstein, 1994a] D. Scharstein. A gradient-based evidence measure for image matching. Department of Computer Science TR 94-1439, Cornell University, Ithaca, NY, August 1994.

[Scharstein, 1994b] D. Scharstein. Matching images by comparing their gradient fields. In *12th International Conference on Pattern Recognition (ICPR'94)*, volume 1, pages 572–575, Jerusalem, Israel, October 1994.

[Scharstein, 1996] D. Scharstein. Stereo vision for view synthesis. In *IEEE Computer Society Conference on Computer Vision and Pattern Recognition (CVPR'96)*, pages 852–858, San Francisco, CA, June 1996. IEEE Computer Society Press.

[Seitz and Dyer, 1995] S. Seitz and C. Dyer. Physically-valid view synthesis by image interpolation. In *IEEE Workshop on Representations of Visual Scenes*, pages 18–25, Cambridge, MA, June 1995.

[Seitz and Dyer, 1996a] S. Seitz and C. Dyer. Toward image-based scene representation using view morphing. In *13th International Conference on Pattern Recognition (ICPR'96)*, volume 1, pages 84–89, Vienna, Austria, August 1996.

[Seitz and Dyer, 1996b] S. Seitz and C. Dyer. View morphing: Synthesizing 3D metamorphoses using image transforms. In *Computer Graphics (SIGGRAPH'96)*, pages 21–30, August 1996.

[Seitz and Dyer, 1997a] S. Seitz and C. Dyer. Photorealistic scene reconstruction by voxel coloring. In *IEEE Computer Society Conference on Computer Vision and Pattern Recognition (CVPR'97)*, pages 1067–1073, San Juan, Puerto Rico, June 1997. IEEE Computer Society Press.

[Seitz and Dyer, 1997b] S. Seitz and C. Dyer. View morphing: Uniquely predicting scene appearance from basis images. In *DARPA Image Understanding Workshop*, pages 881–887, New Orleans, LA, May 1997.

[Seitz and Kutulakos, 1998] S. M. Seitz and K. N. Kutulakos. Plenoptic image editing. In *Sixth International Conference on Computer Vision (ICCV'98)*, pages 17–24, Bombay, India, January 1998. IEEE Computer Society Press.

[Seitz, 1989] P. Seitz. Using local orientation information as image primitive for robust object recognition. In *SPIE Visual Communications and Image Processing IV*, volume 1199, pages 1630–1639, 1989.

[Seitz, 1997] S. Seitz. *Image-Based Transformation of Viewpoint and Scene Appearance*. PhD thesis, University of Wisconsin - Madison, October 1997.

[Shade *et al.*, 1998] J. Shade, S. Gortler, L. He, and R. Szeliski. Layered depth images. In *Computer Graphics (SIGGRAPH'98)*, pages 231–242, July 1998.

[Shah, 1993] J. Shah. A nonlinear diffusion model for discontinuous disparity and half-occlusion in stereo. In *IEEE Computer Society Conference on Computer Vision and Pattern Recognition (CVPR'93)*, pages 34–40, New York, NY, June 1993. IEEE Computer Society Press.

[Shashua and Navab, 1994] A. Shashua and N. Navab. Relative affine structure: Theory and applications to 3D reconstruction from perspective views. In *IEEE Computer Society Conference on Computer Vision and Pattern Recognition (CVPR'94)*, pages 483–489, Seattle, WA, June 1994. IEEE Computer Society Press.

[Shashua, 1993] A. Shashua. Projective depth: A geometric invariant for 3D reconstruction from two perspective/orthographic views and for visual recognition. In *Fourth International Conference on Computer Vision (ICCV'93)*, pages 583–590, Berlin, Germany, May 1993. IEEE Computer Society Press.

[Shashua, 1995] A. Shashua. Algebraic functions for recognition. *IEEE Transactions on Pattern Analysis and Machine Intelligence*, 17(8):779–789, August 1995.

[Shum and Szeliski, 1998] H.-Y. Shum and R. Szeliski. Construction and refinement of panoramic mosaics with global and local alignment. In *Sixth International Conference on Computer Vision (ICCV'98)*, pages 953–958, Bombay, India, January 1998. IEEE Computer Society Press.

[Shum *et al.*, 1995] H.-Y. Shum, K. Ikeuchi, and R. Reddy. Principal component analysis with missing data and its application to polyhedral object modeling. *IEEE Transactions on Pattern Analysis and Machine Intelligence*, 17(9):854–867, September 1995.

[Shum *et al.*, 1998] H.-Y. Shum, M. Han, and R. Szeliski. Interactive construction of 3D models from panoramic mosaics. In *IEEE Computer Society Conference on Computer Vision and Pattern Recognition (CVPR'98)*, pages 427–433, Santa Barbara, CA, June 1998. IEEE Computer Society Press.

[Simoncelli *et al.*, 1991] E. P. Simoncelli, E. H. Adelson, and D. J. Heeger. Probability distributions of optic flow. In *IEEE Computer Society Conference on*

Computer Vision and Pattern Recognition (CVPR'91), pages 310–315, Maui, Hawaii, June 1991. IEEE Computer Society Press.

[Simoncelli, 1994] E. P Simoncelli. Design of multi-dimensional derivative filters. In *First IEEE International Conference on Image Processing (ICIP'94)*, volume I, pages 790–794, Austin, TX, November 1994. IEEE Computer Society Press.

[Skerjanc and Liu, 1991] R. Skerjanc and J. Liu. A three camera approach for calculating disparity and synthesizing intermediate pictures. *Signal Processing: Image Communications*, 4(1):55–64, 1991.

[Skerjanc, 1994] R. Skerjanc. Combined motion and depth estimation based on multiocular image sequences for 3DTV. In *SPIE Stereoscopic Displays and Virtual Reality Systems*, volume 2155, page 35, 1994.

[Slama, 1980] C. Slama, editor. *Manual of Photogrammetry*. American Society of Photogrammetry, Falls Church, VA, fourth edition, 1980.

[Stewart *et al.*, 1996] C. V. Stewart, R. Y. Flatland, and K. Bubna. Geometric constraints and stereo disparity computation. *International Journal of Computer Vision*, 20(3):143–168, December 1996.

[Szeliski and Coughlan, 1994] R. Szeliski and J. Coughlan. Hierarchical spline-based image registration. In *IEEE Computer Society Conference on Computer Vision and Pattern Recognition (CVPR'94)*, pages 194–201, Seattle, WA, June 1994. IEEE Computer Society Press.

[Szeliski and Golland, 1998] R. Szeliski and P. Golland. Stereo matching with transparency and matting. In *Sixth International Conference on Computer Vision (ICCV'98)*, pages 517–524, Bombay, India, January 1998. IEEE Computer Society Press.

[Szeliski and Hinton, 1985] R. Szeliski and G. Hinton. Solving random-dot stereograms using the heat equation. In *IEEE Computer Society Conference on Computer Vision and Pattern Recognition (CVPR'85)*, pages 284–288, San Francisco, CA, June 1985. IEEE Computer Society Press.

[Szeliski and Kang, 1995] R. Szeliski and S. B. Kang. Direct methods for visual scene reconstruction. In *IEEE Workshop on Representations of Visual Scenes*, pages 26–33, Cambridge, MA, June 1995.

[Szeliski and Shum, 1997] R. Szeliski and H.-Y. Shum. Creating full panoramic image mosaics and environment maps. In *Computer Graphics (SIGGRAPH'97)*, pages 251–258, August 1997.

[Szeliski, 1989] R. Szeliski. *Bayesian Modeling of Uncertainty in Low-Level Vision*. Kluwer Academic Publishers, Boston, MA, 1989.

[Szeliski, 1994] R. Szeliski. Image mosaicing for tele-reality applications. In *IEEE Workshop on Applications of Computer Vision (WACV'94)*, pages 44–53, Sarasota, FL, December 1994. IEEE Computer Society Press.

[Szeliski, 1996] R. Szeliski. Video mosaics for virtual environments. *IEEE Computer Graphics and Applications*, 16(2):22–30, March 1996.

[Teodosio and Bender, 1993] L. Teodosio and W. Bender. Salient video stills: Content and context preserved. In *ACM Multimedia '93*, pages 39–46, Anaheim, California, August 1993.

[Terzopoulos, 1986] D. Terzopoulos. Regularization of inverse visual problems involving discontinuities. *IEEE Transactions on Pattern Analysis and Machine Intelligence*, 8(4):413–424, July 1986.

[Thompson, 1959] E. H. Thompson. A rational algebraic formulation of the problem of relative orientation. *Photogrammetric Record*, 3:152–159, 1959.

[Tian and Huhns, 1986] Q. Tian and M. N. Huhns. Algorithms for subpixel registration. *Computer Vision, Graphics, and Image Processing*, 35:220–233, 1986.

[Tomasi and Kanade, 1992] C. Tomasi and T. Kanade. Shape and motion from image streams under orthography: A factorization method. *International Journal of Computer Vision*, 9(2):137–154, November 1992.

[Torborg and Kajiva, 1996] J. Torborg and J. T. Kajiva. Talisman: Commodity realtime 3D graphics for the PC. In *Computer Graphics (SIGGRAPH'96)*, pages 353–363, August 1996.

[Ullman and Basri, 1991] S. Ullman and R. Basri. Recognition by linear combination of models. *IEEE Transactions on Pattern Analysis and Machine Intelligence*, 13(10):992–1006, October 1991.

[Vetter and Poggio, 1997] T. Vetter and T. Poggio. Linear object classes and image synthesis from a single example image. *IEEE Transactions on Pattern Analysis and Machine Intelligence*, 19(7):733–742, July 1997.

[Wandell, 1995] Brian. A. Wandell. *Foundations of Vision.* Sinauer Associates, Inc., Sunderland, MA, 1995.

[Wang and Adelson, 1993] J. Y. A. Wang and E. H. Adelson. Layered representation for motion analysis. In *IEEE Computer Society Conference on Computer Vision and Pattern Recognition (CVPR'93)*, pages 361–366, New York, NY, June 1993. IEEE Computer Society Press.

[Wang and Adelson, 1994] J. Y. A. Wang and E. H. Adelson. Representing moving images with layers. *IEEE Transactions on Pattern Analysis and Machine Intelligence*, 3(5):625–638, September 1994.

[Wei *et al.*, 1998] G.-Q. Wei, W. Brauer, and G. Hirzinger. Intensity- and gradient-based stereo matching using hierarchical Gaussian basis functions. *IEEE Transactions on Pattern Analysis and Machine Intelligence*, 20(11):1143–1160, November 1998.

[Wells, 1986] W. M. Wells, III. Efficient synthesis of Gaussian filters by cascaded uniform filters. *IEEE Transactions on Pattern Analysis and Machine Intelligence*, 8(2):234–239, March 1986.

[Werner *et al.*, 1995] T. Werner, R. Hersch, and V. Hlaváč. Rendering real-world objects using view interpolation. In *Fifth International Conference on Computer Vision (ICCV'95)*, pages 957–962, Cambridge, MA, June 1995. IEEE Computer Society Press.

[Westover, 1990] L. Westover. Footprint evaluation for volume rendering. In *Computer Graphics (SIGGRAPH'90)*, volume 24, pages 367–376, 1990.

[Witkin *et al.*, 1987] A. Witkin, D. Terzopoulos, and M. Kass. Signal matching through scale space. *International Journal of Computer Vision*, 1:133–144, 1987.

[Wolberg, 1990] G. Wolberg. *Digital Image Warping.* IEEE Computer Society Press, Los Alamitos, California, 1990.

[Wolf, 1983] P. R. Wolf. *Elements of Photogrammetry.* McGraw-Hill, second edition, 1983.

[Xiong and Turkowski, 1997] Y. Xiong and K. Turkowski. Creating image-based VR using a self-calibrating fisheye lens. In *IEEE Computer Society Conference on Computer Vision and Pattern Recognition (CVPR'97)*, pages 237–243, San Juan, Puerto Rico, June 1997. IEEE Computer Society Press.

[Yuille and Poggio, 1984] A. L. Yuille and T. Poggio. A generalized ordering constraint for stereo correspondence. A.I. Memo 777, Artificial Intelligence Laboratory, Massachusetts Institute of Technology, Cambridge, MA, May 1984.

[Zabih and Woodfill, 1994] R. Zabih and J. Woodfill. Non-parametric local transforms for computing visual correspondence. In *Third European Conference on Computer Vision (ECCV'94)*, volume II, pages 151–158, Stockholm, Sweden, May 1994. LNCS 801, Springer-Verlag.

[Zabih, 1994] R. Zabih. *Individuating Unknown Objects by Combining Motion and Stereo.* PhD thesis, Stanford University, August 1994.

[Zeller and Faugeras, 1994] C. Zeller and O. Faugeras. Applications of non-metric vision to some visual guided tasks. In *12th International Conference on Pattern Recognition (ICPR'94)*, volume 1, pages 132–136, Jerusalem, Israel, October 1994.

[Zhang *et al.*, 1995] Z. Zhang, R. Deriche, O. Faugeras, and Q.-T. Luong. A robust technique for matching two uncalibrated images through the recovery of the unknown epipolar geometry. *Artificial Intelligence Journal*, 78:87–119, October 1995. INRIA Technical Report No. 2273.

[Zhang *et al.*, 1998] Z. Zhang, K. Isono, and S. Akamatsu. Structure from uncalibrated images using fuzzy domain knowledge: Application to facial images synthesis. In *Sixth International Conference on Computer Vision (ICCV'98)*, pages 784–789, Bombay, India, January 1998. IEEE Computer Society Press.

[Zhang, 1998a] Z. Zhang. Determining the epipolar geometry and its uncertainty: A review. *International Journal of Computer Vision*, 27(2):161–195, March 1998.

[Zhang, 1998b] Z. Zhang. Image-based geometrically-correct photorealistic scene/object modeling (IBPhM): A review. In *Third Asian Conference on Computer Vision (ACCV'98)*, pages 340–349, Hong Kong, January 1998. LNCS 1351/1352, Springer-Verlag.

[Zoghiami *et al.*, 1997] I. Zoghiami, O. Faugeras, and R. Deriche. Using geometric corners to build a 2D mosaic from a set of images. In *IEEE Computer Society Conference on Computer Vision and Pattern Recognition (CVPR'97)*, pages 420–425, San Juan, Puerto Rico, June 1997. IEEE Computer Society Press.

Springer

Lecture Notes in Computer Science

For information about Vols. 1–1537
please contact your bookseller or Springer-Verlag

Vol. 1538: J. Hsiang, A. Ohori (Eds.), Advances in Computing Science – ASIAN'98. Proceedings, 1998. X, 305 pages. 1998.

Vol. 1539: O. Rüthing, Interacting Code Motion Transformations: Their Impact and Their Complexity. XXI,225 pages. 1998.

Vol. 1540: C. Beeri, P. Buneman (Eds.), Database Theory – ICDT'99. Proceedings, 1999. XI, 489 pages. 1999.

Vol. 1541: B. Kågström, J. Dongarra, E. Elmroth, J. Waśniewski (Eds.), Applied Parallel Computing. Proceedings, 1998. XIV, 586 pages. 1998.

Vol. 1542: H.I. Christensen (Ed.), Computer Vision Systems. Proceedings, 1999. XI, 554 pages. 1999.

Vol. 1543: S. Demeyer, J. Bosch (Eds.), Object-Oriented Technology ECOOP'98 Workshop Reader. 1998. XXII, 573 pages. 1998.

Vol. 1544: C. Zhang, D. Lukose (Eds.), Multi-Agent Systems. Proceedings, 1998. VII, 195 pages. 1998. (Subseries LNAI).

Vol. 1545: A. Birk, J. Demiris (Eds.), Learning Robots. Proceedings, 1996. IX, 188 pages. 1998. (Subseries LNAI).

Vol. 1546: B. Möller, J.V. Tucker (Eds.), Prospects for Hardware Foundations. Survey Chapters, 1998. X, 468 pages. 1998.

Vol. 1547: S.H. Whitesides (Ed.), Graph Drawing. Proceedings 1998. XII, 468 pages. 1998.

Vol. 1548: A.M. Haeberer (Ed.), Algebraic Methodology and Software Technology. Proceedings, 1999. XI, 531 pages. 1999.

Vol. 1549: M. Pettersson, Compiling Natural Semantics. XVII, 240 pages. 1999.

Vol. 1550: B. Christianson, B. Crispo, W.S. Harbison, M. Roe (Eds.), Security Protocols. Proceedings, 1998. VIII, 241 pages. 1999.

Vol. 1551: G. Gupta (Ed.), Practical Aspects of Declarative Languages. Proceedings, 1999. VIII, 367 pgages. 1999.

Vol. 1552: Y. Kambayashi, D.L. Lee, E.-P. Lim, M.K. Mohania, Y. Masunaga (Eds.), Advances in Database Technologies. Proceedings, 1998. XIX, 592 pages. 1999.

Vol. 1553: S.F. Andler, J. Hansson (Eds.), Active, Real-Time, and Temporal Database Systems. Proceedings, 1997. VIII, 245 pages. 1998.

Vol. 1554: S. Nishio, F. Kishino (Eds.), Advanced Multimedia Content Processing. Proceedings, 1998. XIV, 454 pages. 1999.

Vol. 1555: J.P. Müller, M.P. Singh, A.S. Rao (Eds.), Intelligent Agents V. Proceedings, 1998. XXIV, 455 pages. 1999. (Subseries LNAI).

Vol. 1556: S. Tavares, H. Meijer (Eds.), Selected Areas in Cryptography. Proceedings, 1998. IX, 377 pages. 1999.

Vol. 1557: P. Zinterhof, M. Vajteršic, A. Uhl (Eds.), Parallel Computation. Proceedings, 1999. XV, 604 pages. 1999.

Vol. 1558: H. J.v.d. Herik, H. Iida (Eds.), Computers and Games. Proceedings, 1998. XVIII, 337 pages. 1999.

Vol. 1559: P. Flener (Ed.), Logic-Based Program Synthesis and Transformation. Proceedings, 1998. X, 331 pages. 1999.

Vol. 1560: K. Imai, Y. Zheng (Eds.), Public Key Cryptography. Proceedings, 1999. IX, 327 pages. 1999.

Vol. 1561: I. Damgård (Ed.), Lectures on Data Security.VII, 250 pages. 1999.

Vol. 1562: C.L. Nehaniv (Ed.), Computation for Metaphors, Analogy, and Agents. X, 389 pages. 1999. (Subseries LNAI).

Vol. 1563: Ch. Meinel, S. Tison (Eds.), STACS 99. Proceedings, 1999. XIV, 582 pages. 1999.

Vol. 1565: P. P. Chen, J. Akoka, H. Kangassalo, B. Thalheim (Eds.), Conceptual Modeling. XXIV, 303 pages. 1999.

Vol. 1567: P. Antsaklis, W. Kohn, M. Lemmon, A. Nerode, S. Sastry (Eds.), Hybrid Systems V. X, 445 pages. 1999.

Vol. 1568: G. Bertrand, M. Couprie, L. Perroton (Eds.), Discrete Geometry for Computer Imagery. Proceedings, 1999. XI, 459 pages. 1999.

Vol. 1569: F.W. Vaandrager, J.H. van Schuppen (Eds.), Hybrid Systems: Computation and Control. Proceedings, 1999. X, 271 pages. 1999.

Vol. 1570: F. Puppe (Ed.), XPS-99: Knowledge-Based Systems. VIII, 227 pages. 1999. (Subseries LNAI).

Vol. 1571: P. Noriega, C. Sierra (Eds.), Agent Mediated Electronic Commerce. Proceedings, 1998. IX, 207 pages. 1999. (Subseries LNAI).

Vol. 1572: P. Fischer, H.U. Simon (Eds.), Computational Learning Theory. Proceedings, 1999. X, 301 pages. 1999. (Subseries LNAI).

Vol. 1574: N. Zhong, L. Zhou (Eds.), Methodologies for Knowledge Discovery and Data Mining. Proceedings, 1999. XV, 533 pages. 1999. (Subseries LNAI).

Vol. 1575: S. Jähnichen (Ed.), Compiler Construction. Proceedings, 1999. X, 301 pages. 1999.

Vol. 1576: S.D. Swierstra (Ed.), Programming Languages and Systems. Proceedings, 1999. X, 307 pages. 1999.

Vol. 1577: J.-P. Finance (Ed.), Fundamental Approaches to Software Engineering. Proceedings, 1999. X, 245 pages. 1999.

Vol. 1578: W. Thomas (Ed.), Foundations of Software Science and Computation Structures. Proceedings, 1999. X, 323 pages. 1999.

Vol. 1579: W.R. Cleaveland (Ed.), Tools and Algorithms for the Construction and Analysis of Systems. Proceedings, 1999. XI, 445 pages. 1999.

Vol. 1580: A. Včkovski, K.E. Brassel, H.-J. Schek (Eds.), Interoperating Geographic Information Systems. Proceedings, 1999. XI, 329 pages. 1999.

Vol. 1581: J.-Y. Girard (Ed.), Typed Lambda Calculi and Applications. Proceedings, 1999. VIII, 397 pages. 1999.

Vol. 1582: A. Lecomte, F. Lamarche, G. Perrier (Eds.), Logical Aspects of Computational Linguistics. Proceedings, 1997. XI, 251 pages. 1999. (Subseries LNAI).

Vol. 1583: D. Scharstein, View Synthesis Using Stereo Vision. XV, 163 pages. 1999.

Vol. 1584: G. Gottlob, E. Grandjean, K. Seyr (Eds.), Computer Science Logic. Proceedings, 1998. X, 431 pages. 1999.

Vol. 1585: B. McKay, X. Yao, C.S. Newton, J.-H. Kim, T. Furuhashi (Eds.), Simulated Evolution and Learning. Proceedings, 1998. XIII, 472 pages. 1999. (Subseries LNAI).

Vol. 1586: J. Rolim et al. (Eds.), Parallel and Distributed Processing. Proceedings, 1999. XVII, 1443 pages. 1999.

Vol. 1587: J. Pieprzyk, R. Safavi-Naini, J. Seberry (Eds.), Information Security and Privacy. Proceedings, 1999. XI, 327 pages. 1999.

Vol. 1590: P. Atzeni, A. Mendelzon, G. Mecca (Eds.), The World Wide Web and Databases. Proceedings, 1998. VIII, 213 pages. 1999.

Vol. 1592: J. Stern (Ed.), Advances in Cryptology – EUROCRYPT '99. Proceedings, 1999. XII, 475 pages. 1999.

Vol. 1593: P. Sloot, M. Bubak, A. Hoekstra, B. Hertzberger (Eds.), High-Performance Computing and Networking. Proceedings, 1999. XXIII, 1318 pages. 1999.

Vol. 1594: P. Ciancarini, A.L. Wolf (Eds.), Coordination Languages and Models. Proceedings, 1999. IX, 420 pages. 1999.

Vol. 1596: R. Poli, H.-M. Voigt, S. Cagnoni, D. Corne, G.D. Smith, T.C. Fogarty (Eds.), Evolutionary Image Analysis, Signal Processing and Telecommunications. Proceedings, 1999. X, 225 pages. 1999.

Vol. 1597: H. Zuidweg, M. Campolargo, J. Delgado, A. Mullery (Eds.), Intelligence in Services and Networks. Proceedings, 1999. XII, 552 pages. 1999.

Vol. 1598: R. Poli, P. Nordin, W.B. Langdon, T.C. Fogarty (Eds.), Genetic Programming. Proceedings, 1999. X, 283 pages. 1999.

Vol. 1599: T. Ishida (Ed.), Multiagent Platforms. Proceedings, 1998. VIII, 187 pages. 1999. (Subseries LNAI).

Vol. 1601: J.-P. Katoen (Ed.), Formal Methods for Real-Time and Probabilistic Systems. Proceedings, 1999. X, 355 pages. 1999.

Vol. 1602: A. Sivasubramaniam, M. Lauria (Eds.), Network-Based Parallel Computing. Proceedings, 1999. VIII, 225 pages. 1999.

Vol. 1603: J. Vitek, C.D. Jensen (Eds.), Secure Internet Programming. X, 501 pages. 1999.

Vol. 1605: J. Billington, M. Diaz, G. Rozenberg (Eds.), Application of Petri Nets to Communication Networks. IX, 303 pages. 1999.

Vol. 1606: J. Mira, J.V. Sánchez-Andrés (Eds.), Foundations and Tools for Neural Modeling. Proceedings, Vol. I, 1999. XXIII, 865 pages. 1999.

Vol. 1607: J. Mira, J.V. Sánchez-Andrés (Eds.), Engineering Applications of Bio-Inspired Artificial Neural Networks. Proceedings, Vol. II, 1999. XXIII, 907 pages. 1999.

Vol. 1609: Z. W. Raś, A. Skowron (Eds.), Foundations of Intelligent Systems. Proceedings, 1999. XII, 676 pages. 1999. (Subseries LNAI).

Vol. 1610: G. Cornuéjols, R.E. Burkard, G.J. Woeginger (Eds.), Integer Programming and Combinatorial Optimization. Proceedings, 1999. IX, 453 pages. 1999.

Vol. 1611: I. Imam, Y. Kodratoff, A. El-Dessouki, M. Ali (Eds.), Multiple Approaches to Intelligent Systems. Proceedings, 1999. XIX, 899 pages. 1999. (Subseries LNAI).

Vol. 1612: R. Bergmann, S. Breen, M. Göker, M. Manago, S. Wess, Developing Industrial Case-Based Reasoning Applications. XX, 188 pages. 1999. (Subseries LNAI).

Vol. 1614: D.P. Huijsmans, A.W.M. Smeulders (Eds.), Visual Information and Information Systems. Proceedings, 1999. XVII, 827 pages. 1999.

Vol. 1615: C. Polychronopoulos, K. Joe, A. Fukuda, S. Tomita (Eds.), High Performance Computing. Proceedings, 1999. XIV, 408 pages. 1999.

Vol. 1617: N.V. Murray (Ed.), Automated Reasoning with Analytic Tableaux and Related Methods. Proceedings, 1999. X, 325 pages. 1999. (Subseries LNAI).

Vol. 1620: W. Horn, Y. Shahar, G. Lindberg, S. Andreassen, J. Wyatt (Eds.), Artificial Intelligence in Medicine. Proceedings, 1999. XIII, 454 pages. 1999. (Subseries LNAI).

Vol. 1621: D. Fensel, R. Studer (Eds.), Knowledge Acquisition Modeling and Management. Proceedings, 1999. XI, 404 pages. 1999. (Subseries LNAI).

Vol. 1622: M. González Harbour, J.A. de la Puente (Eds.), Reliable Software Technologies – Ada-Europe'99. Proceedings, 1999. XIII, 451 pages. 1999.

Vol. 1625: B. Reusch (Ed.), Computational Intelligence. Proceedings, 1999. XIV, 710 pages. 1999.

Vol. 1626: M. Jarke, A. Oberweis (Eds.), Advanced Information Systems Engineering. Proceedings, 1999. XIV, 478 pages. 1999.

Col. 1628: R. Guerraoui (Ed.), ECOOP'99 - Object-Oriented Programming. Proceedings, 1999. XIII, 529 pages. 1999.

Vol. 1629: H. Leopold, N. García (Eds.), Multimedia Applications, Services and Techniques - ECMAST'99. Proceedings, 1999. XV, 574 pages. 1999.

Vol. 1634: S. Džeroski, P. Flach (Eds.), Inductive Logic Programming. Proceedings, 1999. VIII, 303 pages. 1999. (Subseries LNAI).

Vol. 1639: S. Donatelli, J. Kleijn (Eds.), Application and Theory of Petri Nets 1999. Proceedings, 1999. VIII, 425 pages. 1999.